Modern Critical Views

Chinua Achebe
Henry Adams
Aeschylus
S. Y. Agnon
Edward Albee
Raphael Alberti
Louisa May Alcott
A. R. Ammons
Sherwood Anderson
Aristophanes
Matthew Arnold
Antonin Artaud
John Ashbery
Margaret Atwood
W. H. Auden
Jane Austen
Isaac Babel
Sir Francis Bacon
James Baldwin
Honoré de Balzac
John Barth
Donald Barthelme
Charles Baudelaire
Simone de Beauvoir
Samuel Beckett
Saul Bellow
Thomas Berger
John Berryman
The Bible
Elizabeth Bishop
William Blake
Giovanni Boccaccio
Heinrich Böll
Jorge Luis Borges
Elizabeth Bowen
Bertolt Brecht
The Brontës
Charles Brockden Brown
Sterling Brown
Robert Browning
Martin Buber
John Bunyan
Anthony Burgess
Kenneth Burke
Robert Burns
William Burroughs
George Gordon, Lord
 Byron
Pedro Calderón de la Barca
Italo Calvino
Albert Camus
Canadian Poetry: Modern
 and Contemporary
Canadian Poetry through
 E. J. Pratt
Thomas Carlyle
Alejo Carpentier
Lewis Carroll
Willa Cather
Louis-Ferdinand Céline
Miguel de Cervantes

Geoffrey Chaucer
John Cheever
Anton Chekhov
Kate Chopin
Chrétien de Troyes
Agatha Christie
Samuel Taylor Coleridge
Colette
William Congreve & the
 Restoration Dramatists
Joseph Conrad
Contemporary Poets
James Fenimore Cooper
Pierre Corneille
Julio Cortázar
Hart Crane
Stephen Crane
e. e. cummings
Dante
Robertson Davies
Daniel Defoe
Philip K. Dick
Charles Dickens
James Dickey
Emily Dickinson
Denis Diderot
Isak Dinesen
E. L. Doctorow
John Donne & the
 Seventeenth-Century
 Metaphysical Poets
John Dos Passos
Fyodor Dostoevsky
Frederick Douglass
Theodore Dreiser
John Dryden
W. E. B. Du Bois
Lawrence Durrell
George Eliot
T. S. Eliot
Elizabethan Dramatists
Ralph Ellison
Ralph Waldo Emerson
Euripides
William Faulkner
Henry Fielding
F. Scott Fitzgerald
Gustave Flaubert
E. M. Forster
John Fowles
Sigmund Freud
Robert Frost
Northrop Frye
Carlos Fuentes
William Gaddis
Federico García Lorca
Gabriel García Márquez
André Gide
W. S. Gilbert
Allen Ginsberg
J. W. von Goethe

Nikolai Gogol
William Golding
Oliver Goldsmith
Mary Gordon
Günther Grass
Robert Graves
Graham Greene
Thomas Hardy
Nathaniel Hawthorne
William Hazlitt
H. D.
Seamus Heaney
Lillian Hellman
Ernest Hemingway
Hermann Hesse
Geoffrey Hill
Friedrich Hölderlin
Homer
A. D. Hope
Gerard Manley Hopkins
Horace
A. E. Housman
William Dean Howells
Langston Hughes
Ted Hughes
Victor Hugo
Zora Neale Hurston
Aldous Huxley
Henrik Ibsen
Eugène Ionesco
Washington Irving
Henry James
Dr. Samuel Johnson and
 James Boswell
Ben Jonson
James Joyce
Carl Gustav Jung
Franz Kafka
Yasonari Kawabata
John Keats
Søren Kierkegaard
Rudyard Kipling
Melanie Klein
Heinrich von Kleist
Philip Larkin
D. H. Lawrence
John le Carré
Ursula K. Le Guin
Giacomo Leopardi
Doris Lessing
Sinclair Lewis
Jack London
Robert Lowell
Malcolm Lowry
Carson McCullers
Norman Mailer
Bernard Malamud
Stéphane Mallarmé
Sir Thomas Malory
André Malraux
Thomas Mann

Modern Critical Views

Katherine Mansfield
Christopher Marlowe
Andrew Marvell
Herman Melville
George Meredith
James Merrill
John Stuart Mill
Arthur Miller
Henry Miller
John Milton
Yukio Mishima
Molière
Michel de Montaigne
Eugenio Montale
Marianne Moore
Alberto Moravia
Toni Morrison
Alice Munro
Iris Murdoch
Robert Musil
Vladimir Nabokov
V. S. Naipaul
R. K. Narayan
Pablo Neruda
John Henry Newman
Friedrich Nietzsche
Frank Norris
Joyce Carol Oates
Sean O'Casey
Flannery O'Connor
Christopher Okigbo
Charles Olson
Eugene O'Neill
José Ortega y Gasset
Joe Orton
George Orwell
Ovid
Wilfred Owen
Amos Oz
Cynthia Ozick
Grace Paley
Blaise Pascal
Walter Pater
Octavio Paz
Walker Percy
Petrarch
Pindar
Harold Pinter
Luigi Pirandello
Sylvia Plath
Plato

Plautus
Edgar Allan Poe
Poets of Sensibility & the
  Sublime
Poets of the Nineties
Alexander Pope
Katherine Anne Porter
Ezra Pound
Anthony Powell
Pre-Raphaelite Poets
Marcel Proust
Manuel Puig
Alexander Pushkin
Thomas Pynchon
Francisco de Quevedo
François Rabelais
Jean Racine
Ishmael Reed
Adrienne Rich
Samuel Richardson
Mordecai Richler
Rainer Maria Rilke
Arthur Rimbaud
Edwin Arlington Robinson
Theodore Roethke
Philip Roth
Jean-Jacques Rousseau
John Ruskin
J. D. Salinger
Jean-Paul Sartre
Gershom Scholem
Sir Walter Scott
William Shakespeare
  Histories & Poems
  Comedies & Romances
  Tragedies
George Bernard Shaw
Mary Wollstonecraft
  Shelley
Percy Bysshe Shelley
Sam Shepard
Richard Brinsley Sheridan
Sir Philip Sidney
Isaac Bashevis Singer
Tobias Smollett
Alexander Solzhenitsyn
Sophocles
Wole Soyinka
Edmund Spenser
Gertrude Stein
John Steinbeck

Stendhal
Laurence Sterne
Wallace Stevens
Robert Louis Stevenson
Tom Stoppard
August Strindberg
Jonathan Swift
John Millington Synge
Alfred, Lord Tennyson
William Makepeace Thackeray
Dylan Thomas
Henry David Thoreau
James Thurber and S. J.
  Perelman
J. R. R. Tolkien
Leo Tolstoy
Jean Toomer
Lionel Trilling
Anthony Trollope
Ivan Turgenev
Mark Twain
Miguel de Unamuno
John Updike
Paul Valéry
Cesar Vallejo
Lope de Vega
Gore Vidal
Virgil
Voltaire
Kurt Vonnegut
Derek Walcott
Alice Walker
Robert Penn Warren
Evelyn Waugh
H. G. Wells
Eudora Welty
Nathanael West
Edith Wharton
Patrick White
Walt Whitman
Oscar Wilde
Tennessee Williams
William Carlos Williams
Thomas Wolfe
Virginia Woolf
William Wordsworth
Jay Wright
Richard Wright
William Butler Yeats
A. B. Yehoshua
Emile Zola

Modern Critical Views

JOHN KEATS

Modern Critical Views

JOHN KEATS

Edited with an introduction by

Harold Bloom

Sterling Professor of the Humanities
Yale University

CHELSEA HOUSE PUBLISHERS
New York

THE COVER:
The cover depicts the great visionary lyric "La Belle Dame Sans Merci," where a "faery's child," a beautiful enchantress, gazes upon a knight-at-arms, and looks at him "as she did love." This ambiguous gaze may be said to precipitate the knight-at-arm's tragedy, as he is starving to death after she has abandoned him.—H.B.

PROJECT EDITORS: Emily Bestler, James Uebbing
EDITORIAL COORDINATOR: Karyn Gullen Browne
EDITORIAL STAFF: Linda Grossman, Laura Ludwig, Peter Childers
DESIGN: Susan Lusk

Cover illustration by Ken Mitchell

Printed and bound in the United States of America

10   9   8   7   6   5   4   3   2

Library of Congress Cataloging in Publication Data

Keats, modern critical views.
    Bibliography: p.
    Includes index.
    Contents: Negative capability / Walter Jackson Bate—
The negative road / Paul de Man—The world of the
early poems / Morris Dickstein—[etc.]
    1. Keats, John, 1795–1821—Criticism and interpreta-
tion—Addresses, essays, lectures. I. Bloom, Harold.
PR4837.K35 1984   821'.7   84–27425
ISBN 0–87754–608–8

Contents

Editor's Note

This volume gathers together what its editor judges to be the best and most representative criticism devoted to John Keats during the past two decades. The "Introduction" sets Keats in the full context of the Romantic tradition with its attendant anxieties of influence, and so necessarily seeks to isolate Keats's own hard-won originality.

Walter Jackson Bate, the precursor of all Keats criticism subsequent to him, begins the array of essays, which I have arranged chronologically in their order of publication. Negative capability, which Keats named as his ideal poetic stance, is uniquely Bate's subject. A more European and dialectical mode of negation is ascribed to Keats by the late Paul de Man, in a remarkable general overview of Keats's achievement both as poet and as theorist.

The remaining essays range over most of Keats's major poems, starting with Morris Dickstein on the earlier work and Stuart M. Sperry considering the problematical allegory of *Endymion*. Geoffrey Hartman's essay massively reads the ode "To Autumn," while the editor's own essay centers upon the "Ode to Psyche" and *The Fall of Hyperion*. These are followed by a younger generation of critics in the interpretations of the first *Hyperion* by Paul Sherwin and of *Lamia* by Leslie Brisman. Helen Vendler's brilliant recovery of the neglected "Ode on Indolence" and David Bromwich's Hazlittian readings of the "Ode on a Grecian Urn" and the "Ode to a Nightingale" round off this volume's detailed survey of the greatest of Keats's poems.

Introduction

One of the central themes in W. J. Bate's definitive *John Keats* is the "large, often paralyzing embarrassment...that the rich accumulation of past poetry, as the eighteenth century had seen so realistically, can curse as well as bless." As Mr. Bate remarks, this embarrassment haunted Romantic and haunts post-Romantic poetry, and was felt by Keats with a particular intensity. Somewhere in the heart of each new poet there is hidden the dark wish that the libraries be burned in some new Alexandrian conflagration, that the imagination might be liberated from the greatness and oppressive power of its own dead champions.

Something of this must be involved in the Romantics' loving struggle with their ghostly father, Milton. The role of wrestling Jacob is taken on by Blake in his "brief epic" *Milton*, by Wordsworth in *The Recluse* fragment, and in more concealed form by Shelley in *Prometheus Unbound* and Keats in the first *Hyperion*. The strength of poetical life in Milton seems always to have appalled as much as it delighted; in the fearful vigor of his unmatched exuberance the English master of the sublime has threatened not only poets, but the values once held to transcend poetry:

> ...the Argument
> Held me a while misdoubting his Intent,
> That he would ruin (for I saw him strong)
> The sacred Truths to Fable and old Song
> (So *Sampson* grop'd the Temple's Posts in spite)
> The World O'erwhelming to revenge his sight.

The older Romantics at least thought that the struggle with Milton had bestowed a blessing without a crippling; to the younger ones a consciousness of gain and loss came together. Blake's audacity gave him a Milton altogether fitted to his great need, a visionary prototype who could be dramatized as rising up, "unhappy tho' in heav'n," taking off the robe of the promise, and ungirding himself from the oath of God, and then descending into Blake's world to save the later poet and every man "from his Chain of Jealousy." Wordsworth's equal audacity allowed him, after praising

Milton's invocatory power, to call on a greater Muse than Urania, to assist him in exploring regions more awful than Milton ever visited. The prophetic Spirit called down in *The Recluse* is itself a child of Milton's Spirit that preferred, before all temples, the upright and pure heart of the Protestant poet. But the child is greater than the father, and inspires, in a fine Shakespearean reminiscence:

> The human Soul of universal earth,
> Dreaming on things to come.

Out of that capable dreaming came the poetic aspirations of Shelley and of Keats, who inherited the embarrassment of Wordsworth's greatness to add to the burden of Milton's. Yielding to few in my admiration for Shelley's blank verse in *Prometheus*, I am still made uneasy by Milton's ghost hovering in it. At times Shelley's power of irony rescues him from Milton's presence by the argument's dissonance with the steady Miltonic music of the lyrical drama, but the ironies pass and the Miltonic sublime remains, testifying to the unyielding strength of an order Shelley hoped to overturn. In the lyrics of *Prometheus* Shelley is free, and they rather than the speeches foretold his own poetic future, the sequence of *The Witch of Atlas, Epipsychidion* and *Adonais*. Perhaps the turn to Dante, hinted in *Epipsychidion* and emergent in *The Triumph of Life*, was in part caused by the necessity of finding a sublime antithesis to Milton.

With Keats, we need not surmise. The poet himself claimed to have abandoned the first *Hyperion* because it was too Miltonic, and his critics have agreed in not wanting him to have made a poem "that might have been written by John Milton, but one that was unmistakably by no other than John Keats." In the Great Odes and *The Fall of Hyperion* Keats was to write poems unmistakably his own, as *Endymion* in another way had been his own. Individuality of style, and still more of conception, no critic would now deny to the odes, Keats's supreme poems, or to *The Fall of Hyperion*, which was his testament, and is the work future poets may use as Tennyson, Arnold and Yeats used the odes in the past.

That Keats, in his handful of great poems, surpassed the Milton-haunted poets of the second half of the eighteenth century is obvious to a critical age like our own, which tends to prefer Keats, in those poems, to even the best work of Blake, Wordsworth and Shelley, and indeed to most if not all poetry in the language since the mid-seventeenth century. Perhaps the basis for that preference can be explored afresh through a consideration of precisely how Keats's freedom of the negative weight of poetic tradition is manifested in some of his central poems. Keats lost and gained, as each of the major Romantics did, in the struggle with the greatness of Milton. Keats was perhaps too generous and perceptive a critic, too wonderfully balanced a humanist, not to have lost some values of a cultural legacy that both stimulated and inhibited the nurture of fresh values.

Mr. Bate finely says, commenting on Keats's dedication sonnet to Leigh Hunt, that "when the imagination looks to any past, of course, including one's own individual past, it blends memories and images into a denser, more massive unit than ever existed in actuality." Keats's confrontation with this idealized past is most direct from the *Ode to Psyche* on, as Mr. Bate emphasizes. Without repeating him on that ode, or what I myself have written elsewhere, I want to examine it again in the specific context of Keats's fight against the too-satisfying enrichments with which tradition threatens the poet who seeks his own self-recognition and expressive fulfillment.

Most readers recalling the *Ode to Psyche* think of the last stanza, which is the poem's glory, and indeed its sole but sufficient claim to stand near the poet's four principal odes. The stanza expresses a wary confidence that the true poet's imagination cannot be impoverished. More wonderfully, the poet ends the stanza by opening the hard-won consciousness of his own creative powers to a visitation of love. The paradise within is barely formed, but the poet does not hesitate to make it vulnerable, though he may be condemned in consequence to the fate of the famished knight of his own faery ballad. There is triumph in the closing tone of *To Psyche*, but a consciousness also I think of the danger that is being courted. The poet has given Psyche the enclosed bower nature no longer affords her, but he does not pause to be content in that poet's paradise. It is not Byzantium which Keats has built in the heretofore untrodden regions of his mind but rather a realm that is precisely not far above all breathing human passion. He has not assumed the responsibility of an expanded consciousness for the rewards of self-communing and solitary musing, in the manner of the poet-hero of *Alastor*, and of Prince Athanase in his lonely tower. He seeks "love" rather than "wisdom," distrusting a reality that must be approached apart from men. And he has written his poem, in however light a spirit, as an act of self-dedication and of freedom from the wealth of the past. He will be Psyche's priest and rhapsode in the proud conviction that she has had no others before him, or none at least so naked of external pieties.

The wealth of tradition is great not only in its fused massiveness, but in its own subtleties of internalization. One does poor service by sandbagging this profoundly moving poem, yet even the heroic innovators but tread the shadowy ground their ancestors found before them. Wordsworth had stood on that ground, as Keats well knew, and perhaps had chosen a different opening from it, neither toward love nor toward wisdom, but toward a plain recognition of natural reality and a more sublime recognition-by-starts of a final reality that seemed to contain nature.

Wordsworth never quite named that finality as imagination, though Blake had done so and the young Coleridge felt (and resisted) the demonic temptation to do so. Behind all these were the fine collapses of the Age of Sensibility, the raptures of *Jubilate Agno* and the *Ode on the Poetical Character*, and the more forced but highly impressive tumults of *The Bard* and *The Progress of Poesy*. Farther back was the ancestor of all such moments of poetic incarnation, the Milton of the great invocations, whose spirit I think haunts the *Ode to Psyche* and the *Ode to a Nightingale*, and does not vanish until *The Fall of Hyperion* and *To Autumn*.

Hazlitt, with his usual penetration, praises Milton for his power to absorb vast poetic traditions with no embarrassment whatsoever: "In reading his works, we feel ourselves under the influence of a mighty intellect, that the nearer it approaches to others, becomes more distinct from them." This observation, which comes in a lecture Keats heard, is soon joined by the excellent remark that "Milton's learning has the effect of intuition." The same lecture, in its treatment of Shakespeare, influenced Keats's conception of the Poetical Character, as Mr. Bate notes. Whether Keats speculated sadly on the inimitable power of Milton's positive capability for converting the splendor of the past into a private expressiveness we do not know. But the literary archetype of Psyche's rosy sanctuary is the poet's paradise, strikingly developed by Spenser and Drayton, and brought to a perfection by Milton. I am not suggesting Milton as a "source" for Keats's *Ode to Psyche*. Poets influence poets in ways more profound than verbal echoings. The paradise of poets is a recurrent element in English mythopoeic poetry, and it is perhaps part of the critic's burden never to allow himself to yield to embarrassment when the riches of poetic tradition come crowding in upon him. Poets need to be selective; critics need the humility of a bad conscience when they exclude any part of the poetic past from "tradition," though humility is never much in critical fashion. Rimbaud put these matters right in one outburst: "On n'a jamais bien jugé le romantisme. Qui l'aurait jugé? Les Critiques!!"

Milton, "escap't the *Stygian* pool," hails the light he cannot see, and reaffirms his ceaseless wanderings "where the Muses haunt/clear Spring, or shady Grove," and his nightly visits to "*Sion* and the flow'ry Brooks beneath." Like Keats's nightingale, he "sings darkling," but invokes a light that can "shine inward, and the mind through all her powers/Irradiate." The light shone inward, the mind's powers were triumphant, and all the sanctities of heaven yielded to Milton's vision. For the sanctuary of Milton's psyche is his vast heterocosm, the worlds he makes and ruins. His shrine is built, not to the human soul in love, but to the human soul glorious in its solitude, sufficient, with God's aid, to seek and find its own salvation. If Keats had closed the casement, and turned inward, seeking the principle that could sustain his own soul in the darkness, perhaps he could have gone on with the first *Hyperion*, and become a very different kind of poet. He would then have courted the fate of Collins, and pursued the guiding steps of Milton only to discover the quest was:

> In vain—such bliss to one alone
> Of all the sons of soul was known,
> And Heav'n and Fancy, kindred pow'rs,
> Have now o'erturned th'inspiring bow'rs,
> Or curtain'd close such scene from ev'ry future view.

Yeats, in the eloquent simplicities of *Per Amica Silentia Lunae*, saw Keats as having "been born with that thirst for luxury common to many at the outsetting of the Romantic Movement," and thought therefore that the poet of *To Autumn* "but gave us his dream of luxury." Yeats's poets were Blake and Shelley; Keats and Wordsworth he refused to understand, for their way was not his own. His art, from *The Wanderings of Oisin* through the *Last Poems and Plays*, is founded on a rage against growing old, and a rejection of nature. The poet, he thought, could find his art only by giving way to an anti-self, which "comes but to those who are no longer deceived, whose passion is reality." Yeats was repelled by Milton, and found no place for him in *A Vision*, and certainly no poet cared so little as Milton to express himself through an anti-self. In Blake's strife of spectre and emanation, in Shelley's sense of being shadowed by the *alastor* while seeking the epipsyche, Yeats found precedent for his own quest towards Unity of Being, the poet as daimonic man taking his mask from a phase opposite to that of his own will. Like Blake and Shelley, Yeats sought certainty, but being of Shelley's phase rather than Blake's, he did not find it. The way of Negative Capability, as an answer to Milton, Yeats did not take into account; he did not conceive of a poet "certain of nothing but of the holiness of the Heart's affections and the truth of Imagination." (There is, of course, no irritable reaching after mere fact and reason in Yeats: he reached instead for everything the occult sub-imagination had knocked together in place of fact and reason. But his motive was his incapability "of being in uncertainties, mysteries, doubts," and the results are more mixed than most recent criticism will admit.)

Keats followed Wordsworth by internalizing the quest toward finding a world that answered the poet's desires, and he hoped to follow Shakespeare by making that world more than a sublime projection of his own ego. Shakespeare's greatness was not an embarrassment to Keats, but the hard victories of poetry had to be won against the more menacing values of poetic tradition. The advance beyond the *Ode to Psyche* was taken in the *Ode to a Nightingale*, where the high world within the bird's song is an expansion of the rosy sanctuary of Psyche. In this world our sense of actuality is heightened simultaneously with the widening of what Mr. Bate terms "the realm of possibility." The fear of losing actuality does not encourage the dull soil of mundane experience to quarrel with the proud forests it has fed, the nightingale's high requiem. But to be the breathing garden in which Fancy breeds his flowers is a delightful fate; to become a sod is to suffer what Belial dreaded in that moving speech Milton himself and the late C. S. Lewis have taught too many to despise.

Milton, invoking the light, made himself at one with the nightingale; Keats is deliberate in knowing constantly his own separation from the bird. What is fresh in this ode is not I think a sense of the poet's dialogue with himself; it is surprising how often the English lyric has provided such an undersong, from Spenser's *Prothalamion* to Wordsworth's *Resolution and Independence*. Keats wins freedom from tradition here by claiming so very little for the imagination in its intoxicating but harsh encounter with the reality of natural song. The poet does not accept what is as good, and he does not exile desire for what is not. Yet, for him, what is possible replaces what is not. There is no earthly paradise for poets, but there is a time of all-but-final satisfaction, the fullness of lines 35 to 58 of this ode.

I do not think that there is, before Keats, so individual a setting-forth of such a time, anywhere in poetic tradition since the Bible. The elevation of Wordsworth in *Tintern Abbey* still trembles at the border of a theophany, and so derives from a universe centered upon religious experience. The vatic gift of Shelley's self to the elements, from *Alastor* on, has its remote but genuine ancestors in the sibylline frenzies of traditions as ancient as Orphism. Blake's moments of delight come as hard-won intervals of rest from an intellectual warfare that differs little if at all from the struggles towards a revelatory awareness in Ezekiel or Isaiah, and there is no contentment in them. What Keats so greatly gives to the Romantic tradition in the *Nightingale* ode is what no poet before him had the capability of giving—the sense of the human making choice of a human self, aware of its deathly nature, and yet having the will to celebrate the imaginative richness of mortality. The *Ode to a Nightingale* is the first poem to know and declare, wholeheartedly, that death is the mother of beauty. The *Ode to Psyche* still glanced, with high good humor, at the haunted rituals of the already-written poems of heaven; the *Ode to a Nightingale* turns, almost casually, to the unwritten great poem of earth. There is nothing casual about the poem's tone, but there is a wonderful lack of self-consciousness at the poem's freedom from the past, in the poem's knowing that death, our death, is absolute and without memorial.

The same freedom from the massive beliefs and poetic stances of the past is manifested in the *Ode on a Grecian Urn*, where the consolations of the spirit are afforded merely by an artifice of eternity, and not by evidences of an order of reality wholly other than our own. Part of this poem's strength is in the deliberate vulnerability of its speaker, who contemplates a world of values he cannot appropriate for his own, although nothing in that world is antithetical to his own nature as an aspiring poet. Mr. Bate states the poem's awareness of this vulnerability: "In attempting to approach the urn in its own terms, the imagination has been led at the same time to separate itself—or the situation of man generally—still further from the urn." One is not certain that the imagination is not also separating itself from the essential poverty of man's situation in the poem's closing lines. Mr. Bate thinks we underestimate Keats's humor in the Great Odes, and he is probably right, but the humor that apparently ends the *Grecian Urn* is a grim one. The truth of art may be all of the truth our condition can apprehend, but it is not a saving truth. If this is all we need to know, it may be that no knowledge can help us. Shelley was very much a child of Miltonic tradition in affirming the moral instrumentality of the imagination; Keats is grimly free of tradition in his subtle implication of a truth that most of us learn. Poetry is not a means of good; it is, as Wallace Stevens implied, like the honey of earth that comes and goes at once, while we wait vainly for the honey of heaven.

Blake, Wordsworth, and Shelley knew in their different ways that human splendors had no sources but in the human imagination, but each of these great innovators had a religious temperament, however heterodox, and Keats had not. Keats had a clarity in his knowledge of the uniqueness and finality of human life and death that caused him a particular anguish on his own death-bed, but gave him, before that, the imagination's gift of an absolute originality. The power of Keats's imagination could never be identified by him with an apocalyptic energy that might hope to transform nature. It is not that he lacked the confidence of Blake and of Shelley, or of the momentary Wordsworth of *The Recluse*. He felt the imagination's desire for a revelation that would redeem the inadequacies of our condition, but he felt also a humorous skepticism toward such desire. He would have read the prose testament of Wallace Stevens, *Two Or Three Ideas*, with the wry approval so splendid a lecture deserves. The gods are dispelled in mid-air, and leave "no texts either of the soil or of the soul." The poet does not cry out for their return, since it remains his work to resolve life in his own terms, for in the poet is "the increasingly human self."

Part of Keats's achievement is due then to his being perhaps the only genuine forerunner of the representative post-Romantic sensibility. Another part is centered in the *Ode on Melancholy* and *The Fall of Hyperion*, for in these poems consciousness becomes its own purgatory, and the poet learns the cost of living in an excitement of which he affirms "that it is the only state for the best sort of Poetry—that is all I care for, all I live for." From this declaration it is a direct way to the generally misunderstood rigor of Pater, when he insists that "a counted number of pulses only is given to us of a variegated, dramatic life," and asks: "How may we see in them all that is to be seen in them by the finest senses?" Moneta, Keats's veiled Melancholy, counted those pulses, while the poet waited, rapt in an apprehension attainable only by the finest senses, nearly betrayed by those senses to an even more premature doom than his destined one. What links together *The Fall of Hyperion* and its modern descendants like Stevens's *Notes toward a Supreme Fiction* is the movement of impressions set forth by Pater, when analysis of the self yields to the poet's recognition of how dangerously fine the self's existence has become. "It is with this movement, with the passage and dissolution of impressions, images, sensations, that analysis leaves off— that continual vanishing away, that strange, perpetual weaving and unweaving of ourselves."

Though there is a proud laughter implicit in the *Ode on Melancholy*, the poem courts tragedy, and again makes death the mother of beauty. Modern criticism has confounded Pater with his weaker disciples, and has failed to realize how truly Yeats and Stevens are in his tradition. The *Ode on Melancholy* is ancestor to what is strongest in Pater, and to what came after in his tradition of aesthetic humanism. Pater's "Conclusion" to *The Renaissance* lives in the world of the *Ode on Melancholy*:

> Great passions may give us this quickened sense of life, ecstasy and sorrow of love, the various forms of enthusiastic activity, disinterested or otherwise, which come naturally to many of us. Only be sure it is passion—that it does yield you this fruit of a quickened, multiplied consciousness.

The wakeful anguish of the soul comes to the courter of grief in the very shrine of pleasure, and the renovating powers of art yield the tragedy of their might only to a strenuous and joyful seeker. Keats's problem in *The Fall of Hyperion* was to find again the confidence of Milton as to the oneness of his self and theme, but with nothing of the Miltonic conviction that God had worked to fit that self and theme together. The shrines of pleasure and of melancholy become one shrine in the second *Hyperion*, and in that ruin the poet must meet the imaginative values of tradition without their attendant credences, for Moneta guards the temple of all the dead faiths.

Moneta humanizes her sayings to our ears, but not until a poet's courteous dialectic has driven her to question her own categories for mankind. When she softens, and parts the veils for Keats, she reveals his freedom from the greatness of poetic tradition, for the vision granted has the quality of a new universe, and a tragedy different in kind from the tragedy of the past:

Then saw I a wan face,
Not pined by human sorrows, but bright-blanch'd
By an immortal sickness which kills not;
It works a constant change, which happy death
Can put no end to; deathwards progressing
To no death was that visage; it had pass'd
The lily and the snow; and beyond these
I must not think now, though I saw that face.
But for her eyes I should have fled away.
They held me back with a benignant light,
Soft mitigated by divinest lids
Half closed, and visionless entire they seem'd
Of all external things—

Frank Kermode finds this passage a prime instance of his "Romantic Image," and believes Moneta's face to be "alive only in a chill and inhuman way," yet Keats is held back from such a judgment by the eyes of his Titaness, for they give forth "a benignant light," as close to the saving light Milton invokes as Keats can ever get. Moneta has little to do with the Yeatsian concept of the poetic vision, for she does not address herself to the alienation of the poet. M. H. Abrams, criticizing Mr. Kermode, points to her emphasis on the poet as humanist, made restless by the miseries of mankind. Shelley's Witch of Atlas, for all her playfulness, has more to do with Yeats's formulation of the coldness of the Muse.

Moneta is the Muse of mythopoeia, like Shelley's Witch, but she contains the poetic and religious past, as Shelley's capricious Witch does not. Taking her in a limited sense (since she incarnates so much more than this), Moneta does represent the embarrassments of poetic tradition, a greatness it is death to approach. Moneta's perspective is close to that of the Rilkean Angel, and for Keats to share that perspective he would have to cease to depend on the visible. Moneta's is a perfect consciousness; Keats is committed still to the oxymoronic intensities of experience, and cannot un-perplex joy from pain. Moneta's is a world beyond tragedy; Keats needs to be a tragic poet. Rilke dedicated himself to the task of describing a world regarded no longer from a human point of view, but as it is within the angel. Moneta, like this angel, does not regard external things, and again like Rilke's angel she both comforts and terrifies. Keats, like Stevens, fears the angelic imposition of any order upon reality, and hopes to discover a possible order in the human and the natural, even if that order be only the cyclic rhythm of tragedy. Stevens's definitive discovery is in the final sections of *Notes toward a Supreme Fiction*; Keats's similar fulfillment is in his perfect poem, *To Autumn*.

The achievement of definitive vision in *To Autumn* is more remarkable for the faint presence of the shadows of the poet's hell that the poem tries to exclude. Mr. Bate calls the *Lines to Fanny* (written, like *To Autumn*, in October 1819) "somewhat jumbled as well as tired and flat," but its nightmare projection of the imagination's inferno has a singular intensity, and I think considerable importance:

> Where shall I learn to get my peace again?
> To banish thoughts of that most hateful land,
> Dungeoner of my friends, that wicked strand
> Where they were wreck'd and live a wrecked life;
> That monstrous region, whose dull rivers pour,
> Ever from their sordid urns unto the shore,
> Unown'd of any weedy-haired gods;
> Whose winds, all zephyrless, hold scourging rods,
> Iced in the great lakes, to afflict mankind;
> Whose rank-grown forests, frosted, black, and blind,
> Would fright a Dryad; whose harsh herbag'd meads
> Make lean and lank the starv'd ox while he feeds;
> There flowers have no scent, birds no sweet song,
> And great unerring Nature once seems wrong.

This may have begun as a fanciful depiction of an unknown America, where Keats's brother and sister-in-law were suffering, yet it develops into a vision akin to Blake's of the world of experience, with its lakes of menace and its forests of error. The moss-lain Dryads lulled to sleep in the forests of the poet's mind in his *Ode to Psyche*, can find no home in this natural world. This is Keats's version of the winter vision, the more powerful for being so unexpected, and clearly a torment to its seer, who imputes error to Nature even as he pays it his sincere and accustomed homage.

It is this waste land that the auroras of Keats's *To Autumn* transform into a landscape of perfection process. Does another lyric in the language meditate more humanly "the full of fortune and the full of fate"? The question is the attentive reader's necessary and generous tribute; the critical answer may be allowed to rest with Mr. Bate, who is moved to make the finest of claims for the poem: "Here at last is something of a genuine paradise." The paradise of poets bequeathed to Keats by tradition is gone; a tragic paradise of naturalistic completion and mortal acceptance has taken its place.

There are other Romantic freedoms won from the embarrassments of poetic tradition, usually through the creation of new myth, as in Blake and Shelley, or in the thematic struggle not to create a myth, as in the earlier work of Wordsworth and Coleridge. Keats found his dangerous freedom by pursuing the naturalistic implications of the poet's relation to his own poem, and nothing is more refreshing in an art so haunted by aspirations to surpass or negate nature. Shelley, still joined to Keats in the popular though not the critical consciousness, remains the best poet to read in counterpoint to the Great Odes and *The Fall of Hyperion*. There is no acceptance in Shelley, no tolerance for the limits of reality, but only the outrageous desire never to cease desiring, the unflagging intensity that goes on until it is stopped, and never is stopped. Keats did what Milton might have done but was not concerned to do; he perfected an image in which stasis and process are reconciled, and made of autumn the most human of seasons in consequence. Shelley's ode to autumn is his paean to the West Wind, where a self-destroying swiftness is invoked for the sake of dissolving all stasis permanently, and for hastening process past merely natural fulfillment into apocalyptic renewal. Whether the great winter of the world can be relieved by any ode Keats tended to doubt, and we are right to doubt with him, but there is a hope wholly natural in us that no doubt dispels, and it is of this hope that Shelley is the unique and indispensable poet.

WALTER JACKSON BATE

Negative Capability

The "Negative Capability" letter is best understood as a phrasing and extension of several thoughts, with at least three further extensions. First, the problem of form or style in art enters more specifically. Second, the ideal toward which he is groping is contrasted more strongly with the egoistic assertion of one's own identity. Third, the door is further opened to the perception—which he was to develop within the next few months—of the sympathetic potentialities of the imagination.

He begins by telling his brothers that he has gone to see Edmund Kean, has written his review, and is enclosing it for them. Then on Saturday, December 20, he went to see an exhibition of the American painter, Benjamin West, particularly his picture, "Death on the Pale Horse." Keats was altogether receptive to any effort to attain the "sublime," and West's painting had been praised for succeeding. Yet it struck Keats as flat— "there is nothing to be intense upon; no women one feels mad to kiss; no face swelling into reality." Then the first crucial statement appears:

> The excellence of every Art is its intensity, capable of making all disagree-
> ables evaporate, from their being in close relationship with Beauty &
> Truth—Examine King Lear & you will find this exemplified throughout;
> but in this picture we have unpleasantness without any momentous depth
> of speculation excited, in which to bury its repulsiveness.

In the active cooperation or full "greeting" of the experiencing imagination and its object, the nature or "identity" of the object is grasped so vividly that only those associations and qualities that are strictly relevant to the central conception remain. The irrelevant and discordant (the "disagree-ables") "evaporate" from this fusion of object and mind. Hence "Truth" and "Beauty" spring simultaneously into being, and also begin to approximate each other. For, on the one hand, the external reality—otherwise over-looked, or at most only sleepily acknowledged, or dissected so that a particular aspect of it may be abstracted for special purposes of argument or thought—has now, as it were, awakened into "Truth": it has been met by that human recognition, fulfilled and extended by that human agreement with reality, which we call "truth." And at the same time, with the irrelevant "evaporated," this dawning into unity is felt as "Beauty." Nor is it a unity solely of the object itself, emerging untrammeled and in its full significance, but a unity also of the human spirit, both within itself and with what was at first outside it. For in this "intensity"—the "excellence," he now feels, "of every Art"—we attain, if only for a while, a harmony of the inner life with truth. It is in this harmony that "Beauty" and "Truth" come together. The "pleasant," in the ordinary sense of the word, has nothing to do with the point being discussed; and to introduce it is only to trivialize the conception of "Beauty." Hence Keats's reference to *Lear*. The reality disclosed may be distressing and even cruel to human nature. But the harmony with truth will remain, and even deepen, to the extent that the emerging reality is being constantly matched at every stage by the "depth of speculation excited"—by the corresponding release and extension, in other words, of human insight. "Examine King Lear and you will find this exemplified throughout."

Hazlitt's short essay "On Gusto" had aroused his thinking about style when he read it at Oxford in the *Round Table*; and what he is saying now is partly the result of what he has assimilated from Hazlitt. By "gusto," Hazlitt means an excitement of the imagination in which the perceptive identifica-tion with the object is almost complete, and the living character of the object is caught and shared in its full diversity and given vital expression in art. It is "power or passion defining any object." But the result need not be subjective. By grasping sympathetically the overall significance of the object, the "power or passion" is able to cooperate, so to speak, with that significance—to go the full distance with its potentialities, omitting the irrelevant (which Keats calls the "disagreeables"), and conceiving the object with its various qualities coalescing into the vital unity that is the object itself. One result is that the attributes or qualities that we glean through our different senses of sight, hearing, touch, and the rest are not presented separately or piecemeal, but "the impression made on one sense excites by affinity those of another." Thus Claude Lorrain's landscapes, through "perfect abstractions of the visible images of things," lack "gusto": "They do not interpret one sense by another. . . . That is, his eye wanted imagination;

it did not strongly sympathise with his other faculties. He saw the atmosphere, but he did not feel it." Chaucer's descriptions of natural scenery have gusto: they give "the very feeling of the air, the coolness or moisture of the ground." "There is gusto in the colouring of Titian. Not only do his heads seem to think—his bodies seem to feel."

II

This interplay and coalescence of impressions was to become a conscious aim in Keats's own poetry within the next six months and, by the following autumn, to be fulfilled as richly as by any English poet of the last three centuries. Meanwhile, only a few days before he wrote the "Negative Capability" letter to his brothers, he had followed Hazlitt's use of the word "gusto" in his own review "On Edmund Kean as a Shakesperian Actor" (though he later returns to the word "intensity"—"gusto" perhaps suggesting a briskness or bounce of spirit he does not have in mind). He had been trying in this review to describe how "a melodious passage in poetry" may attain a fusion of "both sensual and spiritual," where each extends and declares itself by means of the other:

> The spiritual is felt when the very letters and points of charactered language show like the hieroglyphics of beauty;—the mysterious signs of an immortal free-masonry!...To one learned in Shakespearian hieroglyphics,—learned in the spiritual portion of those lines to which Kean adds a sensual grandeur: his tongue must seem to have robbed "the Hybla bees, and left them honeyless."

Hence "there is an indescribable gusto in his voice, by which we feel that the utterer is thinking of the past and future, while speaking of the present."

Keats is here extending the notion of "gusto" in a way that applies prophetically to his own maturer style—to an imaginative "intensity" of conception, that is, in which process, though slowed to an insistent present, is carried in active solution. So with the lines he had quoted a month before to Reynolds as an example of Shakespeare's "intensity of working out conceits":

> When lofty trees I see barren of leaves
> Which erst from heat did canopy the herd,
> And Summer's green all girded up in sheaves,
> Borne on the bier with white and bristly beard.

Previous functions, and the mere fact of loss itself, are a part of the truth of a thing as it now is. The nature of the "lofty trees" in this season, now "barren of leaves," includes the fact that they formerly "from heat did canopy the herd"; nor is it only the dry, completed gain of the autumn that is "girded up in sheaves," but the "Summer's green" that it once was. This entire way of thinking about style is proving congenial to Keats in the highest degree; for though it has independent developments, it has also touched and is giving content to the ideal briefly suggested a year before in *Sleep and Poetry*—even before he saw the Elgin Marbles for the first time: an ideal of poetry as "might half slumb'ring on its own right arm." The delight in energy caught in momentary repose goes back to the idea he had "when a Schoolboy . . . of an heroic painting": "I saw it somewhat sideways," he tells Haydon, "large prominent round and colour'd with magnificence— somewhat like the feel I have of Anthony and Cleopatra. Or of Alcibiades, leaning on his Crimson Couch in his Galley, his broad shoulders impercep- tibly heaving with the Sea." So with the line in *Henry VI*, "See how the surly Warwick mans the Wall." One of the comments he wrote in his copy of Milton during the next year gives another illustration:

> Milton in every instance pursues his imagination to the utmost—he is "sagacious of his Quarry," he sees Beauty on the wing, pounces upon it and gorges it to the producing his essential verse. . . . But in no instance is this sort of perseverance more exemplified than in what may be called his *stationing or statu[a]ry*. He is not content with simple description, he must station,—thus here, we not only see how the Birds *"with clang despised the ground,"* but we see them *"under a cloud in prospect."* So we see Adam *"Fair indeed and tall—under a plantane"*—and so we see Satan *"disfigured—on the Assyrian Mount."*

The union of the ideal of dynamic poise, of power kept in reserve, with the ideal of range of implication suggests one principal development in his own style throughout the next year and a half. The very triumph of this union—as triumphs often tend to do—could have proved an embarrassment to later ideals and interests had it become an exclusive stylistic aim. However magnificent the result in the great odes, in portions of *Hyperion*, or in what Keats called the "colouring" and "drapery" of *The Eve of St. Agnes*, it carried liabilities in both pace and variety that would have to be circum- vented for successful narrative and, above all, dramatic poetry. But even at the moment, and throughout the next year, what he calls "intensity"—the "greeting of the Spirit" and its object—is by no means completely wedded to a massive centering of image through poise and "stationing." If his instinc- tive delight in fullness was strengthened in one direction by the Elgin Marbles—which he still made visits to see—other, more varied appeals to his ready empathy were being opened and reinforced by his reading of Shake- speare.

III

The second and longer of the crucial parts of the "Negative Capability" letter is preceded by some more remarks about what he has been doing since his brothers left, and the remarks provide a significant preface. He had dinner—"I have been out too much lately"—with "Horace Smith & met his two Brothers with [Thomas] Hill & [John] Kingston & one [Edward] Du Bois."

Partly because he himself was so direct and—as Bailey said— "transparent," he was ordinarily tolerant of the more innocent affectations by which people hope to establish superiority. Moreover, such affectations appealed to his enormous relish for the idiosyncratic. As the next year passed, the very futility of such brief postures—the pointless intricacy of these doomed stratagems—against the vast backdrop of a universe of constantly unfolding "uncertainties, Mysteries, doubts," was also to take on a pathos for him. . . .

So at Horace Smith's dinner, which he describes to George and Tom, where he met five other men of literary interests. Their entire way of talking about literature fatigued him for the moment. The possible uses of literature seemed frozen into posture, into mannerism. Given his attempts to approach his new ideal of "disinterestedness," and the thoughts of "Humility" and of openness to amplitude that had become more specific, even more convinced, within the last few months, the gathering typified the exact opposite of what was wanted:

> They only served to convince me, how superior humour is to wit in respect to enjoyment—These men say things which make one start, without making one feel, they are all alike; their manners are alike; they all know fashionable; they have a mannerism in their very eating & drinking, in their mere handling a Decanter—They talked of Kean & his low company—Would I were with that company instead of yours said I to myself! I know such like acquaintance will never do for me.

But his humor was to return when he found himself again in Kingston's company at Haydon's a week and a half afterwards. The "mannerism" in the "mere handling a Decanter" had caught his fancy as a symbol of the entire evening. At Haydon's, as he gleefully told George and Tom, "I astonished Kingston at supper. . . keeping my two glasses at work in a knowing way."

Shortly after Smith's literary party, he went to the Christmas pantomime at Drury Lane with Charles Brown and Charles Dilke. Walking with them back, to Hampstead, he found himself having

> not a dispute but a disquisition with Dilke, on various subjects; several things dovetailed in my mind, & at once it struck me, what quality went to form a Man of Achievement especially in Literature & which Shake-

speare possessed so enormously—I mean *Negative Capability*, that is when man is capable of being in uncertainties, Mysteries, doubts, without any irritable reaching after fact & reason—Coleridge, for instance, would let go by a fine isolated verisimilitude caught from the Penetralium of mystery, from being incapable of remaining content with half knowledge. This pursued through Volumes would perhaps take us no further than this, that with a great poet the sense of Beauty overcomes every other consideration, or rather obliterates all consideration.

Using what we know of the background, we could paraphrase these famous sentences as follows. In our life of uncertainties, where no one system or formula can explain everything—where even a word is at best, in Bacon's phrase, a "wager of thought"—what is needed is an imaginative openness of mind and heightened receptivity to reality in its full and diverse concreteness. This, however, involves negating one's own ego. Keats's friend Dilke, as he said later, "was a Man who cannot feel he has a personal identity unless he has made up his Mind about every thing. The only means of strengthening one's intellect is to make up one's mind about nothing—to let the mind be a thoroughfare for all thoughts. . . . Dilke will never come at a truth as long as he lives; because he is always trying at it." To be dissatisfied with such insights as one may attain through this openness, to reject them unless they can be wrenched into a part of a systematic structure of one's own making, is an egoistic assertion of one's own identity. The remark, "without any irritable reaching after fact and reason," is often cited as though the pejorative words are "fact and reason," and as though uncertainties were being preferred for their own sake. But the significant word, of course, is "irritable." We should also stress "capable"—"capable of being in uncertainties, Mysteries, doubts" without the "irritable" need to extend our identities and rationalize our "half knowledge." For a "great poet" especially, a sympathetic absorption in the essential significance of his object (caught and relished in that active cooperation of the mind in which the emerging "Truth" is felt as "Beauty," and in which the harmony of the human imagination and its object is attained) "overcomes every other consideration" (considerations that an "irritable reaching after fact and reason" might otherwise itch to pursue). Indeed, it goes beyond and "obliterates" the act of "consideration"—of deliberating, analyzing, and piecing experience together through "consequitive reasoning."

IV

Such speculations could hardly be called more than a beginning. Taken by themselves they could lead almost anywhere. That, of course, was one of their principal assets. Even so, the need for at least some specific and positive procedures, helpful at any period of life, is particularly pressing at twenty-two. Keats understandably wavered throughout the next few months in trying to interpret whatever premises he had attained thus far—premises that were hardly more than the penumbra of the idea of "disinterestedness" as it touched his concrete experience. Such shadows at least involved extensions of a sort; and the thought of this was to give him some consolation as time passed.

But meanwhile he had moments when something close to mere passivity appealed strongly; and the image of the receptive flower, visited and fertilized by the bee, caught his fancy. The relentless labor of writing *Endymion* was producing a natural reaction. Insights, reconsiderations, "speculations" (to use his own word) overlooked during that huge scurry, were now presenting themselves more abundantly than ever before. Because the gains in having written the poem were becoming assimilated, they were at times almost forgotten. Slow development, maturity, rooted strength, leisure for growth, took on a further attraction. But in the very act of urging eloquently—and justly—the virtues of something not far from Wordsworth's "wise passiveness" the limitations would suddenly disclose themselves to him. He would begin to feel that this was not what he meant, or wanted, at all. At least it was not enough by itself. A letter to John Reynolds (February 19) finely illustrates the course of one "speculation." He starts with a now-favorite thought of his that any one point may serve as a fruitful beginning. A man could "pass a very pleasant life" if he sat down each day and

> read a certain Page of full Poesy or distilled Prose and let him wander with it, and muse upon it, and reflect from it and bring home to it, and prophesy upon it, and dream upon it—untill it becomes stale—but when will it do so? Never—When Man has arrived at a certain ripeness in intellect any one grand and spiritual passage serves him as a starting post towards all "the two-and-thirty Pallaces."

The result would be a genuine "voyage of conception." A doze on the sofa, a child's prattle, a strain of music, even "a nap upon Clover," could all engender "ethereal finger-pointings." It would have the impetus, the strength, of being self-directive. "Many have original Minds who do not think it—they are led away by Custom." The insight, substantiated by his own experience, leads him next to turn upside down the old fable of the spider and the bee, especially as Swift used it. The appeal of the spider as a symbol is that the points of leaves and twigs on which it begins its work can be very few, and yet it is able to fill the air with a "circuiting." "Now it appears to me that almost any Man may like the Spider spin from his own inwards his own airy Citadel," which will then be creatively meaningful—it will be "full of Symbols for his spiritual eye." Of course his starting-points, his "circuiting," and the achieved "space for his wandering," would all differ from that of others. If we wish to be militant, complications would result. Here Keats comes to the heart of his thought:

> The Minds of Mortals are so different and bent on such diverse Journeys that it may at first appear impossible for any common taste and fellowship to exist between two or three under these suppositions—It is however quite the contrary—Minds would leave each other in contrary directions, traverse each other in Numberless points, and all [at] last greet each other at the Journey's end—An old Man and a child would talk together and the old Man be led on his Path, and the child left thinking—Man should not dispute or assert but whisper results to his neighbour, and thus by every germ of Spirit sucking the Sap from mould ethereal every human might become great, and Humanity instead of being a wide heath of Furse and Briars with here and there a remote Oak or Pine, would become a grand democracy of Forest Trees.

At no later time would he have disagreed with what he has just said. But he carries the ideal of receptivity further in sentences that are sometimes separated from context and interpreted as a new, fundamental credo:

> It has been an old Comparison for our urging on—the Bee hive—however it seems to me that we should rather be the flower than the Bee . . . Now it is more noble to sit like Jove tha[n] to fly like Mercury—let us not therefore go hurrying about and collecting honey-bee like, buzzing here and there impatiently from a knowledge of what is to be arrived at: but let us open our leaves like a flower and be passive and receptive—budding patiently under the eye of Apollo and taking hints from every noble insect that favors us with a visit.

In this spirit he has just written the fine unrhymed sonnet, "What the Thrush Said," with its refrain "O fret not after knowledge." He had been "led into these thoughts . . . by the beauty of the morning operating on a sense of Idleness—I have not read any Books—the Morning said I was right—I had no Idea but of the Morning and the Thrush said I was right."

But as soon as he copies the poem for Reynolds, he becomes "sensible all this is a mere sophistication, however it may neighbour to any truths, to excuse my own indolence." There is not much chance of rivaling Jove anyway, and one can consider oneself "very well off as a sort of scullion-Mercury or even a humble Bee." Two days later he also tells his brothers that "The Thrushes are singing"; but he himself is now "reading Voltaire and Gibbon, although I wrote to Reynolds the other day to prove reading was of no use."

V

Wherever the more general implications might lead, he was clearer and more certain in his growing interest in the impersonality of genius, "especially in Literature." For here the ideal of "disinterestedness" directly touched an internal fund both of native gift and (considering his age) accumulated experience.

What strikes us most in his capacity for sympathetic identification, starting with the schooldays at Enfield, is its inclusiveness. This is not the volatile empathic range of even the rare actor. For the range is vertical as well as horizontal, and is distinguished more by an adhesive purchase of mind than by volubility. He might, in describing the bearbaiting to Clarke, instinctively begin to imitate not only the spectators but the bear, "dabbing his fore paws hither and thither," and, in diagnosing Clarke's stomach complaint and comparing the stomach to a brood of baby-birds "gaping for sustenance," automatically open his own "capacious mouth." But empathic expressions of this sort were mere side effects—like the self-forgetful fights at Enfield—of an habitual capacity for identification that went deeper. When he picked up styles in the writing of poetry, it was not as a mimic or copyist but as a fellow participator identified even more with the other's aim and ideal than with the individual himself. If, when still a student at Guy's Hospital, he caught elements of Felton Mathew's style, he dignified them; and the result, poor as it is, transcends anything Mathew wrote. So later with Hunt. Except at the very start, and except for a few isolated passages afterwards, we have nothing of the routine mechanism of a copy. If anything, he brings Hunt more to life. Still later, in *Hyperion*, he was to write within little more than two or three months the only poem among all the Miltonic imitations in English that Milton himself might not have been ashamed to write.

Discussion of these larger manifestations would lead to a summary of his entire development as illustration. We can, however, linger for a moment on his delight in empathic imagery itself. For here, quickly and vividly, his ready sympathy appears long before anyone could have called his attention to such a thing or given him a vocabulary with which to describe it. We think back to Clarke's account of the lines and images that most caught Keats's imagination when they first read together at Enfield. Doubtless feeling the weight of the parting billows on his own shoulders, he "*hoisted himself up, and looked burly and dominant*, as he said, 'what an image that is—*sea-shouldering whales.*' " Much later there was the memorable introduction to Chapman's Homer, and the passage in the shipwreck of Ulysses that brought "one of his delighted stares": "Down he sank to death. / The sea had soak'd his heart through." His reading of Shakespeare, now that he was about to write with less sense of hurry, was beginning to encourage his gift for empathic concentration of image; and within two years this was to develop to a degree hardly rivaled since Shakespeare himself. Among the passages he excitedly copied out for Reynolds, a month before the "Negative Capability" letter, is the description of the trembling withdrawal of a snail into its shell:

> He has left nothing to say about nothing or any thing: for look at Snails, you know what he says about Snails, you know where he talks about "cockled snails"—well . . . this is in the Venus and Adonis: the Simile brought it to my Mind.

> Audi—As the snail, whose tender horns being hit,
> Shrinks back into his shelly cave with pain,
>   And there all smothered up in shade doth sit,
>   Long after fearing to put forth again.

So with the comment he later wrote in his copy of *Paradise Lost* (IX. 179–191):

> Satan having entered the Serpent, and inform'd his brutal sense—might seem sufficient—but Milton goes on *"but his sleep disturb'd not."* Whose spirit does not ache at the smothering and confinement—the unwilling stillness—the *"waiting close"?* Whose head is not dizzy at the possible speculations of satan in his serpent prison—no passage of poetry ever can give a greater pain of suffocation.

Finally, before turning to the impact of Hazlitt, we may glance back a few months to Severn's account of his walks with Keats on Hampstead Heath during the preceding summer, while Keats was still working on Book II of *Endymion*. Nothing could bring him so quickly out of "one of his fits of seeming gloomful reverie" as his vivid identification with organic motion in what he called "the inland sea"—the movement of the wind across a field of grain. He "would stand, leaning forward," watching with a "serene look in his eyes and sometimes with a slight smile." At other times, "when 'a wave was billowing through a tree,' as he described the uplifting surge of air among swaying masses of chestnut or oak foliage," or when he could hear in the distance "the wind coming across woodlands,"

> "The tide! the tide!" he would cry delightedly, and spring on to some stile, or upon the low bough of a wayside tree, and watch the passage of the wind upon the meadow-grass or young corn, not stirring till the flow of air was all around him.

Severn, who tended rather toward revery and vagueness, was repeatedly "astonished" at the closeness with which Keats would notice details, until Severn himself began to catch a little of it:

Nothing seemed to escape him, the song of a bird and the undertone of response from covert or hedge, the rustle of some animal, the changing of the green and brown lights and furtive shadows, the motions of the wind—just how it took certain tall flowers and plants—and the wayfaring of the clouds: even the features and gestures of passing tramps, the colour of one woman's hair, the smile on one child's face, the furtive animalism below the deceptive humanity in many of the vagrants, even the hats, clothes, shoes, wherever these conveyed the remotest hint as to the real self of the wearer.

Severn's notice of Keats's delight in whatever conveyed "the remotest hint as to the real self of the wearer" carries us forward to the Chaucerian relish of character that we find increasingly in the longer letters and even in the mere underlinings and marginal notes of Keats's reading. "Scenery is fine," he writes to Bailey (March 13, 1818), "but human nature is finer—The Sward is richer for the tread of a real, nervous [E]nglish foot." Reading a month or so later in an old copy (1634) of Mateo Aleman's *The Rogue: or, the Life of Guzman de Alfarache*, which James Rice had just given him, he underlines the words, "his voice lowd and shrill but not very cleere," and writes in the margin: "This puts me in mind of Fielding's Fanny 'whose teeth were white but uneven'; it is the same sort of personality. The great Man in this way is Chaucer."

VI

A fairly large internal fund was thus available to be tapped when Keats read, undoubtedly at Bailey's suggestion, Hazlitt's *Essay on the Principles of Human Action*, and bought a copy that was still in his library at his death.

Hazlitt's aim in this short book—his first published work—was to refute the contention of Thomas Hobbes and his eighteenth century followers that self-love, in one way or another, is the mainspring of all human action, and to prove instead, as the subtitle states, "the Natural Disinterest-edness of the Human Mind." Since British philosophy for a century had devoted more speculation to this problem than to any other, Hazlitt's youthful aim was quite ambitious (he began the book in his early twenties, and was twenty-seven when it appeared). His procedure was ingenious, and to some extent original. Moralists trying to disprove Hobbes had for fifty years or more been stressing the sympathetic potentialities of the imagina-tion. Adam Smith's influential *Theory of Moral Sentiments* (1759) is the best-known example. The interest spread to the critical theory of the arts; and well over a century before German psychology developed the theory of *Einfühlung*—for which the word "empathy" was later coined as a translation—English critical theory had anticipated many of the insights involved. It was the peculiar fate of many psychological discoveries of the English eighteenth century to be forgotten from the 1830s until the hungry theorization of the German universities in the late nineteenth century led to a rediscovery and a more systematized and subjective interpretation.

In his *Principles of Human Action*, Hazlitt went much further than Adam Smith's *Theory of Moral Sentiments*. His hope was to show that imaginative sympathy was not a mere escape hatch from the prison of egocentricity, but something thoroughgoing, something indigenous and inseparable from all activities of the mind. Sympathetic identification takes place constantly—even if only with ourselves and our own desired future. Hazlitt's psychology, in effect, is a more dynamic version of Locke's. Instead of the image of the mind as a *tabula rasa* on which experience writes, we have an image of it as something more actively adhesive and projective: equally dependent on what is outside itself for its own coloration, so to speak, but actively uniting with its objects, growing, dwindling, even becoming poisoned, by what it assimilates. Hazlitt's argument turns on the nature of "identity." Suppose that I love myself in the thoroughgoing way that the Hobbists claim—that everything I do, or plan, or hope, is in order to help myself or avoid pain in the future: that even what we call generous acts are done solely (as the Hobbists maintained) because I wish to be praised, or because I wish to get along with others, or because I wish—at least—to be able to live with myself. But how can I know, how especially can I "love," this "identity" that I consider myself? If we look at the problem with empirical honesty, we have to admit that any feeling we have that we are one person, the same person, from one moment to the next (that we have, in short, an "identity") comes directly through two means only—"sensation" and "memory." A child who has burned his finger knows only through "sensation" that it is he and not someone else who has done so. In a similar way, he knows only through "memory" that it was he and not someone else who had this experience in the past. If our identities until now depend on sensation and memory, what can give me an interest in my future sensations? Sensation and memory are not enough. I can picture my future identity only through my *imagination*. The child who has been burned will dread the prospect of future pain from the fire because, through his imagination, he "projects himself forward into the future, and identifies himself with his future being." His imagination "creates" his own future to him.

In short, I can "abstract myself from my present being and take an interest in my future being [only] in the same sense and manner, in which I can go out of myself entirely and enter into the minds and feelings of others." The capacity for imaginative identification, in other words, is not instinctively or mechanically obliged to turn in one direction rather than another: the sole means by which "I can anticipate future objects, or be interested in them," throwing "me forward as it were into my future being" and anticipating events that do not yet exist, is equally able to "carry me out of myself into the feelings of others by one and the same process . . . I could not love myself, if I were not capable of loving others." If stronger ideas than those of one's own identity are present to the mind, the imagination can turn more easily to them. Hazlitt here develops the belief of the association-ist psychologists of the time, in whom he was widely read, that the mind instinctively follows and "imitates" what is before it. . . .

The argument for "the natural disinterestedness of the mind" is not, of course, that most people are really disinterested, but that there is no mechanical determinism, such as Hobbes and his followers assumed, toward self-love. The disinterestedness exists as far as the *potential* development of the mind is concerned. Knowledge can direct and habituate the imagination to ideas other than that of our own identity. We commonly see that long acquaintance with another increases our sympathy, provided undesirable qualities in the other person, or sheer monotony, do not work against it. If the child is unsympathetic to others, it is not from automatic self-love but because of lack of knowledge—a lack that also prevents him from identifying himself very successfully with his own future interests. Greatness in art, philosophy, moral action—the "heroic" in any sense—involves losing the sense of "our personal identity in some object dearer to us than ourselves."

VII

Less than three weeks after Keats wrote the "Negative Capability" letter to his brothers around Christmastime, Hazlitt began a course of lectures at the Surrey Institution, just south of Blackfriars Bridge, every Tuesday evening at seven o'clock. These were the famous *Lectures on the English Poets,* the first of which was on January 13 and the last on March 3. Keats looked forward to hearing them all, and, as far as we know, missed only one ("On Chaucer and Spenser," January 20), when he arrived too late. A few sentences at the start of the third lecture, "On Shakespeare and Milton" (January 27), which Keats told Bailey he definitely planned to attend, may have especially struck him. Shakespeare, said Hazlitt,

> was the least of an egotist that it was possible to be. He was nothing in himself; but he was all that others were, or that they could become. He not only had in himself the germs of every faculty and feeling, but he could follow them by anticipation, intuitively, into all their conceivable ramifica-tions, through every change of fortune, or conflict of passion, or turn of thought. . . . He had only to think of anything in order to become that thing, with all the circumstances belonging to it.

By contrast, much modern poetry seems to have become engaged in a competition to "reduce" itself "to a mere effusion of natural sensibility," surrounding "the meanest objects with the morbid feelings and devouring egotism of the writers' own minds."

The immediate effect of Hazlitt's lectures was to open Keats's eyes much sooner than would otherwise have happened to the limitations of the prevailing modes of poetry—limitations that were far from obvious to most writers until a full century had run its course. But the ideal of the "characterless" poet, touching as it did qualities and habits of response intrinsic to himself, gradually took a secure hold of his imagination throughout the months ahead, though still later it was to appear to him as something of an oversimplification. The extent to which it became domesticated in his habitual thinking is shown by a letter the following autumn, at the beginning of the astonishing year (October 1818 to October 1819) when his greatest poetry was written. He is writing to Richard Woodhouse (October 27):

> As to the poetical Character itself (I mean that sort of which, if I am anything, I am a Member; that sort distinguished from the wordsworthian or egotistical sublime; which is a thing per se and stands alone) it is not itself—it has no self—it is everything and nothing—It has no character—it enjoys light and shade; it lives in gusto, be it foul or fair, high or low, rich or poor, mean or elevated—It has as much delight in conceiving an Iago as an Imogen. What shocks the virtuous philosop[h]er, delights the camelion Poet. It does no harm from its relish of the dark side of things any more than from its taste for the bright one; because they both end in speculation. A Poet is the most unpoetical of any thing in existence; because he has no Identity—he is continually in for—and filling some other Body—The Sun, the Moon, the Sea and Men and Women who are creatures of impulse are poetical and have about them an unchangeable attribute—the poet has none; no identity—he is certainly the most unpoetical of all God's Creatures.... When I am in a room with People if I ever am free from speculating on creations of my own brain, then not myself goes home to myself: but the identity of every one in the room begins to press upon me [so] that I am in a very little time annihilated—not only among Men; it would be the same in a Nursery of children.

Woodhouse, who by now had acquired a close knowledge of Keats, found these remarks a good description of Keats's own bent of mind, and wrote to John Taylor,

> I believe him to be right with regard to his own Poetical Character—And I perceive clearly the distinction between himself & those of the Wordsworth School.... The highest order of Poet will not only possess all the above powers but will have [so] high an imag^n that he will be able to throw his own soul into any object he sees or imagines, so as to see feel be sensible of, & express, all that the object itself wo^d see feel be sensible of or

express—& he will speak out of that object—so that his own self will with the Exception of the Mechanical part be "annihilated."—and it is [of] the excess of this power that I suppose Keats to speak, when he says he has no identity—As a poet, and when the fit is upon him, this is true. . . . Shakesp^r was a poet of the kind above ment^d—and he was perhaps the only one besides Keats who possessed this power in an extr^y degree.

Keats had talked with Woodhouse about the subject before, and had thrown himself into it with the fanciful exuberance he found irresistible when he was among serious people. For Woodhouse adds the comment noticed earlier: "He has affirmed that he can conceive of a billiard Ball that it may have a sense of delight from its own roundness, smoothness, volubility & the rapidity of its motion."

VIII

We have been anticipating, of course: the implications of the "Negative Capability" letter have encouraged us to look ahead a few months. Back in December, as he felt himself emerging onto this new plateau of thinking, the memory of *King Lear* kept recurring. When he had begun *Endymion* at the Isle of Wight, it was the sea—remembered from the cliff near Margate the summer before (1816)—that had led him to return to the play on this second venture: "the passage . . . 'Do you not hear the Sea?' has haunted me intensely." Now that *Endymion* was finished, and a third venture or transition lay ahead, he was remembering the play somewhat differently. It was probably in December, certainly by early January, that he bought a copy of Hazlitt's *Characters of Shakespear's Plays* (published late in 1817). With only one exception, all his underscorings and marginal comments are concentrated in the chapter on *Lear*. They provide in their own way a further gloss to that "intensity" of conception—that identification and "greeting of the Spirit"—of which he had been thinking when he wrote to George and Tom ("Examine King Lear & you will find this exemplified throughout"): an identification especially prized when—as Hazlitt said in a passage Keats underlines—"the extremest resources of the imagination are called in to lay open the deepest movements of the heart." "The greatest strength of genius," said Hazlitt, "is shown in describing the strongest passions: for the power of the imagination, in works of invention, must be in proportion to the force of the natural impressions, which are the subject of them." Double-scoring this in the margin, Keats writes:

> If we compare the Passions to different tuns and hogsheads of wine in a vast cellar—thus it is—the poet by one cup should know the scope of any

particular wine without getting intoxicated—this is the highest exertion of Power, and the next step is to paint from memory of gone self storms.

And beside another passage he draws a line, underscoring the italicized words, and writes "The passage has to a great degree hieroglyphic visioning":

> We see the ebb and flow of the feeling, its pauses and feverish starts, its impatience of opposition, its accumulating force when it has time to recollect itself, *the manner in which it avails itself of every passing word or gesture, its haste to repel insinuation, the alternate contradiction and dilatation of the soul.*

Endymion, which he began to copy and correct for the press during the first week of January, seemed remote indeed from the thoughts that now preoccupied him. So in fact did romances generally, though he was to write two more (*Isabella* and *The Eve of St. Agnes*). On Thursday, January 22, he finished copying the first book of *Endymion*; and then, as he told his brothers the next day, "I sat down . . . to read King Lear once again the thing appeared to demand the prologue of a Sonnet, I wrote it & began to read." It is hardly one of his best sonnets—he never even bothered to publish it— but the occasion meant something to him. For he was approaching the play with a new understanding of how much lay beyond the "old oak Forest" of "Romance."

It was only another beginning, and it would have to proceed much more slowly than the other beginnings. But he was prepared, he thought, for "a very gradual ripening of the intellectual powers"; and all he can say now is that "I think a little change has taken place in my intellect lately." Then he turns to the sonnet, copies it out for George and Tom, and adds: "So you see I am getting at it, with a sort of determination & strength, though verily I do not feel it at this moment—this is my fourth letter this morning & I feel rather tired & my head rather swimming."

PAUL DE MAN

The Negative Road

In the course of time, the reputations of the main English romantic poets have undergone considerable and revealing fluctuations. It would nowadays be considered eccentric to rate Byron above Wordsworth or Blake, yet during his lifetime Byron's fame far surpassed that of his contemporaries. Not till the end of the nineteenth century did Blake begin to receive full recognition, and we are now no longer surprised to find critics give him a central position that none of his contemporaries would have remotely suspected. We may have some difficulty in sharing the excitement with which the young Yeats discovered the audacities of Shelley's more speculative poems, but, on the other hand, Arnold's judgment in rating Wordsworth above Spenser, Dryden, Pope and Coleridge might again find some support, albeit for reasons that have little in common with Arnold's.

These fluctuations reflect changes in critical temper that are themselves the result of a continued reinterpretation of romanticism. Time and again, literary and critical movements set out with the avowed aim of moving beyond romantic attitudes and ideas; in America alone, Pound's imagism, Irving Babbitt's neo-humanism and the New Criticism of T. S. Eliot are relatively recent instances of such a trend; the same anti-romantic (or anti-idealist) bias underlies neo-realist and neo-Marxist tendencies here and abroad. But time and again, it turns out that the new conceptions that thus assert themselves were in fact already present in the full context of European romanticism; instead of moving beyond these problems, we are merely becoming aware of certain aspects of romanticism that had remained

From *Selected Poetry of John Keats*, edited by Paul de Man. Copyright © 1966 by Paul de Man. New American Library, 1966.

hidden from our perception. We certainly have left behind the Victorian image of Wordsworth, but Wordsworth himself is far from having been fixed and determined by a poetic or critical itinerary that went beyond him. What sets out as a claim to overcome romanticism often turns out to be merely an expansion of our understanding of the movement, leading inevitably to changes in our images of individual poets.

The poetry of Keats is no exception. As the amount of biographical and critical studies augments in quantity and in quality, our knowledge of Keats has increased considerably, yet many questions remain unresolved, as if the work had not yielded all the possibilities of significance that it may contain. The curve of his reputation shows perhaps less dramatic ups and downs than in the case of Blake or even Shelley: it has constantly risen since his death at the age of twenty-five in 1821. He had already earned the enthusiastic appreciation of several close and loyal friends during his lifetime, but his career was too short to give him the real critical recognition that would have been so useful: Wordsworth paid little attention to him; for all his apparent sympathy, Shelley was deeply uncongenial and remained aloof; Coleridge was already in the decline and Keats hardly knew him; Hazlitt was the object of his admiration rather than a full admirer, and even Hunt's ultimate loyalty went to Shelley rather than to the earlier disciple. Later in the century, the Victorians were never able to forgive Keats his plebeian birth and the unbridled erotic despair of the love letters to Fanny Brawne; Arnold has to strain a great deal to find in the life and letters traces of the moral high-seriousness that he cannot fail to detect in the greater poems. Some of this Victorian snobbishness still echoes in Yeats's reference to Keats as a "coarse-bred son of a livery-stable keeper" who made "luxuriant song" out of his frustrations. But the poetry had always found considerable appreciation, not only for its decorative aspects that so delighted the Pre-Raphaelites, but for its thematic depth as well. In our own century, when the relationship between life and work is understood in a somewhat less literal manner, a considerable exegetic effort has been directed especially toward the elucidation of the shorter poems. Continued interest in the biography and in the letters—a new edition of the letters edited by Hyder E. Rollins appeared in 1958 and W. J. Bate's biography appeared in 1963— indicates that the problem that preoccupied the Victorians, the contrast between the banality of Keats's life and the splendor of his work, has not been fully resolved. Arnold's remarks about an element of vulgarity in Keats have cut so deep that recent biographers are still writing polemically in an effort to dispel their effect. This almost always results, even among Keats's warmest admirers, in a trace of condescension or defensiveness, as if one were forced to look for attenuating circumstances. The facts are distorted either by making the life appear darker and more tragic than it was, or by exalting Keats's very genuine courage and self-sacrifice to the point where it obscures his poetry. Except for the last few months, the life is in fact more banal than tragic; it is one of Keats's most engaging traits that he resists all temptation to see himself as the hero of a tragic adventure. The unfavorable circumstances of his birth—he was the eldest of four orphaned children cheated out of their modest inheritance by an unscrupulous guardian—were such that he lived almost always oriented toward the future, keeping his capacity for personal happiness in reserve, so to speak, for the better days he saw ahead. The pathos, of course, is that he never reached these days, but he was no longer able to write by the time he realized this. In reading Keats, we are therefore reading the work of a man whose experience is mainly literary. The growing insight that underlies the remarkably swift development of his talent was gained primarily from the act of writing. In this case, we are on very safe ground when we derive our understanding primarily from the work itself.

The pattern of Keats's work is prospective rather than retrospective; it consists of hopeful preparations, anticipations of future power rather than meditative reflections on past moments of insight or harmony. His poems frequently climax in questions—"Was there a poet born?", "Did I wake or sleep?"—or in statements such as: "and beyond these/I must not think now...", "but now no more,/My wand'ring spirit must not further soar"— that suggest he has reached a threshold, penetrated to the borderline of a new region which he is not yet ready to explore but toward which all his future efforts will be directed. *I Stood Tiptoe* announces *Endymion*, *Endymion* announces *Hyperion*, *Hyperion* prefigures *The Fall of Hyperion*, etc.; Keats is steadily moving forward, trying to pull himself up to the level and the demands of his own prospective vision. None of the larger works—and we know that the larger works mattered most to him—can in any sense be called finished. The circle never seems to close, as if he were haunted by a dream that always remains in the future.

The dream is dramatically articulated from the very start, in a naïve but clear mythological outline that even the awkward diction of the early poems cannot altogether hide from sight. It reveals Keats's original concep- tion of the poet's role and constitutes the thematic center around which the history of his development is organized.

In one of Keats's longer early poems, the title line as well as the last word suggest a soaring, Icarus-like urge to "burst our mortal bars" and leave the human world behind. But nothing could be less like Shelley's skylark, a "scorner of the ground," than Keats's young poet. Icarus's rise as well as his fall are acts of overbearing that destroy balance and "burst" beyond natural limits. Even in the earliest poems, Keats never conceives of poetry in this manner: to the contrary, poetry is always the means by which an excess is tempered, a flight checked, a separation healed. In terms of the material sensations toward which Keats's imagery naturally tends, this tendency is expressed in the impression of a temperate breeze that cools excessive heat, but never chills—a sensation so all-pervading throughout the early poems that it cannot be considered merely conventional or derivative:

> . . . pebbly beds;
> Where swarms of minnows show their little heads, . . .
> To taste the luxury of sunny beams
> Tempered with coolness.
> (I Stood Tiptoe, ll. 71 ff.)

> Where had he been, from whose warm head outflew
> That sweetest of all songs, that ever new,
> That aye refreshing, pure deliciousness . . .
> (Idem., ll. 181 ff.)

> The breezes were ethereal, and pure,
> And crept through half-closed lattices to cure
> The languid sick; it cooled their fevered sleep . . .
> (Idem., ll. 221 ff.)

The early Keats discovers the narrative equivalence of this restoring, balancing power of poetry in the Greek myths, which he interprets at the time as tales in which the distance between mortals and immortals is overcome by an act of erotic union. As a story of love between a goddess and a mortal shepherd, Endymion attracts him even more than Psyche or Narcissus, and he announces it as his main theme before embarking on the narrative poem *Endymion* itself. But the symbolic function of the poet as a narrator of myths immediately widens in significance: since he can "give meek Cynthia her Endymion," he not only restores the natural balance of things, but his exemplary act extends to the whole of mankind. The union between the goddess and the shepherd prefigures directly the communal celebration of mankind liberated from its suffering. By telling "one wonder of [Cynthia's] bridal night," the poet causes the "languid sick" to awake and

> Young men, and maidens at each other gazed
> With hands held back, and motionless, amazed
> To see the brightness in each other's eyes;
> And so they stood, filled with a sweet surprise,
> Until their tongues were loosed in poesy.
> Therefore no lover did of anguish die:
> But the soft numbers, in that moment spoken,
> Made silken ties, that never may be broken.
> (Idem., ll. 231 ff.)

Here we have Keats's original dream in all its naïve clarity: it is a dream about poetry as a redeeming force, oriented toward others in a concern that is moral but altogether spontaneous, rooted in the fresh sensibility of love and sympathy and not in abstract imperatives. The touching tale of a lovelorn goddess replaces the Ten Commandments, a humanized version of Hellenic myth replaces biblical sternness, in an optimistic belief that the universe naturally tends toward the mood of temperate balance and that poetry can always recapture the freshness of ever-rising springs.

The optimism of this myth is tempered, however, by the negative implications it contains: if poetry is to redeem, it must be that there is a need for redemption, that humanity is indeed "languid sick" and "with temples bursting." The redemption is the happier future of a painful present. One of the lines of development that Keats's poetry will follow reaches a deeper understanding of this pain which, in the earlier texts, is merely a feverish restlessness, a discordance of the sensations that creates a tension between warring extremes of hot and cold. Some of his dissatisfaction with the present is transposed in Keats's image of his own situation as a beginning poet on the contemporary literary scene: the greatness of the major predecessors—Spenser, Shakespeare and Milton—measures his own inadequacy and dwarfs the present:

> Is there so small a range
> In the present strength of manhood, that the high
> Imagination cannot freely fly
> As she was wont of old?
> (Sleep and Poetry, ll. 162 ff.)

Totally oriented toward the future, Keats cannot draw strength from this past grandeur; his use of earlier models will always be more a sympathetic imitation than a dialogue between past and present, as between Milton and Wordsworth in The Prelude. Hence that Keats's use of earlier poets is more technical than thematic: however Spenserian or Miltonic the diction of The Eve of St. Agnes and Hyperion may be, Spenser and Milton are not present as such in the poems; Keats has to derive all his power from energy he finds in himself or in his immediate vicinity. But he experiences his own times as literarily deficient: a curious passage from Sleep and Poetry, where the entire movement of the poem, as well as the allegiance to Leigh Hunt, would demand the unmixed praise of contemporary poetry, turns into a criticism of Byron and Wordsworth for failing to deliver the message of hope that Keats would like to hear. As a criticism of The Excursion the observation would be valid enough, but it is presented instead as a source of personal discouragement. A certain form of despondency and stagnation seems to threaten Keats from the start and forces him to take shelter in falsely idyllic settings like the one at the end of *Sleep and Poetry,* where the problem that concerns him can be temporarily forgotten but not resolved.

Retreats of this kind recur throughout the work, but they gain in poetic significance as the predicament from which he retreats grows in universality. This progression can be traced in the changed use of Ovidian myth from *Endymion* on, as compared to the earliest poems. Originally, the myths serve to gain access to the idyllic aspects of nature: they are "delightful stories" about "the fair paradise of Nature's light." The sad tales alternate with joyful ones merely for the sake of variety. This, of course, is by no means the dominant mood in Ovid himself, who often reports acts of refined cruelty with harsh detachment. From *Endymion* on, the movement of mythical metamorphosis, practically absent from the early poems, achieves a striking prominence that will maintain itself to the end; the very narrative pattern of *Endymion,* of *Lamia* and, in a more hidden way, of *Hyperion* and the Odes, is based on a series of transformations from one order of being into another. The various metamorphic combinations between the inanimate, the animal, human and divine world keep appearing, and the moment of transformation always constitutes the dramatic climax toward which the story is oriented. Far from being merely picturesque, the metamorphoses acquire an obsessive intensity in which one recognizes a more mature version of the original, happy dream of redemption.

The erotic contact between the gods and man in Ovid is anything but the idyllic encounter between Cynthia and Endymion in *I Stood Tiptoe*; it results instead in the brutal degradation of the human being to a lower order of life, his imprisonment in the rigid forms of the inanimate world: Niobe's "very tongue frozen to her mouth's roof" (*Met.* VI, 1. 306), Daphne's "swift feet grown fast in sluggish roots" (I, l. 551), Myrrha, the mother of Adonis, watching her skin change to hard bark (X, l. 494). This state of frozen immobility, of paralysis under the life-destroying impact of eternal powers, becomes the obsessive image of a human predicament that poetry is to redeem. A long gallery of human beings thus caught in poses of frozen desire appear throughout the work: the lovers in Book III of *Endymion* imprisoned in a sea cave "vast, and desolate, and icy-cold" (III, 1. 632), the figures on the Grecian Urn, the knight-at-arms of "La Belle Dame sans Merci" caught "On the cold hillside," the knights and ladies at the beginning of *The Eve of St. Agnes* "sculptured dead, on each side, [who] seem to freeze,/Emprisoned in black, purgatorial rails," Saturn at the beginning of *Hyperion* "quiet as a stone,/Still as the silence round about his lair." There hardly exists a single of Keats's important poems in which a version of this recurrent theme fails to appear, though the outward form may vary. It is most frequently associated with the sensation of cold, as if the cooling breeze of I *Stood Tiptoe* heralding the benevolent arrival of the gods had suddenly turned icy and destructive. The myth is a paradoxical version of the mutability theme: the passage of time, the loss of power, death, are the means by which the gods announce their presence; time is the only eternal force and it strips man of his ability to move freely in the direction of his own desire; generations are wasted by old age, "youth grows pale, and specter-thin, and dies" and "Everything is spoiled by use" ("Fancy," l. 68). Under the impact of this threat, mankind is made powerless in the stagnation that Keats felt at times in himself and saw around him. Mutability causes paralysis.

His dream then becomes a kind of reversal of the Ovidian metamorphosis, in which man was frozen into a natural form: the poet is the one who can reverse the metamorphosis and reanimate the dead forms into life. Again, Book III of *Endymion* gives a clear mythological outline of this process: by a mere touch of his wand, warmth is restored to the frozen lovers and the reanimated figures rejoice in an exact repetition of the redemption scene from I *Stood Tiptoe* (*Endymion*, III, ll. 780 ff.). This dream, by which dead nature is restored to life and refinds, as it were, the human form that was originally its own, is Keats's fondest reverie. A large measure of his poetical power stems from this. It allows him to give nature such an immediate and convincing presence that we watch it take on effortlessly human form: the ode "To Autumn" is the supreme achievement of this Ovidian metamorphosis in reverse. His ability to make his conceits and metaphors spring out of a genuine identity of nature with man, rather than out of an intellectual awareness of an analogy between both, is also rooted in this dream. It is so strong that it forces itself upon the narrative of his longer poems, even when the original story does not allow for it. In *Hyperion*, one can never conceive of Apollo as the warring opponent of the Titans. Instead, the story inevitably turns toward a repetition of the Glaucus episode in *Endymion*: Apollo tends to become the young man whose task it is to free and rejuvenate Saturn, the victim of old age. We are dealing with still another version of Keats's humanitarian dream. He will reach maturity at the end of a rather complicated itinerary, when the last trace of naïveté is removed from this vision.

The power by means of which the poet can redeem the suffering of mankind is called love, but love, in Keats, is a many-sided force. On the simplest level, love is merely the warmth of sensation: Endymion's ardor is such that it seems to melt the curse of time away at sheer contact. Till the later "Ode to Psyche" when love has been internalized to such an extent that it bears only the remotest relationship to anything physical, the epithet "warm," associated with Eros, preserves the link with sensation in a world that is otherwise entirely mental.

A bright torch, and a casement ope at night,
To let the warm Love in!
("Ode to Psyche," ll. 66–67)

The importance of sensuality to Keats has been abundantly stressed; when some biographers, with the laudable intention of rescuing Keats from the Victorian reproach of coarseness, have tried to minimize the importance of erotic elements in his poetry, they present an oddly distorted picture. Yet, even his most straightforward eroticism easily turns into something more than sensation. First of all, sensuous love for him is more readily imagined than experienced; therefore it naturally becomes one of the leading symbols for the workings of the imagination. One of his most elaborate conceits on the activity of the mind, the final stanza of the "Ode to Psyche," spontaneously associates Eros with fancy; the same is true of the poem "Fancy," in which Eros is present as an activity of the mind. Moreover, since Keats is the least narcissistic of romantic poets, love is easily transferred by him to others and becomes a communal bond: one remembers how the union of Cynthia and Endymion spontaneously turns into a public feast, the kind of Rousseauistic brotherhood that recurs in romantic poetry as a symbol of reconciliation. In *Endymion* also, one passes without tension from love to a communal spirit of friendship with social and political overtones; something of the spirit of the French Revolution still echoes in these passages. In the optimistic world of *Endymion*, love and history act together as positive forces and historical redemption goes hand in hand with sensuous fulfillment.

Another aspect of the love experience, however, leads to more complex involvements. Aside from sensation, love also implies sympathy, a forgetting of the self for the sake of others, especially when the other is in a state of suffering. In the earlier poems, when the poet's sympathy goes out to Narcissus, to Psyche or to Pan, or even when Endymion is moved to tears over the sad fate of the wood-nymph Arethusa, these movements of the heart could still be considered a conventional form of sensibility. But in the recurrent image of frozen immobility, the suffering is not just an arbitrary trick of fate or a caprice of the gods: it becomes the generalized statement of the human predicament, man stifled by the awareness of his mortality. Sympathetic understanding of these threatened figures, the attempt "To think how they may ache in icy hoods and mails" (*St. Agnes*, l. 18), tears us away from the safety of everyday experience and forces us to enter a realm that is in fact the realm of death. The ordinary life of consciousness is then suspended and its continuity disrupted. Hence that the experience can only be expressed in metaphors such as "trance" or "sleep," suspended states of consciousness in which the self is momentarily absent. The "romantic" setting of certain dream episodes in *Endymion* or in "La Belle Dame sans Merci" should not mislead us into misunderstanding the connection between love and death that prevails here: love is not a temptation to take us out of the finite world of human experiences, still less an impulse toward a platonic heaven. Keats's love impulse is a very human sense of sympathy and pity, chivalrous perhaps, but devoid of transcendental as well as escapist dimensions. Endymion cannot resist the "sorrow" of the Indian maiden, Glaucus is taken in by the feigned tears of Circe, the knight of "La Belle Dame..." is definitely lulled to sleep only after his lady has "wept, and sighed full sore," and Lamia, also, woos her lover Lucius by appealing to his pity as well as to his senses. Keats's imagination is fired by a mixture of sensation and sympathy in which the dual nature of love is reunited. The sympathy, however, is even more important than the sensation: love can exist without the latter but not without the former, and some of Keats's heroes are motivated by sympathy alone. This adds an important dimension to our understanding of the relationship between love, poetry and death in his work: because poetry is essentially an act of sympathy, of human redemption, it must move through the death-like trances that abound in Keats. One misunderstands these moments altogether if one interprets them as a flight from human suffering; to the contrary, they are the unmistakable sign of a sympathetic identification with the human predicament. There are moments of straightforward escape in Keats: we mentioned the end of *Sleep and Poetry* as one instance; several of the more trivial poems fulfill the same function. But the "tranced summer night" of *Hyperion*, the Cave of Quietude in Book IV of *Endymion*, the "drowsy numbness" of the Nightingale Ode, the "cloudy swoon" of *The Fall of Hyperion*, do not stand in opposition to human sympathy; as the subsequent dramatic action of these poems indicates, they represent a necessary first step toward the full unfolding of humanitarian love as it grows into a deeper understanding of the burden of mortality.

This expansion of the theme of love, which takes place without entering into conflict with the other, sensuous aspect of love, leads to a parallel deepening of the theme of history. In the easy simplicity of *Endymion*, Keats can herald, at the opening of Book II, the "sovereign power of love" over history: love suffices to bring about universal reconciliation and to make the slow labor of history superfluous. By the time of *Hyperion*, a considerable change has already taken place: the myth of the defeat of the Titans by a new generation of gods is interpreted as the very movement of history. Oceanus's speech (*Hyperion*, III, ll. 114 ff.) as well as Mnemosyne's initiation of Apollo to

> Names, deeds, gray legends, dire events, rebellions,
> Majesties, sovran voices, agonies,
> Creations and destroyings...
> (*Hyperion*, III, ll. 114 ff.)

make very clear the increased importance of the theme. But it is not till the late *Fall of Hyperion* that Keats's historical consciousness is fully developed. In *Hyperion*, it remains obscure why the knowledge of the historical past which "pours into the wide hollows of [Apollo's] brain" suffices to "make a god of [him]." The corresponding scene in *The Fall of Hyperion* may be confused in some respects, but not as far as the poet's attitude toward history is concerned: history, in its most general aspects, is for him a privileged subject, because the gift of sympathy which he possesses to a larger degree than any other man allows him to understand the sacrificial nature of all historical movement, as epitomized in the downfall of Saturn. Far from reasserting the consoling law stated by Oceanus "That first in beauty should be first in might" (*Hyperion*, II, 1. 229), the historical awareness in *The Fall* returns to the deeper theme of man's temporal contingency. The poet is the chosen witness of the damage caused by time; by growing in consciousness he gains no new attributes of beauty or might, merely the negative privilege of witnessing the death of those who surpassed him in greatness. The suggestion of a conquering, youthful Apollo has entirely disappeared. The dynamic thrust of history itself is frozen into immobility by the deadly power of time and the poet now has to expand his capacity for sympathy until it encompasses the full range of this tragedy:

> Without stay or prop
> But my own weak mortality, I bore
> The load of this eternal quietude,
> The unchanging gloom...
> (*The Fall of Hyperion*, I, ll. 388 ff.)

History can only move by becoming aware of its own contingency. From his earliest poems on, Keats had conceived of his own work as a movement of becoming, a gradual widening of his consciousness by successive stages. The pattern is present in the prefigured outline of his own career in *Sleep and Poetry*, in the structure of *Endymion* which, for all its apparent disorder, is nevertheless organized as a consistent "growth of a poet's mind," in the famous letter to Reynolds of May 3, 1818, on the poet's progress from the thoughtless Chamber to the "Chamber of Maiden-Thought." This prospective scheme now no longer appears as a reassuring projection, since every step in the progression takes on the form of a tragedy beyond redemption, though not beyond the power of understanding. Nowhere does Keats come closer to a historical consciousness that recognizes and names the full power of negativity. Traveling entirely by his own pathways, he comes upon some of the insights that will shape the destiny of the nineteenth and twentieth centuries.

Yet it seems that Keats never achieves an authority that is commensurate with the quality of this perception. The conception of the poet's role, in *The Fall of Hyperion*, appears at once so lofty in its impersonality and disinterestedness, yet so humane in its concern for the grief of others, that we would expect a more serene tone in Keats's later work. Instead, he frequently sounds the strident note of someone who sees through the fallacy of his own certainties. There seems to be little room for self-deception in the stern wisdom of *The Fall of Hyperion*; where are we to find the point where Keats lies open to his own reproof?

Nothing could be more genuine than the positive aspect of Keats's concern for others: neither in the poetry nor in the letters can one discover a jarring tone that would reveal the presence of affectation or pose in his humanitarian attitude. Keats's generosity is total and all the more admirable since it is never based on an idealization of himself or of others, or on an attempt to emulate a chosen mode. Perfect good faith, however, does not shelter us from the intricacies of moral inauthenticity. Keats's gift for sympathy has a negative aspect, and the significance of his complete evolution can only be understood if one takes this into account.

Already in *Endymion*, when Keats is speaking of love and friendship as central formative experiences, he refers to these experiences as "self-destroying":

> But there are
> Richer entanglements, enthrallments far
> More self-destroying, leading, by degrees,
> To the chief intensity: the crown of these
> Is made of love and friendship...
> (*Endymion*, I, ll. 797 ff.)

"Self-destroying" is obviously used in a positive sense here, to designate the moral quality of disinterestedness—yet "destroying" is a curiously strong term. The phrase is revealing, for a recurrent pattern in the poetry indicates a strong aversion to a direct confrontation with his own self; few poets have described the act of self-reflection in harsher terms. For Endymion, the most miserable condition of man is that in which he is left to consider his own self in solitude, even when this avowedly takes him close to teaching the "goal of consciousness" (II, l. 283):

> There, when new wonders ceased to float before,
> And thoughts of self came on, how crude and sore
> The journey homeward to habitual self!
> A mad pursuing of the fog-born elf,
> Whose flitting lantern, through rude nettle-brier,

> Cheats us into a swamp, into a fire,
> Into the bosom of a hated thing.
> (*Idem.* II, ll. 274 ff.)

The inward quest for self-knowledge is described here in the very terms used by Milton to represent the triumph of Satanic temptation (*Paradise Lost*, IX, ll. 633 ff.). The "hated thing" to which Keats refers is the situation, rather than the content of his own consciousness: the condition of the "sole self" is one of intolerable barrenness, the opposite of all that imagination, poetry and love can achieve. The experience of being "tolled back to one's sole self" is always profoundly negative. He almost succeeds in eliminating himself from his poetry altogether. There is, of course, much that is superficially autobiographical in *Endymion* and even in *Hyperion*, but one never gains an intimate sense of Keats's own selfhood remotely comparable to that conveyed by other romantic poets. The "I" of the Nightingale Ode, for instance, is always seen in the movement that takes it away from its own center. The emotions that accompany the discovery of the authentic self, feelings of guilt and dread as well as sudden moments of transparent clarity, are lacking in Keats. Poetic "sleep" or "trance" is a darkening, growing opacity of the consciousness. Suffering plays a very prominent role in his work, but it is always the suffering of others, sympathetically but objectively perceived and so easily generalized into historical and universal pain that it rarely appears in its subjective immediacy: a passage such as the opening scene of *Hyperion* gains its poetic effectiveness from the controlled detachment of an observer who is not directly threatened. The only threat that Keats seems to experience subjectively is that of self-confrontation.

Keats's sympathetic love thus appears less simple than it may seem at first sight: his intense and altogether genuine concern for others serves, in a sense, to shelter him from the self-knowledge he dreads. He is a man distracted from the awareness of his own mortality by the constant spectacle of the death of others. He can go very far in participating in their agony: he is indeed one "to whom the miseries of the world/Are misery and will not let [him] rest" (*Fall of Hyperion*, I, ll. 148–49). But the miseries are always "of the world" and not his own, a distinction that should disappear when the suffering referred to is so general that it designates a universal human predicament. Although it would be entirely false to say of Keats that he escaped out of human suffering into the idealized, trance-like condition of poetry, one can say, with proper caution, that he moves away from the burden of self-knowledge into a world created by the combined powers of the sympathetic imagination, poetry and history, a world that is ethically impeccable, but from which the self is excluded.

The tension resulting from this ambivalence does not remain entirely hidden. It comes to the surface, for instance, in the difficult choice he has to make in his literary allegiances, when he has to reconcile his admiration for Shakespeare and Milton with his consideration for Wordsworth, whom he considered his greatest contemporary. His own term for the "self-destroying" power of the poetic imagination is "negative capability," the ability of the mind to detach itself from its own identity, and he associates this characteristic of the poetic temperament primarily with Shakespeare. It is typical, in this respect, that he would consider Shakespeare's life as exemplary: "Shakespeare led a life of Allegory..." (letter to George Keats, February 19, 1819) in the full figural and Christian sense of the term, when it is precisely a life so buried under the wealth of its own inventions that it has ceased to exist as a particular experience. This stands, of course, in total contrast to what we find in Wordsworth, for whom the determining moment occurs when the mind exists in and for itself, in the transparency of an inwardness entirely focused upon the self. Even in the absence of the posthumously published *Prelude*, Keats knew the direction of Wordsworth's thought and felt the challenge it offered to his own orientation. W. J. Bate, in his biography of Keats, has well seen the decisive importance of this confrontation when, in the letter of May 3, 1818, to Reynolds, Keats rates Wordsworth above Milton ("who did not think into the human heart") because he is the poet of the conscious self. But Keats did not choose, at that time, to follow Wordsworth into the "dark passages" which he had begun to explore. The poem that stems from these meditations, the first *Hyperion*, is certainly not Wordsworthian and not altogether Miltonic either: the emphasis on characterization, the deliberate variety of tones, the pageant-like conception of history, are all frankly Shakespearian, and in many ways *Hyperion* resembles an optimistic, humanized version of *Troilus and Cressida* more than *Paradise Lost*. It definitely is a poem founded on negative capability. The sense of human sympathy has grown considerably since *Endymion*, but we are even further removed from real self-awareness than in the early poem. Only at the very end of his career will these unresolved tensions come fully into the open and disrupt the continuity of his development—but this happened, not as a result of literary influence but under the pressure of outward circumstances.

Interpreters of Keats have difficulty agreeing on the significance of his latest work: after the almost miraculous outburst of creative activity in May, 1819, when he wrote practically all the great odes in quick succession, there still followed a period of nearly six months until the final onset of his illness. *The Fall of Hyperion, Lamia* and several other shorter poems were written at that time. There is some logic in considering the entire period from June till the end of the year as one single unit—the "late" Keats—that includes the poems to Fanny Brawne, dating from the fall of 1819, and frequently considered as poetically unimportant and slightly embarrassing documents written when he was no longer in full control of his faculties. In truth, it is from *The Fall of Hyperion* on that a sharp change begins to take place; it is also from that moment on that the differences among the commentators begin to increase. For all the divergences in the interpretation of the main odes, there exists a clear consensus about the general meaning and merit of these poems; the differences refer to matters of detail and are certainly to be expected in the case of rich and complex poems studied in such great detail. But *The Fall of Hyperion* is considered by some as "the culmination of Keats's work" and the dialogue between Moneta and the poet as a "dialectical victory" over Moneta's attack on poetry; for others, however, the same passage is read as symbolizing "exhaustion and despair" at "seeing the world of poetry doomed to destruction." *Lamia* has also given rise to incompatible readings and to general puzzlement. The hesitations of the critics are the unmistakable sign of a change that is so far-reaching that it requires a radical readjustment on the part of the readers. The particular difficulty and obscurity of *The Fall of Hyperion* and *Lamia* stems from the fact that they are works of transition toward a new phase that is fully revealed only in the last poems Keats wrote.

The striking fact about Keats's last poems is that they contain an attack on much that had been held sacred in the earlier work; one is reminded, at moments, of Yeats's savagely derisive treatment of his own myths in some of the *Last Poems*. There is something indecorous in the spectacle of a poet thus turning against himself and one can understand the desire of commentators to play down this episode in Keats's history, all the more since illness, poverty and increased bitterness invaded his life at the time, offering a convenient explanation for this radical change in tone. It would be a reflection, however, on the strength of Keats's earlier convictions if they had not been able to stand up under the pressure of these events, however damaging they may have been. Even among his near contemporaries—one thinks of Hölderlin, Maurice de Guérin and Gérard de Nerval—some of the most assertive poems are written in a comparable state of physical and mental distress. We must understand that, far from detracting from his stature, the negativity of Keats's last poems shows that he was about to add another dimension to a poetic development that, up till then, had not been altogether genuine.

We can take as an example the poem dated October, 1819, and entitled "To ——," sometimes referred to as "Ode" or "Second Ode to Fanny Brawne." The term "Ode" in the title is fitting, for the dramatic organization of the poem is very similar to that of the famous great odes; it is, in fact, the exact negative counterpart of the "Ode to a Nightingale." The paradox that was partly concealed by the richness of the language in the earlier odes is now fully revealed: the poems in fact set out to destroy the entities they claim to praise; or, to put it less bluntly, the ambiguity of feeling toward these entities is such that the poems fall apart. In the October poem, the absurdity of the dramatic situation is apparent from the first lines, in which Keats begs Fanny to assist him, by her presence, in curing a suffering of which this very presence is the sole cause:

> What can I do to drive away
> Remembrance from my eyes? for they have seen,
> Aye, an hour ago, my brilliant queen!
> Touch has a memory. O say, love, say,
> What can I do to kill it and be free
> In my old liberty?
>
> ("To ——," ll. 1 ff.)

The prospective character of Keats's poetry, which we stressed from the start, stands out here in its full meaning. The superiority of the future over the past expresses, in fact, a rejection of the experience of actuality. Memory, being founded on actual sensations, is for Keats the enemy of poetic language, which thrives instead on dreams of pure potentiality. In the last stanzas, the poem turns from past to future, with all the ardor of the sensuous desire that tormented Keats at the time, and with an immediacy that produces the kind of language that already proved so cumbersome in the erotic passages of *Endymion*:

> O, let me once more rest
> My soul upon that dazzling breast!
> Let once again these aching arms be placed,
> The tender gaolers of thy waist! . . .
> Give me those lips again!
>
> (*Idem.*, ll. 48 ff.)

The interest of the passage is that the desire it names has already been canceled out by the statement made at the onset of the poem. The passion that produces these lines is precisely what has been rejected at the start as the main obstacle to the "liberty" of poetic creation. Before Fanny's presence had put the poet within "the reach of fluttering love," his poetic faculties could grow unimpaired:

> My muse had wings
> And ever ready was to take her course
> Whither I bent her force, . . .
>
> (*Idem.*, ll. 11 ff.)

This belongs to a past that preceded his involvement; the movement toward the future is checked by the awareness of a contradiction that opposes love to poetry as memory is opposed to dream. Contradicting the prayer for her return, the poem concludes by stating a preference for imaginary passion over actual presence:

> Enough! Enough! it is enough for me
> To dream of thee!

It is certainly true that the poem destroys itself in a hopeless conflict between temptation and rejection, between praise and blame, that no language can hope to resolve. What is so revealing, however, is that the contradiction so crudely manifest here is potentially present in the earlier odes as well.

The difference in situation between this late poem and the odes "On a Grecian Urn" and "To a Nightingale" is obvious enough: the urn and the nightingale are general, impersonal entities, endowed with significance by an act of the poet's imagination; Fanny Brawne, on the other hand, is a highly distinct and specific person whose presence awakens in him an acute sense of threatened selfhood. The temptation she incarnates clashes directly with his desire to forget his own self. In the earlier odes, this conflict is avoided by keeping carefully apart what the urn and the nightingale signify for Keats himself, and what they signify for Keats in relation to humanity in general. The poetic effectiveness of the odes depends entirely on the positive temptation that emanates from the symbolic entities: the world to which they give access is a world of happiness and beauty, and it is by the suggestive evocation of this world that beauty enters the poems. This, in turn, allows for the dramatic contrast with the world of actual experience, caught in the destructive power of mutability and described throughout, in the Grecian Urn as well as in the Nightingale Ode, in terms that appeal directly to our moral sympathy:

> Here, where men sit and hear each other groan;
>   Where palsy shakes a few, sad, last gray hairs,
>   Where youth grows pale, and specter-thin, and dies;
>   Where but to think is to be full of sorrow
>   And leaden-eyed despairs...
>   ("Ode to a Nightingale," ll. 24 ff.)

The mixture of emotions, in these texts, is subtle and self-deceiving. On the one hand, the poet's sympathy for the suffering of mankind gives him the kind of moral authority that allows him to call authoritatively for a lucid acceptance of human limitations. It is this morally responsible voice that warns his fellow men against the danger of giving in to the deceptive quality of poetic symbols: they "tease" and "deceive" in foreshadowing an eternity that is not within our reach; the urn and the nightingale finally act as powers of death and, in that sense, these poems are also written against the objects they set out to praise. But Keats does not remain in the barren, impoverished world of human contingency, the world of gray rocks and stones that is the landscape of Wordsworth's *Prelude*. As a poet, he does not seem to share in the torments of temporality. The youth that "grows pale, and specter-thin, and dies" in Stanza 3 of the Nightingale Ode could not possibly be the same voice that evokes so magnificently the change that comes over the world by losing oneself in the "embalmèd darkness" of the bird's song:

> I cannot see what flowers are at my feet,
>> Nor what soft incense hangs upon the boughs,
> But, in embalmèd darkness, guess each sweet
>> Wherewith the seasonable month endows
> The grass, the thicket, and the fruit-tree wild...
>> *(Idem., ll. 41 ff.)*

The richness of these most un-Wordsworthian lines can only come into being because Keats's self is in fact dissociated from the suffering mankind with which he sympathizes. As a humanist, he can lay claim to a good conscience and write poems that have reassured generations of readers, willing to be authoritatively told about the limits of their knowledge ("that is all/Ye know on earth, and all ye need to know"); but as a poet, he can indulge in the wealth of a soaring imagination whose power of metamorphosis knows no limits. The poet of the Grecian Urn would hardly be able to evoke the happy world on the urn if he were himself the creature "lowing at the skies" about to be sacrificed.

We can see, from the poem "To ——" what happens when this distance between the private self and its moral stance vanishes: the late poem is the "Ode to a Nightingale" with the metamorphic power of the imagination destroyed by a sense of real selfhood. This destruction now openly coincides with the appearance of love on the scene, in an overt admission that, up to this point, the moral seriousness of the poems had not, in fact, been founded on love at all:

> How shall I do
> To get anew
> Those molted feathers, and so mount once more
>> Above, above
>> The reach of fluttering Love
> And make him cower lowly while I soar?
>> ("To ——," ll. 18 ff.)

The violence of the feeling is reminiscent of the hostile language in which Endymion refers to solitary self-knowledge. In the experience of love, the self comes to know itself without mask, and when this happens the carefree movement of the poetic imagination falters. Before, as we know from the Nightingale Ode, the intoxication of the imagination, like that of wine, was able to fuse the familiar Keatsian tension between heat and cold into one single sensation:

> O, for a draught of vintage! that hath been
>   Cooled a long age in the deep-delved earth,
> Tasting of Flora and the country green,
>   Dance, and Provençal song, and sunburned mirth!
>   ("Ode to a Nightingale," ll. 11 ff.)

But now, in a world ruled by the law of love, such easy syntheses are no longer within our power:

> Shall I gulp wine? No, that is vulgarism,
> A heresy and schism,
>   Foisted into the canon law of love;—
> No—wine is only sweet to happy men; . . .
>   ("To ——," ll. 24 ff.)

Consequently, the metamorphosis of the landscape, achieved in Stanza 5 of the Nightingale Ode under the impact of the trancelike song, fails, and we are confronted instead with the bleakness of a totally de-mythologized world:

> That monstrous region, whose dull rivers pour,
> Ever from their sordid urns unto the shore,
> Unowned of any weedy-hairèd gods;
> Whose winds, all zephyrless, hold scourging rods,
> Iced in the great lakes, to afflict mankind;
> Whose rank-grown forests, frosted, black, and blind,
> Would fright a Dryad; whose harsh herbaged meads
> Make lean and lank the starved ox while he feeds;
> There bad flowers have no scent, birds no sweet song,
> And great unerring nature once seems wrong.
>   (Idem., ll. 34 ff.)

The landscape, at last, is that of Keats's real self, which he had kept so carefully hidden up till now under poetic myth and moral generosity. It is still an imagined landscape, but rooted this time in an experience that is both intimate and painful: his brother's financial disaster near the very "Great Lakes" here evoked was caused by such a landscape and it is certain that Keats equated his own miseries with the calamitous misadventures of his brother in America. This does not make this landscape less "symbolic" than the world of the nightingale or the Grecian Urn, but it dramatizes the distinction between a symbol rooted in the self and one rooted in an abstract dream.

The power which forces a man to see himself as he really is, is also called "philosophy" in the later Keats; the term receives the same ambiguous value-emphasis as does the word "love." In the same poem "To ———," the previous poetry, written when he was free of the burden of love, is called "unintellectual" and the confining power of self-awareness is stressed again in the rhetorical question:

> What seabird o'er the sea
> Is a philosopher the while he goes
> Winging along where the great water throes?
> (*Idem.*, ll. 15 ff.)

We have come a long way since the early days of *Endymion* when Keats thought of philosophy as a means to help him carry out his generous dream of human redemption. Apollonius, the philosopher in *Lamia*, has all the outward attributes of villainy, yet there can be no doubt that truth is on his side: Lucius is about to mistake the seductiveness of a serpent for real love and it is, after all, his own weakness that is to blame for his inability to survive the revelation of the truth. In this poem, Truth and Beauty are indeed at odds, but one may well conjecture that, as Keats's sense of truth grew, he would have been able to discover a beauty that would have surpassed that of Lamia. Fanny Brawne may well have looked to him more like Moneta than like La Belle Dame sans Merci.

With the development that stood behind him, this final step could only take the violently negative form of his last poems. It is morally consistent that he would have rebelled against a generosity that offered more protection than it cost him. After having acted, in all his dreams of human redemption, as the one who rescues others from their mortal plight, his last poem reverses the parts. Taking off from an innocuous line in *The Fall of Hyperion* ("When this warm scribe my hand is in the grave") he now offers his hand no longer in a gesture of assistance to others, but as the victim who defies another to take away from him the weight of his own death:

> This living hand, now warm and capable
> Of earnest grasping, would, if it were cold
> And in the icy silence of the tomb,
> So haunt thy days and chill thy dreaming nights
> That thou wouldst wish thine own heart dry of blood
> So in my veins red life might stream again,
> And thou be conscience-calmed—see here it is—
> I hold it towards you.
> ("This Living Hand," ll. 1–8)

Romantic literature, at its highest moments, encompasses the greatest degree of generality in an experience that never loses contact with the individual self in which it originates. In the *Confessions*, Rousseau tells how an injustice committed at his expense during his youth awakened within him a universal moral sense: "I feel my pulse quicken as I write this; I shall never forget these moments if I live a hundred thousand years. This first experience of violence and injustice remained so deeply engraved on my soul that all ideas related to it take me back to this initial emotion; this experience which, at its origin, existed only for me, has acquired such a strong consistency in itself, and has grown so far away from my own self-interest, that my heart flares up at the sight or at the report of an unjust deed, committed anywhere at anyone's expense, as if it concerned me personally." It is the scope of this generalized passion which makes it possible for Rousseau to be at the same time the poet who wrote *Julie* and the moral philosopher who wrote the *Social Contract*. The same scope is present in Wordsworth and also, at times, in Blake and Coleridge. Nowadays, we are less than ever capable of philosophical generality rooted in genuine self-insight, while our sense of selfhood hardly ever rises above self-justification. Hence that our criticism of romanticism so often misses the mark: for the great romantics, consciousness of self was the first and necessary step toward moral judgment. Keats's last poems reveal that he reached the same insight; the fact that he arrived at it by a negative road may make him all the more significant for us.

MORRIS DICKSTEIN

The World of the Early Poems

... to somewhere
Virginal perhaps, less fragmentary, cool.
—HART CRANE, "For the Marriage of Faustus and Helen"

No part of Keats' work is more vulnerable to the charge of escapism than the early poems. Dr. Leavis summed up his case against Shelley by attacking his "weak grasp upon the actual," but in so much of the 1817 *Poems* and *Endymion* Keats like Shelley is in explicit flight from the actual. He seeks out "places of nestling green for poets made," womblike enclosures "sequestered, wild, romantic," far away from the world and all its troubles. Or he longs to "burst our mortal bars" by receiving "shapes from the invisible world, unearthly singing / From out the middle air." He envisions the death of a poet as a kind of transcendental junket beyond this "dull, and earthly mould," to become "enskyed" like Endymion:

> "Fair world, adieu!
> Thy dales, and hills, are fading from my view:
> Swiftly I mount, upon wide spreading pinions,
> Far from the narrow bounds of thy dominions."
> ("To My Brother George," 103–6)

Corresponding to these motifs is a conception of poetry which in its refusal

---

to take any account of the darker side of experience, as Lionel Trilling says half ironically, "puzzles and embarrasses us," for it seems "the essence of Philistinism." In "Sleep and Poetry" Keats attacks poetry that "feeds upon the burrs / And thorns of life." Poetry, he tells us, should provide "trains of peaceful images," should "sooth the cares, and lift the thoughts of man" (244–47, 340):

> And they shall be accounted poet kings
> Who simply tell the most heart-easing things.
>
> (267–68)

This is inept verse, but the problems it raises are more substantive than technical. Many critics have pinpointed the vulgarities of diction and chastised Keats' models, secure in the knowledge that he was shortly to find better ones. It is less easy to deal with the substance of these poems. In this respect "To Sleep" and "In Drear-Nighted December" are less troublesome for they are not escapist poems so much as poems about the desire or compulsion to escape. They are born of anguish and mental division, highly self-conscious in their very attack on self-consciousness.

The divisions of Keats in his early poems do not pertain to self-consciousness. The troubled, almost desperate tone of the sonnet "To Sleep" places it firmly in the period that produced the "Ode to a Nightingale" and the "Ode on Melancholy." But if "Sleep and Poetry" and "I stood tip-toe" are troubled by anything, it is the pain of youth and inexperience, and Keats' sense of not yet having written great verse. They are poems of celebration, and are mainly about poetry itself, the "end and aim" of which, in the perspective of youthful ardor, seems clear enough. The complexity of awareness that is the glory and the torment of the later Keats is absent from these poems. Yet in a naive and spontaneous way they undertake many of the strategies that we have seen to be characteristic of Keats at a later, more sophisticated period.

Sleep and death in "To Sleep" and the natural cycle in "In Drear-Nighted December" are envied not for their own sake but have rather a special meaning for Keats. He appeals to them as antidotes to consciousness, modes of self-transcendence, even to the point of self-annihilation, which the all-too-conscious poet seizes upon. Yet such forms of self-transcendence are no sudden discovery that Keats makes late in his career. They have always been important, particularly to the poet of the 1817 volume and the more complex *Endymion*.

Earlier generations, that took more pleasure in descriptive verse, could be indulgent toward Keats' first volume for what Leigh Hunt in his still interesting review called the young poet's "close observation of nature."

But Hunt's sensitive illustration of their descriptive accuracy provided authority for a distortion of critical emphasis. Hunt takes it for granted that the reader will find evidence of sufficient (and probably excessive) imaginative liberty, exquisite proof of a "most luxuriant fancy." Therefore, starting on the first page of the book, he sets out to show that it "presents us with a fancy, founded, as all beautiful fancies are, on a strong sense of what really exists or occurs." Yet this delicate polarity is lost when Graham Hough says of the same volume that

> Keats, like Gautier, was "un homme pour qui le monde visible existe." And the visible world meant chiefly the world of nature; not nature with all the mystical and moral overtones that Wordsworth found in it, but simply the unanalysed delightfulness of living and growing things.

Citing several passages from the opening poem, he goes on to say that "there is nothing here that could not be seen in a summer afternoon on Hampstead Heath."

A close look at that first poem proves Keats to be less than satisfied with "le monde visible." The very first line—"I stood tip-toe upon a little hill"—puts a double emphasis on upward movement, hinting at the higher flights that the poem will later undertake. The "natural description" that follows tends to break away from nature, to make mental constructions upon it. Line after line yields extreme examples of the pathetic fallacy. The sweet buds pull in their stems "with a modest pride" (3). The dew on the buds forms "starry diadems / Caught from the early sobbing of the morn." The clouds are likened to "flocks new shorn" sleeping "on the blue fields of heaven" (8–10),

> ...and then there crept
> A little noiseless noise among the leaves,
> Born of the very sigh that silence heaves.
> (10–12)

Personification is here bolstered by oxymoron with such effect that the literal object ("a gentle air in solitude," Leigh Hunt tells us) is almost obliterated by the power of the formulation. We have Hunt's assurance that the poem originated with an actual morning on Hampstead Heath, but as it progresses the poet seems less and less content with the natural scene. The "greediest eye" extends itself farther and farther, moves toward the horizon, and beyond it:

> Far round the horizon's crystal air to skim,
> And trace the dwindled edgings of its brim;
> (17–18)

Gradually, the natural landscape turns into an imagined one, food for speculation.

> To picture out the quaint, and curious bending
> Of a fresh woodland alley, never ending;
> Or by the bowery clefts, and leafy shelves,
> Guess where the jaunty streams refresh themselves.
>
> (19–22)

The visual (to use Geoffrey Hartman's terms) gives way to the visionary. The mind, which began by observing nature, proceeds to contemplate it and be liberated from it.

> I gazed awhile, and felt as light, and free
> As though the fanning wings of Mercury
> Had play'd upon my heels: I was light-hearted,
> And many pleasures to my vision started.
>
> (23–26)

"The 'posey' of luxuries that he then proceeds to pluck," J. R. Caldwell says, "that is the images of beauty which he jumbles out, are items not present to his actual sense, but mere ideas floating across his inward eye as he gazes on the generative scene around him." The seemingly random lines that follow are not primarily objective or descriptive. As Caldwell has shown, they are structured only by a loose process of association in the mind of the living subject.

But Keats' contemplation of nature is not indiscriminate. One motif which recurs so frequently that it seems the epitome of his sense of nature is the bower—the enclosed, sheltered nook, the place of nestling green. Behind this "little space, with boughs all woven round," stands Hunt, but more importantly the poet whom Keats considered Hunt's master and for a time his own, Spenser. In *The Faerie Queene* the bower, especially the famous Bower of Bliss, is dialectically linked to an opposing motif, that of the traveler or the quest, and both embody values that are important for the poem as a whole. The quest in Spenser connotes growth and moral development, what the Germans call *Bildung*, and no matter how fantastic or allegorical the landscape it always supposes a world of time, toil, and change. The Bower of Bliss, on the other hand, embodies a timeless world of desire, the instinctual life that seems impervious to change and development. For the moral traveler it represents the dangerous temptation of shelter and rest. Just before reaching the Bower of Bliss, the boat of Guyon and the Palmer passes "a still / And calmy bay," sheltered on both sides to make a "plesaunt port." Here Siren-like mermaids call out to Guyon:

O turne thy rudder hither-ward awhile:
Here may thy storme-bet Vessell safely ryde;
This is the Port of rest from troublous toyle,
The worlds sweet In, from paine and wearisome turmoyle.

(II, xii, 32)

The Bower itself passes before the moving Guyon as a series of static scenes, and it is largely the firmness of purpose of the Palmer, his moral Virgil, that keeps the knight from stopping or turning aside from his course. At the risk of schematic simplification, we can see the same dichotomy reflected in Spenser's style. From the bower, or the principle of pleasure, springs the famous lushness and sensuousness that so appealed to the Romantics. From the quest, or the principle of *Bildung*, proceeds the complex structure of the poem, its Arthurian epic material, and allegorical method.

The Bower of Bliss well illustrates one of the fundamental ambiguities of the bower motif. Both in pastoral poetry and in the Genesis story the enclosed, sheltered *locus amoenus* usually symbolizes some kind of innocence, the imagined innocence of nature itself, or of our childhood, or of some prelapsarian sexual paradise, free of shame, guilt, and domineering lust. Sometimes all these fantasies are combined, fed as they are by common memories of a lost paradise of total infantile gratification; after all, Freud's announcement of infantile sexuality, like his theory of the unconscious, has many mythic, poetic, and religious antecedents. In any case, the sexual significance of the bower is highly variable, especially in relation to our notions of human innocence, of human nature and purpose. But to the quest-hero of Spenserian epic, who must accomplish his mission in the world of experience, the pleasures of innocence are as regressive and dangerous as the pleasures of sex. Spenser at once exploits the bower tradition and moralizes it when he turns the emblem of innocence into a myth of sexual temptation for the ascetic hero.

In the Romantic period the duality of the bower motif is preserved and developed. Wordsworth's beautiful fragment "Nutting" describes a scene which seems to combine unspoiled innocence and sexual temptation:

The hazels rose
Tall and erect, with tempting clusters hung,
A virgin scene!—A little while I stood,
Breathing with such suppression of the heart
As joy delights in; and, with wise restraint
Voluptuous, fearless of a rival, eyed
The banquet.

(19–25)

In this poem Wordsworth's boy reenacts Sir Guyon's destruction of the Bower of Bliss, but with an important difference. No one is more deeply concerned with, and committed to, the idea of *Bildung* than Wordsworth. The Immortality ode, as Lionel Trilling has told us, is a poem about "growing up"; in fact his whole treatment of time, memory, and childhood reveals a careful avoidance of the dangers of nostalgia. "Nutting" was originally intended as part of his autobiographical poem on the growth of a poet's mind, and Wordsworth, like Spenser, apparently sees the boy's destruction of the bower as a necessary step in that growth. The Bower of Bliss, however, is wholly inimical to the knight's mission: its destruction is a positive moral gesture. But the boy's act, detailed with striking narrative restraint and neutrality, is shot through with moral ambiguity. As he turns away, his exultation is mingled with "a sense of pain" as he observes the "deformed and sullied" being that lies before him. Wordsworth seeks to overcome the crude antithesis that the episode in Spenser proposes between the exigencies of moral development and the turbid claims of the instinctual life. Wordsworth is often accused of being the most asexual of the English poets, but nothing is more important to his sense of nature than the "vital feelings of delight" that animate it. In "Lines Written in Early Spring" he contrasts the idyllic bower with the evil of "what man has made of man":

> Through primrose tufts, in that green bower,
> The periwinkle trailed its wreaths;
> And 'tis my faith that every flower
> Enjoys the air it breathes.
>
> The birds around me hopped and played,
> Their thoughts I cannot measure:—
> But the least motion which they made,
> It seemed a thrill of pleasure.
>
> The budding twigs spread out their fan,
> To catch the breezy air;
> And I must think, do all I can,
> That there was pleasure there.
>
> (9–20)

The emphasis of these lines, like the "thousand blended notes" of the opening of the poem, is on a harmonious reciprocity so great that Wordsworth in the end associates it with the "holy" and unfallen sexuality of Eden, the first of the bowers. In a closely connected poem ("To My Sister") he turns this perception into a virtual manifesto; he promises to restore this natural joy and harmony to the life of man:

No joyless forms shall regulate
Our living calendar:
We from to-day, my Friend, will date
The opening of the year.

Love, now a universal birth,
From heart to heart is stealing,
From earth to man, from man to earth:
—It is the hour of feeling.

(17–24)

The act of the boy in "Nutting" has none of this utopian simplicity and fervor. It is a violent rather than harmonious intercourse, and it takes place in a post-Edenic world of experience and consciousness, a world in which "a sense of pain" may be attendant on pleasure. But Wordsworth is careful not to moralize or condemn it. It is a necessary initiation, and a sexual one, that brings the boy into contact with the vital spirit of nature.

Keats, too, as early as "Sleep and Poetry," foresaw the need to go beyond the bower, to bid farewell to "the realm . . . of Flora, and old Pan." But unlike Wordsworth he shows a truly Spenserian tendency to linger a while, even at the risk of inconsistency. Keats' early poems remain deeply committed to the bower; yet his use of the motif is strikingly rich and picks up many of the varied strands of meaning that had become attached to it. Like Wordsworth he reads Spenser in his diabolical sense (as Blake and Shelley read Milton) and ignores the Spenserian moral. Wordsworth rejects the Spenserian dichotomy of pleasure and *Bildung*: he emphasizes experiences of pleasure that are also integral to human growth. He tries to free the bower of its regressive element and integrate it into a richer conception of the moral life. The early Keats does nothing so complex. He accepts the Spenserian dichotomy but inverts it. The bower remains regressive and inimical to moral growth, but he embraces it nonetheless. For the Keats of "Sleep and Poetry" a bowery nook is indeed elysium, and the "nobler life, / Where I may find the agonies, the strife / Of human hearts" is no more than a pious intention.

The bower is the central image of all Keats' early poems, but it is no longer necessarily a literal *locus amoenus*, the beautiful spot in nature. Sleep, which shelters and refreshes, is itself a bower "more healthful than the leafiness of dales." The heroes of liberty that appear in the early poems are not treated politically at all. The "patriotic lore" of Milton and Sidney delights Keats' soul only after he finds "with easy quest, / A fragrant wild, with Nature's beauty drest." The name of Kosciusko or Alfred is itself a bower, "a full harvest whence to reap high feeling." The recurrent natural imagery here is more important than the separate objects that evoke it. The work of art is another bower. Keats calls the Chaucerian poem *The Floure and the Lefe* "a little copse: / The honied lines do freshly interlace / To keep the reader in so sweet a place. . . ." In Hunt's *Story of Rimini*, says Keats, the reader will find "a region of his own, / A bower for his spirit." This generalizing tendency culminates in the opening lines of *Endymion*, in which any "thing of beauty" becomes a bower for the spirit:

> . . . it will never
> Pass into nothingness; but still will keep
> A bower quiet for us, and a sleep
> Full of sweet dreams, and health, and quiet breathing.

The list that follows mixes examples from nature, art, and history ("the grandeur of the dooms / We have imagined for the mighty dead"). Keats culminates by transforming the bower completely from a spatial concept to a temporal and psychological one, akin to Wordsworth's "spots of time":

> Nor do we merely feel these essences
> For one short hour;

but rather they

> Haunt us till they become a cheering light
> Unto our souls.

We can mostly readily characterize the bower by borrowing the adjectives that Keats applies to Sleep at the beginning of "Sleep and Poetry": gentle, soothing, tranquil, healthful, secret, serene, and full of visions. In the lines describing the realm of Flora and old Pan it is also overtly erotic, though with an innocence that recalls, as Wordsworth does, the undifferentiated instinctual fulfillment of childhood. We are reminded of the explicitly sexual account of the flower and the bee, which is much more suggestive and general in its reference. After defending the passive feminine pleasure of the flower against the active exertions of the bee ("and who shall say between Man and Woman which is the most delighted?"), Keats goes on to attach a moral:

> let us not therefore go hurrying about and collecting honey-bee like, buzzing here and there impatiently from a knowledge of what is to be arrived at: but let us open our leaves like a flower and be passive and receptive—budding patiently under the eye of Apollo and taking hints from every noble insect that favors us with a visit—sap will be given us for Meat and dew for drink.

> (1:232)

In this letter of 1818, Keats is making explicit what remained only a large implication in his "regressive" early poems. He is attacking what has been called the main tendency of all of Western culture—the Faustian impulse. It was Goethe who grasped the modern expression of this spirit when at the end of *Faust* he turned the medieval necromancer into an engineer. He saw that the direction of man's quest to subdue nature had shifted from magic to technology. It is no accident then that the terms that Keats chooses for his attack are partly economic and social. The bee is the epitome of the modern *homo economicus*, "collecting honey-bee like, buzzing here and there impatiently from a knowledge of what is to be arrived at." The bee's activity is not really pleasurable at all, but rather utilitarian: teleologically oriented toward economically useful ends. Keats justifies the passive and feminine against the active and masculine not out of a decadent refinement of sensibility or simple preference for inertia. He is defending enjoyment against productivity and consumption, pleasure against utility. Against the rationality of the *telos* or end, Keats opposes that mode of being which, though economically irresponsible ("sap will be given us for Meat and dew for drink"), needs no further justification, for it is an end in itself. It is not simply out of inexperience or a sense of propriety that the erotic activity in Keats' early poems often shades off into harmless and innocent play, such as biting the white shoulders of nymphs. Keats can combine innocence and erotic activity not because he has a theory of infantile sexuality (though on one level both he and Wordsworth here anticipate Freud), or even because, like Wordsworth in "Lines Written in Early Spring," like Blake, like many of the mystics, he does not accept the Christian association of the Fall with sexuality. It is rather because play for the child, like love-making for the adult, is an irresponsible end in itself, and thus when forbidden by utilitarian rationality from every other area of adult life, it can retain its sway in sexual activity. Keats' mature masculinity, Trilling suggests, "grew easily and gently out of his happy relation with his infant appetites."

It would be a mistake to make too much of the moral originality of Keats' early poems, or to impute to them any direct social consciousness. But the Romantic poets rarely expressed their social values as the novelist did, by dealing directly with historical or social conflicts. Instead their poetry responds to a nascent urban and industrial society by withdrawing from it, by cultivating much that it denies and negates. The almost untroubled sensuality of Keats' early poems, their "exquisite sense of the luxurious" (1:271), does not announce itself polemically as the abolition of repression, or the end of sublimation, nor does it even reveal many marks of internal conflict. It nevertheless remains a sharp though implicit attack on the reality principle and on the utilitarian ideal of productivity, which Herbert Marcuse in *Eros and Civilization* calls "one of the most strictly protected values of modern culture." By this standard, he says, man is evaluated according to his ability to make, augment, and improve socially useful things. Productivity thus designates the degree of the mastery and transformation of nature: the progressive replacement of an uncontrolled natural environment by a controlled technological environment. However, the more the division of labor was geared to utility for the established productive apparatus rather than for the individuals—in other words the more the social need deviated from the individual need—the more productivity tended to contradict the pleasure principle and to become an end-in-itself. The very word came to smack of repression or its philistine glorification: it connotes the resentful defamation of rest, indulgence, receptivity—the triumph over the "lower depths" of the mind and body, the taming of the instincts by exploitative reason.

"Rest, indulgence, receptivity": these are almost Keats' very words. "Let us open our leaves like a flower and be passive and receptive—budding patiently under the eye of Apollo." Not to master nature but to be mastered by it, almost to become a part of it and participate in its rhythms.

This immersion in the natural process may be an escape but it is not born of despair or envy as in "In drear-nighted December." In the early poems it is a sheer fanciful act of exuberance. Keats even constructs an only half-serious aesthetic upon it:

> For what has made the sage or poet write
> But the fair paradise of Nature's light?
> In the calm grandeur of a sober line,
> We see the waving of the mountain pine;
> And when a tale is beautifully staid,
> We feel the safety of a hawthorn glade:
> When it is moving on luxurious wings,
> The soul is lost in pleasant smotherings.
> ("I stood tip-toe," 125–32)

With the "fair paradise" and the "hawthorn glade" we are at the heart of the bower world. Keats can celebrate the identity of the aesthetics of nature and the aesthetics of poetry only because nature and poetry are both bowers for the spirit. But although the passage begins and continues in simple celebration, a darker undertone gradually can be heard. The motif of shelter and safety so important to Keats' bowers brings to mind the threatening world without. Even the motif of sensuous delight suddenly implies the promise of escape: "the soul is lost in pleasant smotherings." This culminates when

> ... at our feet, the voice of crystal bubbles
> Charms us at once away from all our troubles:
> So that we feel uplifted from the world ...
> (137–39)

Between this poem and the similar gestures of escape in "In drear-nighted December" or "To Sleep" lies a chasm of self-consciousness. Yet here we find the early promptings of their tragic view of the world and the self, both seen as troublesome burdens to be sloughed off. In their rudimentary way these poems, so transparent at first glance, are as dialectical as the later ones; they seem facile only because Keats hardly seems to *earn* his yearnings for the annihilation of self. The soul that is lost in "pleasant smotherings" is being trivialized as well as lost, and could not have been much to begin with.

    We do not recognize in this the poet who was to call the world "the vale of Soul-making" (2:102). Yet this yearning is so rooted in his mind that we find it expressed in one of the first poems he ever wrote:

> Fill for me a brimming bowl
> And let me in it drown my soul
>
> . . . I want not the stream inspiring
> That fills the mind with fond desiring,
> But I want as deep a draught
> As e'er from Lethe's wave was quaff'd.
>   ("Fill for me a brimming bowl,"
>   1–2, 5–8)

This is the first gesture toward "the feel of not to feel it," the first expression of that desire for insentience as an antidote to consciousness. But in the 1817 volume and *Endymion* the characteristic means of annihilating self is not insentience but pleasure,

> Richer entanglements, enthralments far
> More self-destroying, leading, by degrees,
> To the chief intensity. . . .
>   (*End.*, I, 798–800)

In his address to Poesy in "Sleep and Poetry" he offers himself up for a hedonistic ritual of self-sacrifice:

> . . . to my ardent prayer,
> Yield from thy sanctuary some clear air,
> Smoothed for intoxication by the breath
> Of flowering bays, that I may die a death
> Of luxury, and my young spirit follow
> The morning sun-beams to the great Apollo
> Like a fresh sacrifice.
>   (55–61)

The common Elizabethan pun on "die" testifies that there is nothing novel in Keats' association of loss of self with an intensity of pleasure. Yet in the lines that follow, Keats begins to recognize that poetic creation is an active process, that only if he resists the loss of self can he become a poet. Only if he "can bear / The o'erwhelming sweets" rather than be sacrificed will he be granted "fair / Visions of all places."

To resist loss of self is not yet to have a complex or mature awareness of self. Similarly, to surmise an active notion of the creative process is not yet to have an adequate theory of the imagination. When Wordsworth in *The Prelude* discovers within himself a "plastic power," a force that rises from the mind's abyss, which he names Imagination, there is no more talk of "wise passiveness." What makes "Sleep and Poetry" so exciting as a transitional poem (along with the almost simultaneously written last part of "I stood tiptoe") is Keats' incipient discovery of Imagination as a creative agency. For the early Keats "vision" amounts to no more than reverie or musings: "I was light-hearted / And many pleasures to my vision started." Sleep is "more full of visions than a high romance." The "fair / Visions of all places" that Poesy offers amount to "an eternal book / Whence I may copy many a lovely saying / About the leaves, and flowers." Here he goes no further than a trivialized version of eighteenth-century neoclassic theory. The poet is a copyist rather than an original creator. The "sayings" preexist him. Instead of Imagination we get "imaginings," which hover round and need only be plucked out of the air: "Also imaginings will hover / Round my fire-side, and haply there discover / Vistas of solemn beauty" ("Sleep and Poetry," 62–73). But this is not the final word of the younger Keats on poetic creation.

Keats never gives himself up entirely to the languorous passivity of sleep and the bower. Even in the meandering catalogue of "Nature's gentle doings" (early in "I stood tiptoe") a contrary principle begins forcibly to assert itself.

> What next? A tuft of evening primroses,
> O'er which the mind may hover till it dozes;
> O'er which it well might take a pleasant sleep,
> But that 'tis ever startled by the leap
> Of buds into ripe flowers; or by the flitting
> Of diverse moths, that aye their rest are quitting;
> Or by the moon lifting her silver rim
> Above a cloud, and with a gradual swim
> Coming into the blue with all her light.
>
> (107–15)

Keats suddenly realizes that nature can be seen as a locus of energy as well as rest, of self-assertion as well as unconscious process. The emergence of flowers from buds, which elsewhere epitomizes the untroubled progress of the organic cycle, here strikes the sleep-prone observer as a startling "leap," with a violence that almost denotes volition. The same quality of self-determining strength is present in Keats' description of the moon, forcefully coming into her own, with a remarkable balance of languorous restraint and energy (e.g., "a gradual swim"). Most significant, however, in view of the long poem soon to follow, is Keats' choice of the moon as a focus for these energies.

At the beginning of our discussion we discerned in "I stood tip-toe" an important upward movement by which Keats seemed to resist assimilation into empirical and objective nature. In the moon this movement finds a high symbolic goal. Running through all of Keats' early poems is a persistent theory of visionary inspiration and a desire for transcendental flight. Often, in earlier poems, this motif is conventional enough, as Keats exuberantly imitates the external trappings of romance:

> A sudden glow comes on them, naught they see
> In water, earth, or air, but poesy.

> ... when a Poet is in such a trance,
> In air he sees white coursers paw, and prance,
> Bestridden of gay knights, in gay apparel,
> Who at each other tilt in playful quarrel.
> ("To My Brother George," 21–22, 25–28)

Later in the poem we have that horrendous apotheosis of the dead poet, which I quoted at the start of this essay. But when in the same poem the moon makes a brief appearance, it seems to offer a much more genuine and enchanting enticement:

> Ah, yes! much more would start into his sight—
> The revelries, and mysteries of night.
>
> (63–64)

Here Keats approaches the vein of the true Romantic night-poem. Mystery and enchantment are not ornamental details of romance machinery but offer visionary access to new realities, occasions for original creation.

The real breakthrough does not come until the second half of "I stood tip-toe," where Keats, as Leigh Hunt first pointed out, echoes Wordsworth's discussion of mythology in the fourth book of The Excursion. In a passage that Hazlitt had singled out for special praise in his review, Wordsworth, who with Coleridge had long sought to prune English poetic diction of the dead wood of personification and mythological reference, gave a sympathetic account of ancient mythology and the pagan gods, as an anthropomorphic product of man's own imagination. Blake, with pithy brilliance, had developed a similar notion in The Marriage of Heaven and Hell, concluding that "All deities reside in the human breast." Wordsworth has no such heterodox intentions, nor does he seem interested like Blake in mythology as a manifestation of the visionary power of the poetic genius. He uses mythology, as Keats sometimes will, as part of a polemic against analytic modes of thought, the tendency to view "all objects unremittingly / In disconnection dead and spiritless; / And still dividing, and dividing still, / Break down all grandeur" (*Excursion*, IV, 961–64). He exalts the opposite tendency of man in an otherwise alien and inhuman world to find "a spiritual presence," which links pagan misconceptions to Christian verities. Wordsworth, growing steadily more orthodox and more suspicious of the free imagination, sees this consoling presence not as a life granted to nature by man's perception, but as a true intuition of the divine. In "I stood tip-toe" Keats, though liberated by Wordsworth, stands closer to Blake. The myth-making poet whom he conceives inventing the story of Narcissus or Endymion (out of his humanizing perception of the flower or the moon) is not in search of consolation, nor do his findings confirm any creative power but his own. ("That which is creative must create itself," Keats was to write [1:374] apropos of the composition of his later Endymion poem.)

> Where had he been, from whose warm head out-flew
> That sweetest of all songs, that ever new,
> That aye refreshing, pure deliciousness,
> Coming ever to bless
> The wanderer by moonlight? to him bringing
> Shapes from the invisible world, unearthly singing
> From out the middle air, from flowery nests,
> And from the pillowy silkiness that rests
> Full in the speculation of the stars.
> Ah! surely he had burst our mortal bars;
> Into some wond'rous region he had gone,
> To search for thee, divine Endymion!
>   ("I stood tip-toe," 181–92)

Here the short upward flight of the beginning of the poem, a mild release from nature into reverie, gives way to a notion of the creative imagination that involves a higher visionary flight, even transcendence. The poet seeks not merely a "spiritual presence" in the external world; if Wordsworth aims to "see into the life of things," then Keats in this poem stands closer to Coleridge, who insists in "Dejection" that the "fountains are within." Within his own spirit, yet for Keats also involving escape toward another place, a refuge for the spirit, possession almost. "Into what Regions was his spirit gone / When he first thought of thee Endymion?" Keats wrote in an earlier variant. But this expanse of spirit does not make for an experience narrowly spiritual: it is sensuous to the height of synaesthetic intensity. Criticism halts in alarm and wonder at such lines as "the pillowy silkiness that rests / Full in the speculation of the stars." One can take note with Professor Fogle of Keats' juxtaposition of a lush tactile image with an abstract visual one, or admire with Professor Trilling Keats' ability to move "from the sensual to the transcendent, from pleasure to knowledge, and knowledge of an ultimate kind." Yet one is not sure of what that knowledge is, and it seems that some blatant, peculiarly Keatsian excess has been perpetrated in order to achieve it.

Yet this moment is not exceptional, for "flowery nests" indicates that we have come upon another bower. The opposition between the enclosed place and the upward flight is only an apparent one, because the bower and the visionary "middle air" are cities of refuge from the tyranny of what Keats in *Endymion* calls "habitual self" (II, 276). But here the element of escape and self-transcendence, while present and significant ("Ah! surely he had burst our mortal bars"), is subordinate to the achievement of a new creative consciousness. One element of the bower in Keats is always that it offers "fair / Visions of all places," but here Keats goes beyond this sort of reverie. Just as he seeks escape not merely from the phenomenal world but from our mortal condition itself, so his vision will involve not random imaginings but a genuinely original myth-making, one that will offer access to new modes of being, that will encompass spiritual experience without denying physical, that will, in Blake's terms, approach and perceive the infinite through "an improvement of sensual enjoyment." For the early Keats, as for Blake, the autonomy of the poetic imagination will be established by cleansing the doors of perception.

Keats' main attempt in the 1817 volume to find a concrete symbol to represent his new sense of the visionary power of the imagination is a disappointment. The passage in "Sleep and Poetry" in which a mysterious airborne chariot appears has been little understood and even less admired. It follows the well-known lines in which Keats promises to bid farewell to the joys of Flora and old Pan, to "pass them for a nobler life, / Where I may find the agonies, the strife / Of human hearts." Miss Lowell, taking this for a renunciation of the pleasure principle and an embrace of reality, was distressed to see it followed not by a full-fledged manifesto for a new humanist poetry but by an obscure vision. Keats, as almost all critics of "Sleep and Poetry" have noted, was indeed deeply influenced by Wordsworth's account of the stages of human growth, especially by his belief that the human bonds and responsibilities of maturity could provide compensation for loss of the prereflective natural pleasures of childhood. There was a strong tendency on Keats' part, particularly later in his career, to see his own development in terms of stages of growth, and like Donne to provide himself with little imaginative autobiographies. And he was later, on one such occasion, to commend Wordsworth for having "martyr[ed] himself to the human heart" (1:278–79). But in "Sleep and Poetry" Keats is not yet prepared to present himself for martyrdom. The acute Wordsworthian sense of time is absent here; Keats longs somehow to possess all the stages of growth simultaneously.

In some respects Keats is describing aesthetic choices rather than life-choices, not a passage from selfish pleasure to social conscience—the context partly belies this—but the traditional Virgilian progress from pastoral to epic, which for Keats here means from nature to vision. But even these are not exclusive alternatives for him. In the succeeding lines that help us interpret the appearance of the car and charioteer Keats wonders whether

> . . . the high
> Imagination cannot freely fly
> As she was wont of old? prepare her steeds,
> Paw up against the light, and do strange deeds
> Upon the clouds? Has she not shown us all?
> From the clear space of ether, to the small
> Breath of new buds unfolding? From the meaning
> Of Jove's large eye-brow, to the tender greening
> Of April meadows?
>
> (163-71)

The important fact about the car then, which we now know to represent "the high / Imagination," is its upward flight—to the epic realm of the gods, Jove, and "the clear space of ether." These lines introduce the polemic against the school of Pope, which in measured couplets "sway'd about upon a rocking horse / And thought it Pegasus," a contrast which pointedly recalls the flying steeds of the Imagination. "The small / Breath of buds unfolding" and "the tender greening / Of April meadows," however, refer back to none other than the supposedly abandoned realm of Flora and old Pan. Keats seems to be saying that true imagination can encompass both epic and pastoral, can possess both the visionary ether and the natural pleasures of the bower. Both this higher and lower flight he contrasts, unfairly or not, with the deadly middle range of Augustan *vers de société*, with its technical precision, urbane (and urban) wit, and willing insensitivity to the natural world. Keats' charioteer, on the other hand, is able somehow "with wond'rous gesture" to speak to the natural world, to animate the landscape with the very energy of his response to it (an intercourse which recalls Wordsworth's "Prospectus" to *The Recluse*, with its vision of the marriage of mind and nature). But aside from the "shapes of delight, of mystery, and fear," which recalls motifs often associated in these early poems with the moon, there is unfortunately little that is vivid about Keats' description of the car. He experiences nothing about this vision so intensely as the loss of it, and the lines which describe that loss are perhaps the most important in the whole 1817 volume:

The visions all are fled—the car is fled
Into the light of heaven, and in their stead
A sense of real things comes doubly strong,
And, like a muddy stream, would bear along
My soul to nothingness: but I will strive
Against all doubtings, and will keep alive
The thought of that same chariot, and the strange
Journey it went.

(155–62)

In one minor sense the reference of these lines is historical and polemical. The visionary car is the great poetry of the sixteenth and seventeenth centuries, the heir (in Keats' view) to the classical tradition of Homer and Virgil, and the muddy stream is the poetry of the century that followed, trapped in an unimaginative "sense of real things." Keats is dedicating himself to the older tradition and to its sense of the powers of the imagination. This passage and the lines about "the high / Imagination" that follow provide a transition to the attack on the Augustans and the account of the state of poetry in his own time. ("Sleep and Poetry," though associative and uneven, is a more unified poem than anyone has been willing to grant.)

But the important reference of the lines is personal rather than public or discursive. This is the first of many crucial passages of disintoxication or disenchantment—perhaps the German *Entzauberung* describes it best—when Keats, after the largest imaginative projects, is brought suddenly back, in a moment of lonely and naked lucidity, to his sole self. It is not simply that imagination or vision, seen as positive quantities, fail him and leave him bereft. As Keats made the car his first symbol of the power of the imagination, he also made it, perhaps less intentionally, the first symbol of his suspicion of the imagination. Keats' "doubtings" are from within; the "sense of real things comes *doubly* strong" only because it must have remained strong even at the height of vision. Yet he preserves a remarkable balance and tension. The sense of real things can also be a muddy stream, can mean the restoration of the tyranny of the merely external object-world, which would darken the waters of inspiration and annihilate the creative ego. The passage expresses poignant loss as well as lucid self-consciousness, and Keats' final resolution is appropriately Wordsworthian. The visionary gleam, Wordsworth had taught, could yet glimmer in the eye of the philosophic mind, naive vision could survive within the self as memory, could bear the buffets of the world by being raised to thought ("The thought of that same chariot, and the strange / Journey it went").

Nature, pleasure, vision—these mean much to the early Keats; they are more than escapist fantasies. Yet they exhibit a common movement of flight from painful realities and arise out of a common impulse to annihilate the self that is the locus of such realities. But this movement and impulse in themselves imply a tragic awareness, in their very resistance to tragedy. In these lines of "Sleep and Poetry" especially, Keats briefly assumes that burden of selfhood, that divided consciousness, which Matthew Arnold called the characteristic modern predicament: "the dialogue of the mind with itself."

STUART M. SPERRY

The Allegory of "Endymion"

E*ndymion* presents particular chal-
lenges to the critic. The poem is by far the longest Keats wrote and has,
among his longer pieces, the notable advantage of completeness. He devoted
almost a year of his brief career to it and learned much from its composition. It seems to merit the fullest critical attention. Yet the poem is
labyrinthine and overgrown, a little wilderness amid whose tangles one can
wander happily but at the risk of becoming lost. Keats was himself aware
both of the fascinations and the dangers of the longer work. "I have heard
Hunt say and may be asked," he wrote George at about the time he began
Endymion, "why endeavour after a long Poem? To which I should answer—
Do not the Lovers of Poetry like to have a little Region to wander in where
they may pick and choose, and in which the images are so numerous that
many are forgotten and found new in a second Reading: which may be food
for a week's stroll in the Summer?" A long poem could provide the reader
with room to move about in, "full of Symbols for his spiritual eye, of softness
for his spiritual touch, of space for his wandering of distinctness for his
Luxury," as he later put it. Nevertheless certain further guidelines and
objectives were, if only by implication, necessary. "Besides," he went on to
George, "a long Poem is a test of Invention which I take to be the Polar Star
of Poetry, as Fancy is the Sails, and Imagination the Rudder." Not long
earlier he had pictured himself as drifting on the stream of rhyme "With
shatter'd boat, oar snapt, and canvass rent." It remained to be seen what

---

navigational skill he could bring to the task of piloting the ship of poetry on a substantial "voyage of conception."

Such different needs—the desire for imaginative flexibility and amplitude together with the concern for some emerging pattern of realization—were ones Keats sought to reconcile within the broader outlines of romance. (When it appeared, his poem was subtitled "A Poetic Romance.") They go far toward explaining the considerable disagreement that has, over the years, separated critics who have sought to define more exactly the category of romance to which the poem belongs. One need only return to such older critics of the poem as Sir Sidney Colvin, Robert Bridges, and Ernest de Selincourt to recall that for many years it was traditional to read the work as a deliberate allegory, conceived more or less upon Platonic lines, of the poet's longing for and eventual union with the spirit of ideal beauty. While differing with respect to minor points of interpretation, these critics resolved the action of the poem into a series of gradually ascending stages of human development, beginning with the love of sensuous beauty, leading in time to humanitarian service and active sympathy for fellow man, and ending with the recognition that these, rightly perceived, are one with the ideal. The argument of the poem was both sustained and coherent in development, essentially a dramatic working-out, culminating in the union of Cynthia and the Indian Maiden, of the conviction Keats expressed the very month he put an end to his first draft: "I am certain of nothing but of the holiness of the Heart's affections and the truth of Imagination—What the imagination seizes as Beauty must be truth."

More recently the allegorical interpretation of the poem has come increasingly under attack. Critics like Newell Ford and E. C. Pettet have drawn attention to a notable discrepancy between Keats's supposed allegorical intention and the discursiveness and incoherence of his narrative, together with the strongly erotic character of much of the episode and imagery. These inconsistencies were, of course, evident to older critics, who explained them as the result of a gap between conception and execution understandable in a young poet distracted and at times misled by a powerfully sensuous nature. Such reasoning, however, is for Ford and Pettet mere rationalization evolved by critics unwilling or unable to confront the frank expression of Keats's longing for an "everlasting erotism," or, more simply, the sexual fantasies of a maturing young man. With the possible exception of a few passages, the poem is for them an instance of romance in the simplest sense—a frank love poem powerfully energized by Keats's adolescent desires. It would be difficult to imagine two interpretations more at odds. Is the work a fable intended to convey certain settled conclusions as to the nature of beauty, truth, and poetic experience? Or is it rather a chain of daydreams and reveries, best interpreted as a psychiatrist interprets the free associations of a patient and useful primarily for what it reveals concerning the quality of Keats's unconscious life?

It would be wrong to imply that critics of the poem have necessarily embraced one view or the other, the traditional and allegorical or the erotic. Nevertheless the two approaches have to date proved most influential and have polarized debate around certain questions of crucial importance. In weighing the merits of such different arguments, one must begin by admitting that Keats never confided, even to friends with whom he was intimate, that he wrote the poem with any allegorical plan in mind. He wrote to George of having to "make 4000 Lines of one bare circumstance and fill them with Poetry," and, divided equally between four books, the mark was one he approximated with extraordinary accuracy. Nor do his habits of composition suggest an allegorical scheme. Bailey, with whom Keats spent the month of September 1817 when he was at work on his third book, reported that Keats "sat down to his task,—which was about 50 lines a day,—with his paper before him, & wrote with as much regularity, & apparently with as much ease, as he wrote his letters." If Keats intended his poem to be read as allegory in any strict sense, the key to its meaning was a well-kept secret among his friends throughout his lifetime and after his death.

Yet for all this it remains impossible to read the whole of Keats's narrative, regardless of how aimless and confusing much of it seems, as a mere play of erotic fantasy. Endymion's speech on happiness, the central argument of Book One, outlines an ascending order of imaginative values, beginning with a love of natural objects, leading on to sympathy and friendship, and culminating in human and divine love, a hierarchy of intensities that is both developed and put to trial in the books to come. Later in the poem Endymion's sympathy for Alpheus and Arethusa, Glaucus's pity for the drowned lovers and their joint service in restoring Circe's victims to life, and the ultimate revelation that Cynthia and the Indian Maiden are one are too clearly turning points within the narrative to be dismissed as random bits of episode. Even those critics most opposed to reading the poem as allegory are forced, in one way or another, to grant such episodes a calculated significance. There was, moreover, the example set by Shelley, a fellow protégé of Hunt's whose progress Keats followed and measured himself against throughout his career and whose *Alastor or the Spirit of Solitude* had appeared only a year earlier. The latter work, a poem of quest containing passages as erotic as any in *Endymion*, had taken as its theme both the ennobling heroism and the fatal self-absorption of visionary pursuit as set off by the contradictory dialectics of its preface. The dilemma Shelley depicted was one Keats found himself engrossed by: the plight of the artist who envisions to himself an image that "unites all of wonderful, or wise, or beautiful, which the poet, the philosopher, or the lover could depicture" but that can be pursued only at the expense of an enervating introspection that isolates and kills. What was particularly impressive was the combination of openness and subtlety with which Shelley developed various aspects of the paradox into a parable of complex thematic significance. More broadly, however, one cannot ignore the whole larger tradition on which Keats drew for the major handling of his narrative: the main line of Elizabethan pastoral-didactic verse that runs from Spenser to Milton and includes such writers as George Sandys, the translator and interpreter of Ovid. It is a tradition of mythological verse in which one discovers, along with a prodigality and confusion of detail, and instinctive drift toward allegory, in Colvin's words an "habitual wedding of allegory and romance."

It is, in fact, allegory in its broadest and most general sense that characterizes *Endymion*. There is no reason for believing Keats began his poem with a plan for its development or its ultimate significance clearly in view. Quite the opposite is, in all likelihood, the case. Yet, at the same time, there is every reason to believe that he looked upon the composition as a necessary "test, a trial," as he himself put it, not merely of his "Powers of Imagination," but of his deepest instincts and beliefs. The poem must crystallize, if only for himself, the most important of his poetic convictions. Above all it must confront the whole question of visionary experience that had emerged throughout the early verse, concentrated in his fascination with the legend of Endymion. For the latter is obviously no simple love story. In its involvement with dreams and visions, its contrast between mortality and immortality, and its culmination in transcendence, the Endymion myth is unmistakably connected with the visionary concerns of the earlier poetry. As one who has "burst our mortal bars" to ascend into "some wond'rous region," Endymion offered an unmistakable analogue for the poet who gains "Wings to find out an immortality" of poetic inspiration and fulfillment. The legend provided Keats a means for dramatizing his fundamental conviction of "the truth of imagination." At the same time it possessed the flexibility to permit him to elaborate and test the reality of that belief as he proceeded.

Yet what form, more exactly, would the elaboration take? Beyond the necessity of treating the "one bare circumstance" of his fable, Keats was bound only by the otherworldly bias of the legend—its ending in transcendence of mortality—and by the expectation of some joyous, triumphant conclusion like the marriage celebrations he had touched on briefly at the end of "I Stood Tip-toe." Otherwise his plan for proceeding was pliable, even disconcertingly vague. Nevertheless his determination to adhere to his own methods of composition carried with it the necessity of trusting to his powers of invention, his ability to improvise the kind of episode that would keep his poem moving forward dramatically. As for its further significance, that would have to come organically, "as naturally as the Leaves to a tree" or not at all. The poem must communicate knowledge and conviction but, in Arnold's phrase, "insensibly, and in the second place, not the first," and through what would be essentially an act of self-discovery both for poet and reader. Much later, when his mind was "pick'd up and sorted to a pip," he was to look back on the author of *Endymion* as one "whose mind was like a pack of scattered cards." Nevertheless the experience of writing the poem, however "slip-shod" it might later seem to him, was one he could not entirely regret. As he wrote his publisher, James Hessey, in one of the most candid and noble paragraphs of self-criticism any poet has written:

> I will write independently.—I have written independently *without Judgment*—I may write independently *& with judgment* hereafter.—The Genius of Poetry must work out its own salvation in a man: It cannot be matured by law & precept, but by sensation & watchfulness in itself— That which is creative must create itself—In Endymion, I leaped headlong into the Sea, and thereby have become better acquainted with the Soundings, the quicksands, & the rocks, than if I had stayed upon the green shore, and piped a silly pipe, and took tea & comfortable advice.
>
> (Keats's italics)

As he instinctively realized, the poem represented a headlong plunge into the sea, into the reaches of his own unconsciousness and creativity, the region from which, as in his sonnet "On the Sea," some voice or harmony would have in its own way to come. In working out the destiny of his hero he was in fact working out his own.

II

It was only natural that, faced with the necessity of making a beginning, he should start his poem with what was most fundamental: his commitment to his notion of the creative process. Following its initial declaration, the opening paragraph of *Endymion* proceeds to an enumeration of particular "thing[s] of beauty"—the sun, moon, trees, sheep, flowers, rills, and forest brakes. However its real concern is with the process by which these forms are converted, partly through the agency of sleep and dreams, into "essences" that are well-nigh spiritual. The progression proceeds from the images of the natural world to their inclusion in works of imagination ("All lovely tales that we have heard or read") only to engross them all collectively within an image of supernal energy and delight—"An endless fountain of immortal drink, / Pouring unto us from the heaven's brink." The process is the now familiar one by which the images of nature are spiritualized in imagination and put into "etherial existence" for man's enduring enjoy-ment. It is a process that both exalts and liberates man in imagination and at the same time "binds" him ever more closely to the earth—the particular tension that Keats was to become steadily more preoccupied with as he proceeded.

The same progression dominates the poem's finest lyric, the "Hymn to Pan," early in Book One. In the first four stanzas the god is celebrated as the presiding deity of the world of natural process, only to emerge in the final stanza as a symbol for something more:

> Be still the unimaginable lodge
> For solitary thinkings; such as dodge
> Conception to the very bourne of heaven,
> Then leave the naked brain: be still the leaven,
> That spreading in this dull and clodded earth
> Gives it a touch ethereal—a new birth:
> Be still a symbol of immensity;
> A firmament reflected in a sea;
> An element filling the space between;
> An unknown—but no more.
>
> (i.293–302)

Ultimately Pan is something more than just a god of huntsmen, a god of the harvest. He is the symbol of a form of *thinking*. Yet he represents at most a tendency, a kind of thought that is only latent, as "a touch ethereal," throughout the universe of natural life. He remains inscrutable, something "unimaginable," precisely because he is too diverse and inexhaustible in his implications ever to be perfectly defined or brought to full "conception." He remains the symbol of a source of speculation that can have no limit, that can never be finally grasped or formulated. He endures as a symbol of the ultimate mystery of life but considered positively, as a source of endless investigation and discovery.

The principal argument of Book One, the lines Keats likened in effect to "a kind of Pleasure Thermometer," has already been discussed at length within the context of his early notion of the creative process. However, it is important to observe that within the dramatic structure of his poem Keats does not allow his hero's expression of faith in the validity of the imagina-tion and its intensifying power to go unchallenged. Endymion may cling to his intimations of divinity as "A hope beyond the shadow of a dream" (i.857), as something more than mere "atomies / That buzz about our slumbers, like brain-flies, / Leaving us fancy-sick" (i.851–53). Nevertheless from our first glimpse of him in the poem he seems pale and wan, alienated from the healthful pursuits of his fellow Latmians by his strange fits of abstraction. Indeed it is not long before Keats himself addresses him as

"Brain-sick shepherd-prince" (ii.43). More important, Endymion's affirmations of the truth of his visionary experiences are directly opposed by the counterarguments of his sister, Peona, who warns him against deceiving fantasies:

> The Morphean fount
> Of that fine element that visions, dreams,
> And fitful whims of sleep are made of, streams
> Into its airy channels with so subtle,
> So thin a breathing, not the spider's shuttle,
> Circled a million times within the space
> Of a swallow's nest-door, could delay a trace,
> A tinting of its quality: how light
> Must dreams themselves be; seeing they're more slight
> Than the mere nothing that engenders them!
> Then wherefore sully the entrusted gem
> Of high and noble life with thoughts so sick?
> Why pierce high-fronted honour to the quick
> For nothing but a dream?
>
> (i.747–60)

Her argument is a plea for Endymion to return to the world of action from the life of solitary contemplation that has absorbed him. But more than this, her speech uses several of Keats's favorite metaphors for imaginative creation only to deny their validity. The whole process of associative interweaving and etherealization is too subtle and attenuating to permit any genuine connection with reality to exist.

Thus from an early point in the poem Endymion's faith in the truth of his visionary pursuit is challenged by the warnings of his sister. Two attitudes toward his quest for happiness have emerged, one affirmative, the other skeptical. No doubt this complication was useful and even necessary to Keats for dramatic reasons, a part of the test his hero would have to undergo; but there is no reason to assume the conflict was entirely unconnected with important questions of his own. Keats was clearly committed to dramatizing his hero's struggles and ultimate reward by union with his goddess and the achievement of immortality: the conclusion was one largely determined by the fable he had chosen. Indeed we are reminded of this basic expectation from time to time along the way. At the beginning of Book Two, Endymion is informed that, like his namesake in "I Stood Tiptoe," he

> ...must wander far
> In other regions, past the scanty bar
> To mortal steps.
>
> (ii.123–25)

Again at the end of Book Three, after many disappointments, he is mysteriously reassured of his coming reward and of his love's intent to "snatch" him "into endless heaven" (iii.1026–27). Yet the deeper poetic elaboration of this intention is neither steady nor consistent. For one thing, as Endymion's dream-journeys toward his immortal love become more ecstatic, the end of the cycle—the fading of the dream, the return to earth, and the sense of loss and despondency—grows in intensity. The major action of the poem does not follow the pattern of gradual ascent but resembles more the parabolic structure we have seen emerge for the first time in the central vision of "Sleep and Poetry," a pattern of longing, momentary fulfillment, then loss, despondency, and doubt.

In dealing with the love interludes that provide the chief narrative involvement of the earlier books, it is necessary to examine the erotic character of the poem in closer detail. As I have indicated, it is for a number of reasons impossible to agree with critics who read *Endymion* as no more than a simple tale of sexual passion, the gratification of its author's suppressed desires. For time and again critics have failed to see that Keats's use of erotic imagery is integrally related to the visionary concerns of his poem, that it habitually calls into play instincts and feelings that, while connected with the sexual impulse, run deeper. Beginning with "I Stood Tip-toe," he had been drawn to the Endymion legend as a search for "endless bliss," an "immortality of passion." Yet in tracing the love-adventures of his hero, he was necessarily led to work out the implications of the quest at a deeper psychological level than any he had yet explored. At the height of his rapturous embrace with Cynthia in Book Two, Endymion exclaims:

> O known Unknown! from whom my being sips
> Such darling essence, wherefore may I not
> Be ever in these arms?
>
> (ii.739–41)

She is a "second self," his "breath of life," who promises him that

> I will tell the stories of the sky,
> And breathe thee whispers of its minstrelsy.
> My happy love will overwing all bounds!
> O let me melt into thee; let the sounds
> Of our close voices marry at their birth;
> Let us entwine hoveringly—O dearth
> Of human words! roughness of mortal speech!
> Lispings empyrean will I sometime teach
> Thine honied tongue—lute-breathings, which I gasp
> To have thee understand, now while I clasp
> Thee thus.
>
> (ii.812–22)

To read such passages as mere sexual description is to fail to see that something more than sensual passion is involved. The images of mouth and lips, of kissing, sipping, speech, possess a more than physical significance. Endymion draws emotional vitality and life from the unknown form he embraces who seems almost a part of his own unconscious being, the source of feelings that cannot be readily expressed in words. The imagery, that is to say, suggests not so much the physical passion of real lovers as the communion of the poet with the vital springs of his imaginative life. The larger context of the love-embrace suggests an ecstasy of imaginative fulfillment conveyed metaphorically through the details of bodily passion.

To interpret the love theme in *Endymion* as a part of Keats's broader visionary concern is not to explain away the erotic elements in the poem (or in Keats's nature) but to restore them to their proper perspective. For one thing, the sexual drive in any individual is never self-contained but overlaps with and is inseparable from a broad range of imaginative preoccupations. In the brief, awkwardly apologetic preface Keats published with the poem he wrote: "The imagination of a boy is healthy, and the mature imagination of a man is healthy; but there is a space of life between, in which the soul is in a ferment, the character undecided, the way of life uncertain, the ambition thick-sighted." The passage, in the kind of immaturity and indecisiveness it admits, possesses unmistakable sexual overtones; nevertheless, it is the imagination in its larger sense of which he writes.

In Book One Keats had boldly outlined the scale of various degrees of imaginative involvement leading to the "chief intensity" of love. Yet it was primarily through the longing of Endymion for Cynthia and his pursuit of the goddess that he possessed the means of dramatizing the psychological reality of visionary experience and thus of translating the terms of an abstract progression into action that is vital, fluid, and emotionally meaningful. In one sense Cynthia exists as a symbol, a mere abstraction. Yet she is a value that is variously defined and given significance by a powerful sensuality of imagination, a sensuality that itself develops and changes in implication as the poem proceeds. Even from the first our attention is not drawn to the love interludes for their own sake but for their part in the whole cycle of Endymion's visionary experience—of which the union with Cynthia is the culminating moment, but nevertheless only a part. As in the earlier poetry the process begins with a gradual withdrawal from the natural world; Endymion retreats through mossy caves and bowers until, feeling "endued / With power to dream deliciously" (ii.707–708), he falls asleep. Following the exclusion of the outer world, the dream begins through which a state of intense imaginative awareness is conveyed that underlies, at some far deeper level, the rational, conceptual functions of the mind:

Yet it was but a dream: yet such a dream
That never tongue, although it overteem
With mellow utterance, like a cavern spring,
Could figure out and to conception bring
All I beheld and felt.

(i.574–78)

The dream is not characterized merely by images of sensual gratification but by synesthesia and effortless movement, by warmth and the sudden flowering of foliage, and by the vital, flowing quality that we associate with certain states of intense imaginative experience. It is a world of fluent harmony, the expression of a primitive experience and knowledge that forever seeks yet defies precise articulation or the power of human intelligence to arrest and define.

Endymion's love for Cynthia is the expression of Keats's romance with his muse. It represents the poet's need to explore, through the metaphor of carnal knowledge, his own relation to the hidden springs of inspiration on which the life of his art depends. Nevertheless it is necessary to see that, virtually from the outset of the poem, Endymion's desire for Cynthia is neither a simple nor an unqualified attraction. The emphasis on the goddess's inviolable chastity is evident, while the note of dire warning and taboo that extends even to the Indian Maiden in the final book (iv.751–58) is both explicit and implicit throughout the earlier love sections of the poem. Beyond the alluring warmth and security of Cynthia's embrace there extends a phantasmagoric world of meteors and falling stars, of chilling airs and awesome dens and caverns; and the "dizzy sky," the hints of madness, and the threat of a precipitous fall (ii.185ff.) reintroduce the theme of the Daedalian overreacher Keats had touched on in "Sleep and Poetry." As the successful lover, Endymion is united with the source of all sweetness and joy; but he is also, like an infant, "*lapp'd* and *lull'd* along the *dangerous* sky" (i.646). Moreover the pleasures he experiences are too intense to be long enjoyed. At or near their climax a counter-movement toward earth begins, the fabric of the dream collapses, and Endymion is left in mere slumber, in "stupid sleep" (i.678). The power of the dream destroys, by force of contrast, all the natural beauty of the Latmian glades and meadows, leaving Endymion with a waking vision that, in its surrealistic horror, Keats never surpassed:

> . . . deepest shades
> Were deepest dungeons; heaths and sunny glades
> Were full of pestilent light; our taintless rills
> Seem'd sooty, and o'er-spread with upturn'd gills

Of dying fish; the vermeil rose had blown
In frightful scarlet, and its thorns out-grown
Like spiked aloe.

(i.692–98)

Despite the apparent logic of the "Pleasure Thermometer," the destructive
and inhibiting aspects of Endymion's passion do not diminish as the poem
advances; they increase.

Such shifts and changes in the presentation of Endymion's quest
reflect more than Keats's need to complicate and extend the interest of his
narrative. They express, rather, genuine ambiguities and qualifications that
came to mind only as he proceeded and as he grasped the deeper significance his treatment of the myth had begun to assume. No doubt he had
from the first foreseen certain obstacles and difficulties in his hero's way.
Endymion's isolation and neglect of his proper role as leader of his people are
manifest. Similarly the fundamental message of the Alpheus and Arethusa
episode and of that of Glaucus in Book Three seems unmistakable: in his
pursuit of visionary beauty Endymion was not to be permitted to forget the
need for sympathy and active service on behalf of fellow man. Yet in the
implications they present such episodes resist reduction to any easy "allegoric" reading. One can take as an example the Bower of Adonis in Book
Two, which traditional critics of the poem have never been comfortable in
discussing. With its accumulated store of cream and ripened fruit, the
Bower represents a perfectly self-contained world of sensuous and imaginative luxury, idealized beyond all threat of interruption, where the sleeper
dreams of his coming joys with Venus. Indeed the episode may directly
prefigure, as proponents of the erotic interpretation have argued, the very
apotheosis Keats intended for his hero. Yet the Bower, in its dream-like
isolation from the world of process and change, seems strangely etherized
and shrouded in the quiet of a deathwatch. Although grown to a man, the
sleeping Adonis resembles, as much as anything, the infant in the womb or
cradle whose every need is gratified. The episode may portray an ideal of
imaginative realization; but it is at the same time enveloped in an air of
sickliness and self-indulgence.

Such questions of nuance, and, more important, of interpretation,
multiply throughout the second half of the poem. The story of Glaucus
occupies almost the whole of Book Three and is the only sustained narrative
interlude in *Endymion*; yet its relation to the thematic center of the poem is
far from simple. On the most basic level its relevance to the themes of
sympathy and humanitarian service is clear. However, the episode seems to
bear upon the nature and the goal of Endymion's quest in a deeper way.
More specifically, how is one to interpret Glaucus's misadventure in pursuit
of his nymph Scylla? Does his failure merely serve to heighten the triumph

and superior powers of his liberator, Endymion? Or does the episode possess a further significance? Does it serve as something of a warning to Keats's hero, a premonition that the search for fulfillment in imaginative experience can end in deception and enslavement rather than in happiness and truth? Does the episode stand in sharp contrast to, or does it subtly qualify, the ambition and significance of Endymion's own pursuit? The more one studies the episode, the more difficult it becomes to narrow its significance to any single implication in the thread of Keats's "allegory."

Like Endymion, Glaucus has longed for passionate joys beyond his reach and taken the plunge "for life or death" into a denser element.

> Why was I not contented? Wherefore reach
> At things which, but for thee, O Latmian!
> Had been my dreary death? Fool! I began
> To feel distemper'd longings: to desire
> The utmost privilege that ocean's sire
> Could grant in benediction: to be free
> Of all his kingdom. Long in misery
> I wasted, ere in one extremest fit
> I plung'd for life or death. To interknit
> One's senses with so dense a breathing stuff
> Might seem a work of pain; so not enough
> Can I admire how crystal-smooth it felt,
> And buoyant round my limbs. At first I dwelt
> Whole days and days in sheer astonishment;
> Forgetful utterly of self-intent;
> Moving but with the mighty ebb and flow.
> Then, like a new fleg'd bird that first doth shew
> His spreaded feathers to the morrow chill,
> I tried in fear the pinions of my will.
> 'Twas freedom!
>
> (iii.372–91)

His plunge into the ocean brings to mind the way Keats himself "leaped headlong into the Sea" (I, 374) in committing himself to the act of self-discovery his poem represented. The description also recalls, in its new-found liberation, the same initial sense of release and exhilaration that animates the dream voyages of Keats's hero. Like Endymion, Glaucus soon becomes enamored of an otherworldly creature, the nymph Scylla, who becomes the object of his desire and whom he pursues, much as Alpheus pursues Arethusa, until, in a moment of confusion, he falls prey to the charms of the enchantress Circe. The division in his affections has no counterpart in the earlier account of Endymion's quest, although it prefigures the hero's dilemma when, at the outset of Book Four, he suddenly finds himself in love with both the Indian Maiden and his immortal goddess.

It is possible to regard Circe, like Acrasia (Keats's obvious model), as an embodiment of false sensual attraction and Glaucus's infatuation for her as a betrayal of his loyalty to Scylla that must not go unpunished. Yet once again such a pat rendering of Keats's allegory does little justice to our sense of the complexity the Glaucus episode introduces into the poem. The rose-canopied bower where Circe promises him the supreme enjoyment of "a long love dream" (iii.440) seems to reflect ironically on both the Bower of Adonis and certain aspects of the love-making between Endymion and Cynthia. Glaucus is enraptured:

> Who could resist? Who in this universe?
> She did so breathe ambrosia; so immerse
> My fine existence in a golden clime.
> She took me like a child of suckling time,
> And cradled me in roses.
>
> (iii.453–57)

We remember that only a little earlier Endymion, clasped in his goddess's embrace, had "swoon'd / Drunken from pleasure's nipple" (ii.868–69). Glaucus, however, has confused Scylla with Circe, the Bower of Adonis with the Bower of Bliss, and one morning he awakes to find his "specious heaven" transformed to "real hell" (iii.476). Amid bursts of cruel, ironic laughter the enchantress, revealed in her true ugliness, proceeds to parody the whole conception of the love-nest and to mock the lassitude and self-indulgence of her victim:

> Ha! ha! Sir Dainty! there must be a nurse
> Made of rose leaves and thistledown, express,
> To cradle thee my sweet, and lull thee: yes,
> I am too flinty-hard for thy nice touch:
> My tenderest squeeze is but a giant's clutch.
> So, fairy-thing, it shall have lullabies
> Unheard of yet: and it shall still its cries
> Upon some breast more lily-feminine.
>
> (iii.570–77)

Glaucus has discovered not Cynthia but La Belle Dame. His infatuation and its end in powerlessness and withered age represents a caricature of the whole notion of the romantic quest which inevitably raises certain questions concerning Endymion's own pursuit. One senses again that the larger meaning of the poem, the real "allegory" of *Endymion*, lies in the way such episodes as those of Alpheus and Arethusa, Endymion's love-encounters with his goddess, the Bower of Adonis, and Glaucus's confusion between Scylla and Circe play off against and qualify each other. Together they reflect the gradual emergence of Keats's deeper attitude toward visionary experience rather than the elaboration of any settled plan.

Our suspicion that Endymion's dilemma has fully become Keats's own increases with Book Four. The induction to this book is the shortest and weakest of the four and introduces a note of despondency that virtually every commentator has in one way or another observed. Keats has now thoroughly tired of the poem and is already looking forward to *Hyperion* as a work that will accomplish what he knows *Endymion* cannot. More significant is the appearance of the Indian Maiden, an event that is sudden and altogether unprepared for. At the very time when he should be struggling upward on the final lap of his journey toward the "chief intensity," Endymion is unexpectedly confronted with the choice between two quite different and opposing ideals of love—the one transcendent, ecstatic, and immortal; the other warm, earthly, and filled with the passion of the human heart. The dilemma, touched on by Shelley in *Alastor*, is one that from the first had fascinated Keats. Yet the struggle, crystallizing ambiguities latent in the earlier part of the narrative, now begins to achieve the proportions of a crisis demanding a new and more profound kind of resolution than any he could have possibly foreseen. As Book Four progresses, the conflict between the two ideals for possession of Endymion's soul becomes steadily more intense and divisive, up until the abrupt conclusion. When, for example, Endymion and the Indian Maiden mount two winged steeds and soar into the region of the skies—the obvious dramatization of Endymion's urge to reconcile his earthly and his heavenly loves—the moon appears from behind a cloud.

> While to his lady meek the Carian turn'd,
> To mark if her dark eyes had yet discern'd
> This beauty in its birth—Despair! despair!
> He saw her body fading gaunt and spare
> In the cold moonshine. Straight he seiz'd her wrist;
> It melted from his grasp: her hand he kiss'd,
> And, horror! kiss'd his own—he was alone.
> Her steed a little higher soar'd, and then
> Dropt hawkwise to the earth.
>
> (iv.504–12)

Beautiful as it first appears, the moon assumes an openly destructive role, withering in its chill light the warm beauty by Endymion's side. The baleful part of Cynthia's influence is now fully evident. Attempting to kiss the Indian Maiden, Endymion kisses his own hand, an act of autoeroticism that clearly suggests the solipsistic dangers of the visionary ideal and its ability to dissolve the ties of real human love. From his lofty perch Endymion is plunged into the Cave of Quietude, a kind of Keatsian Center of Indifference. Here he regains his presence of mind but only to reassess, a few lines later, the significance of his quest in a new and startling way:

> I have clung
> To nothing, lov'd a nothing, nothing seen
> Or felt but a great dream! O I have been
> Presumptuous against love, against the sky,
> Against all elements, against the tie
> Of mortals each to each, against the blooms
> Of flowers, rush of rivers, and the tombs
> Of heroes gone!
>   (iv.636–43)

The very intensity of Endymion's otherworldly longing has fatally overtaxed the sustaining, elemental power of those bands of natural association and human affection that prompt man's higher intimations even while they bind him more securely to the earth. Gaining conviction, he proceeds to reject the whole reality and worth of his heavenly pursuit:

> Caverns lone, farewel!
> And air of visions, and the monstrous swell
> Of visionary seas! No, never more
> Shall airy voices cheat me to the shore
> Of tangled wonder, breathless and aghast.
>   (iv.651–55)

With such words he has, as it were, come round to agreeing with his sister's judgment, and the whole value and meaning of his pilgrimage is brought into question.

For critics of the older school such speeches are only the final darkness before the onrushing dawn, Endymion's last moment of doubt before the revelation that the conflicting attractions that confront him are in fact but different aspects of a single ideal. Such a reading, whatever its validity as an ex post facto judgment, betrays the deeper meaning of the poem considered as a process of creative self-discovery. For it ignores the tone of real conviction and dramatic urgency that characterizes the struggle in Book Four and, by contrast, the brief and remarkably spiritless conclusion. The final resolution arrives in the last hundred lines with the bewildering speed of anticlimax. Cynthia's light, once so hostile and destructive, irradiates the features of the Indian Maiden with the force of a maternal blessing. There is no time for rejoicing or acclaim or the marriage festivities Keats had contemplated celebrating in "I Stood Tip-toe." The two lovers simply bless Peona, then flee away into the night. Endymion's dilemma is thus disposed of, but it is never really resolved. The point of the identification Keats brings about in the closing lines is intellectually unmistakable; but as Douglas Bush has written, it "is only a bit of 'Platonic' algebra, not an equation felt on the pulses."

Reasons can be cited, virtually without end, to explain the manifestly disappointing and unsatisfactory state of the conclusion—Keats's boredom and fatigue with the ordeal the completion of the poem had become, his eagerness to pass on to other projects, his lack of concern for or want of experience in creating an effective ending. Such explanations must, however, be subordinated to the poem's underlying honesty, an honesty that marks so much of Keats's writing and that springs from genuine commitment to the act of composition itself. The point can best be made by turning to a curious passage not far from the end of Book Four. Momentarily abandoning the turbulence and uncertainty of the action, Keats intervenes as narrator to address some words of apology to his hero which are, however, intended chiefly for the reader:

> Endymion! unhappy! it nigh grieves
> Me to behold thee thus in last extreme:
> Ensky'd ere this, but truly that I deem
> Truth the best music in a first-born song.
> (iv.770–73)

Obviously it is Keats himself who is most of all unhappy, embarrassed by the tangled involvements of his narrative and aware that his poem should by now have achieved its resolution. Yet the difficulty he faces is surely not that of literally carrying out the conclusion required by his fable. Endymion would have been "Ensky'd ere this" were it not, Keats tells us, that a kind of truth forbids, and the reason deserves to be taken with full seriousness.

The "truth" seems to be not only that Keats had become genuinely involved in the allegory of his poem but that, as Glen O. Allen has argued, the emphasis of the allegory had changed significantly in the course of composition and that the "enskying" of his hero had lost much of its climactic importance. Endymion is not apotheosized in Cynthia's visionary heaven. There is no ascension to the skies. The two lovers merely slip quietly away together through the woods. The conclusion his poem demanded, Keats realized, was not his hero's elevation to the "chief intensity" but rather some balance between light and shade, desire and restraint, mortality and immortality that he could only intimate in the union of Cynthia and the Indian Maiden. Yet the need for such a larger reconciliation was one he had only gradually become aware of and did not lend itself to the old climactic design and structure of his legend. Nor was it one that, for deeper reasons, he could dramatize in any genuinely satisfying or "truthful" way. This is not to argue that toward the end of his poem Keats suddenly lost faith in visionary experience. It is to say, rather, that the obstacles to Endymion's success, as Keats elaborated them, had so qualified the nature of his goal as to become themselves part of a new and more complex solution than any he had, however dimly, foreseen.

Such a hypothesis can be verified by examining within the course of the poem itself certain shifts of emphasis that reveal a remarkable change and maturing in Keats's aesthetic assumptions. The theoretical keystone of the structure of the work is the central passage in Book One, Endymion's speech on happiness which Keats likened to a "Pleasure Thermometer." Yet it is impossible to ignore the growing emphasis on disappointment and unhappiness as an integral part of human experience both as the poem proceeds and as a theme reflected increasingly in Keats's letters of the autumn of 1817, when he was at work on his last book. As early as Book Two the lovers' ecstasy is broken by Cynthia's cry, "Endymion: woe! woe! is grief contain'd / In the very deeps of pleasure, my sole life?" (ii.823–24). In the roundelay of the Indian Maiden in Book Four the perception of sorrow is for the first time admitted as an unavoidable and creative element in the experience of beauty. In his letter to Bailey of November 22, 1817, written when he was halfway through his final book, Keats cited *both* Book One and "O Sorrow" as demonstrations of his "favorite Speculation" as to the truth of the imagination. Yet he must himself have been aware of important differences between them, and if we return to look more carefully at the famous passage in his letter, we can see his concern to bring the two parts of his poem more fully into accord. "I am certain of nothing," he wrote, "but of the holiness of the Heart's affections and the truth of Imagination—What the imagination seizes as Beauty must be truth—whether it existed before or not—for I have the *same* Idea of *all* our Passions *as of Love* they are *all* in their sublime, creative of essential Beauty" (I, 184; my italics). Keats, in other words, had already begun to move toward that deeper conception of beauty springing from intense awareness of the whole of human life in all its mingled joy and sorrow that was to become a major theme of *Hyperion*. This is not to say that the "Ode to Sorrow" is much more than a weak and sentimental approximation to that ideal, but, insofar as it attempts to reconcile sorrow within a deeper apprehension of beauty, the shift it marks in the direction of Keats's allegory is clear. One might say, perhaps, that by the end of the poem the pleasure principle expounded in the first book had at least been qualified by a recognition of the need for a broader and deeper participation in the whole of human experience. In the same way the earlier idea of Endymion's quest as a search for "oneness" or ecstatic self-annihilation in sympathetic feeling has in the end become partly modified (through the working out of Keats's fable) by an awareness much closer to a simultaneous apprehension of joy and sorrow, mortality and immortality, desire and human limitation.

Endymion, then, is a work whose scope and meaning to a large extent evolved during the months Keats worked on it and which is, therefore, not fully coherent as an allegory for the reason that it embodies new truths and insights Keats discovered only in the course of composition which could not be perfectly expressed within its old design. This is not to say, of course, that the poem is any less meaningful; it is to argue, rather, that its real significance lies as much in the questions it raises as in those it solves. Foremost among these was the whole problem for Keats of the adequacy of his habits and method of composition. In *Endymion* he had begun with a set of vague affirmations and a number of equally vague doubts and misgivings concerning the nature of visionary experience. His method for progressing had been to trust his own powers of improvisation, to let the poem find its own way, create its own involvements, and derive its own solutions. A clear, premeditated plan, even had he been able to conceive of one, was alien to the spirit and larger purpose of his undertaking. It was enough to "send / My herald thought into a wilderness," as he wrote at the outset of Book One, "and quickly dress / My uncertain path with green, that I may speed / Easily onward" (i.58–62). His progress with the work had taken him from the long, increasingly complicated dream-involvements of the earlier books to the apparent digression of the Glaucus episode and to his innovation of the Indian Maiden as a necessary rival and counterpart of Cynthia in Book Four. But in the end he had finished with a work lacking real definition or coherence, having had to extricate himself through the patent device of a *dea ex machina* conclusion. Somewhat like his hero, he had become trapped in the convolutions of the poem without the ability to transcend it.

The irony was hardly lost on him. "J.S. is perfectly right in regard to the slip-shod Endymion," he wrote Hessey. "That it is so is no fault of mine.—No!—though it may sound a little paradoxical. It is as good as I had power to make it—*by myself*" (i, 374). He would continue to write in the way he knew he must—"independently." He would continue faithful to the principles of "sensation & watchfulness," to his belief that "that which is creative must create itself." He must, however, learn to write *"with judgment,"* with greater deliberation and purpose. The realization lies behind his first, somewhat puzzling, reference to *Hyperion* in a letter in which he declares a major contrast he intends between the two works. In *Hyperion*, he wrote Haydon several months before *Endymion* was published, "the march of passion and endeavour will be undeviating—and one great contrast between them will be—that the Hero of the written tale being mortal *is led on*, like Buonaparte, *by circumstance*; whereas the Apollo in Hyperion *being a foreseeing God will shape his actions like one.*" The comment reflects more light on his own poetic intentions than it does on the character of either hero. The question was, could he maintain his allegiance to Pan, his symbol for that generative mystery from which all that was truly valuable in poetry sprang, and at the same time cultivate the prescience and control of Apollo? He would continue to write in the only way he could, from within himself; but he must acquire the clearness and finality of utterance he knew he must achieve for greatness.

GEOFFREY HARTMAN

Poem and Ideology:
A Study of "To Autumn"

"Most English great poems have little or nothing to say." Few do that nothing so perfectly, one is tempted to add, as Keats's "To Autumn." Our difficulty as interpreters is related to the way consciousness almost disappears into the poem: the mind, for once, is not what is left (a kind of sublime litter) after the show is over. "To Autumn" seems to absorb rather than extrovert that questing imagination whose breeding fancies, feverish overidentifications, and ambitious projects motivate the other odes.

It is not that we lack terms to describe the poem. On the contrary, as W. J. Bate has said, "for no other poem of the last two centuries does the classical critical vocabulary prove so satisfying." We can talk of its decorum, "the parts...contributing directly to the whole, with nothing left dangling or independent," of its lack of egotism, "the poet himself...completely absent; there is no 'I', no suggestion of the discursive language that we find in the other odes," and finally of a perfect concreteness or adequacy of symbol, the union in the poem of ideal and real, of the "greeting of the Spirit" and its object.

Yet terms like these point to an abstract perfection, to something as pure of content as a certain kind of music. They bespeak a triumph of form that exists but not—or not sufficiently—the nature of that form: its power to illumine experience, to cast a new light, a new shadow maybe, on things. In what follows I suggest, daringly, that "To Autumn" has something to say:

From *Literary Theory and Structure*, edited by F. Brady, J. Palmer and M. Price. Copyright © 1975 by Yale University Press.

that it is an ideological poem whose very form expresses a national idea and a new stage in consciousness, or what Keats himself once called the "gregarious advance" and "grand march of intellect."

There are problems with *ideological*, a word whose meaning is more charged in Marxist than in general usage. Marxism thinks of ideology as a set of ideas that claim universality while serving a materialistic or class interest. "Ideology is untruth, false consciousness, lie. It shows up in failed works of art . . . and is vulnerable to criticism. . . . Art's greatness consists in allowing that to be uttered which ideology covers up." The attack on ideology in Marxism resembles that on "unearned abstractions" in Anglo-American formalistic theory, except that it engages in "depth politics" to uncover these abstractions. Formalistic criticism can worry overt ideas, or idealisms, Keats's "Beauty is Truth, Truth Beauty," for example, yet it accepts gladly the disappearance of ideas, or disinterestedness of form in "To Autumn." There is no attempt to demystify this form by discovering behind its decorum a hidden interest. In a low-risk theory of this kind the presence of ideas can be disturbing but not, obviously, their absence.

The great interpretive systems we know of have all been interest-centered, however; they have dug deep, mined, undermined, removed the veils. The Synagogue is blind to what it utters, the Church understands. The patient dreams, the doctor translates the dream. The distant city is really our city; the *unheimlich* the *heim-lich*; strange, uncanny, and exotic are brought home. Like those etymologies older scholars were so fond of, which showed us the fossilized stem of abstract words, so everything is slain, in interest-theories, on the stem of generational or class conflict.

Yet like nature itself, which has so far survived man's use of it, art is not polluted by such appropriations. Some works may be discredited, others deepened—the scandal of form remains. From Kant through Schopenhauer and Nietzsche, the aesthetic element proper is associated with disinterestedness, impersonality, and resistance to utilitarian concepts. Beauty of this undetermined kind becomes an itch: the mind, says Empson, wants to scratch it, to see what is really there, and this scratching we call interpretation. Most men, says Schopenhauer, seek in objects "only some relation to their will, and with everything that has not such a relation there sounds within them, like a ground-bass, the constant, inconsolable lament, 'It is of no use to me.'" Though the link between art and impersonality is often acknowledged—in New Criticism as well as Neoclassic theory—no very successful *interpretive* use of the principle exists. The notion of impersonality is vulnerable because so easily retranslated into unconscious interest or the masked presence of some *force majeure*.

I try to face this problem of the ideology of form by choosing a poem without explicit social context and exploring its involvement in social and historical vision. This would be harder, needless to say, if Keats had not elsewhere explicitly worried the opposition of dreamer and poet or poet and thinker. Even if "To Autumn" were a holiday of the spirit, some workday concerns of the poet would show through. My use of the concept of ideology, at the same time, will seem half-way or uncritical to the Marxist thinker. In uncovering Keats's ideology I remain as far as possible within terms provided by Keats himself, or furnished by the ongoing history of poetry. This is not, I hope, antiquarianism, but also not transvaluation. It should be possible to consider a poem's *geschichtlicher Stundenschlag* (Adorno)—how it tells the time of history—without accepting a historical determinism. Keats's poetry is indeed an event in history: not in world-history, however, but simply in the history of fiction, in our awareness of the power and poverty of fictions.

My argument runs that "To Autumn," an ode that is hardly an ode, is best defined as an English or Hesperian model which overcomes not only the traditional type of sublime poem but the "Eastern" or epiphanic consciousness essential to it. The traditional type was transmitted by both Greek and Hebrew religious poetry, and throughout the late Renaissance and eighteenth century, by debased versions of the Pindaric or cult-hymn. Only one thing about epiphanic structure need be said now: it evokes the presence of a god, or vacillates sharply between imagined presence and absence. Its rhetoric is therefore a crisis-rhetoric, with priest or votary, vastation or rapture, precarious nearness or hieratic distance ("Ah Fear! Ah frantic Fear! I see, I see thee near!"). As these verses by William Collins suggest, epiphanic structure proceeds by dramatic turns of mood and its language is ejaculative (Lo, Behold, O come, O see). Keats's "Hesperianism" triumphs, in "To Autumn," over this archaic style with its ingrained, superstitious attitude toward power—power seen as external and epochal. The new sublimity domesticates with the heart; the poet's imagination is neither imp nor incubus. Though recognizably sublime, "To Autumn" is a poem of *our* climate.

Climate is important. It ripens wits as well as fruits, as Milton said in another context. The higher temperature and higher style of the other odes are purged away: we have entered a temperate zone. What is grown here, this "produce of the air," is like its ambience: Hesperian art rather than oriental ecstasy or unnatural flight of the imagination. Autumn is clearly a mood as well as a season, and Stevens would have talked about a weather of the mind. Yet "mood" and "weather" have an aura of changeableness, even of volatility, while the Autumn ode expresses something firmer: not, as so often in Stevens or in the "Beulah" moments of other poets, a note among notes but, as in Spenser, a vast cloud-region or capability. The very shape of the poem—firm and regular without fading edges but also no overdefined contours—suggests a slowly expanding constellation that moves as a whole, if it moves at all.

Its motion is, in fact, part of the magic. Time lapses so gently here; we pass from the fullness of the maturing harvest to the stubble plains without experiencing a cutting edge. If time comes to a point in "To Autumn" it is only at the end of the poem, which verges (more poignant than pointed) on a last "gathering." The scythe of time, the sense of mortality, the cutting of life into distinct, epochal phases is not felt. We do not even stumble into revelation, however softly—there is no moment which divides before and after as in the "Ode to Psyche" with its supersoft epiphany, its Spenserian and bowery moment which makes the poet Psyche's devotee despite her "shadowy thought" nature. The Autumn ode is nevertheless a *poesis*, a shaped segment of life coterminous with that templar "region of the mind" which the other poems seek, though they may honor more insistently the dichotomy of inside and out, fane and profane. Poetry, to change "the whole habit of the mind," changes also our view of the mind's habitat. To say that "To Autumn" is ideological and that its pressure of form is "English" has to do with that also.

I begin with what is directly observable, rather than with curious knowledge of archaic ode or hymn. In the odes of Keats there is a strong, clearly marked moment of disenchantment, or of illusion followed by disillusion. Fancy, that "Queen of shadows" (Charlotte Smith), becomes a "deceiving elf"—and although the deception remains stylized, and its shock releases pathos rather than starker sentiments, it is as pointed as the traditional turn of the Great Ode. (Compare the turn, for example, from one mode of music to another in Dryden's *Alexander's Feast* or the anastrophe "He is not dead, he lives" in pastoral elegy.) The transition leading from stanzas 7 to 8 in the Nightingale ode is such a turn, which results in calling imagination a "deceiving elf." An imaginative fancy that has sustained itself despite colder thoughts is farewelled.

There is, exceptionally, no such turn in "To Autumn." The poem starts on enchanted ground and never leaves it. This special quality becomes even clearer when we recall that "La Belle Dame sans Merci," with its harvest background and soft ritual progression, ends in desolation of spirit on the cold hillside. But because the final turn of the Nightingale ode, though clear as a bell, is not gross in its effect, not productive of coital sadness, a comparison with Autumn's finale is still possible. In "To Autumn" birds are preparing to fly to a warmer clime, a "visionary south," though we do not see them leave or the cold interrupt. In "To a Nightingale" the poet is allowed a call—adieu, adieu—which is birdlike still and colors the darker "forlorn," while his complete awakening is delayed ("Do I wake or sleep?") and verbal prolongations are felt. There is no complete disenchantment even here.

"To Autumn," moreover, can be said to have something approaching a strophic turn as we enter the last stanza. With "Where are the songs of

Spring? Aye, where are they?" a plaintive anthem sounds. It is a case, nevertheless, where a premise is anticipated and absorbed. The premise is that of transience, or the feel of winter, and the rest of the stanza approaches that cold threshold. The premise is absorbed because its reference is back to Spring instead of forward to Winter; by shifting from eye to ear, to the music-theme, Keats enriches Autumn with Spring. We remain within a magical circle where things repeat each other in a finer tone, as Autumn turns into a second Spring: "While barred clouds *bloom* the soft-dying day." The music now heard is no dirge of the year but a mingling of lullaby and aubade. For the swallows a second summer is at hand (aubade). For us—if we cannot follow them any more than the elusive nightingale—what comes next is not winter but night (lullaby). We go gently off, in either case, on extended wings.

Thus "To Autumn," like Stevens's "Sunday Morning," becomes oddly an Ode to Evening. The full meaning of this will appear. But in terms of formal analysis we can say that the poem has no epiphany or decisive turn or any absence/presence dialectic. It has, instead, a *westerly drift* like the sun. Each stanza, at the same time, is so equal in its poetical weight, so loaded with its own harvest, that westering is less a natural than a poetic state—it is a mood matured by the poem itself. "To Autumn," in fact, does not explicitly evolve from sunrise to sunset but rather from a rich to a clarified dark. Closely read it starts and ends in twilight. "Season of mists and mellow fruitfulness"—though the mists are of the morning, the line links fertility and semidarkness in a way that might be a syntactical accident were it not for the more highly developed instance of "I cannot see what flowers are at my feet...," that famous stanza from the Nightingale ode where darkened senses also produce a surmise of fruitfulness. The Autumn ode's twilight is something inherent, a condition not simply of growth but of imaginative growth. Westering here is a spiritual movement, one that tempers visionariness into surmise and the lust for epiphany into finer-toned repetitions. We do not find ourselves in a temple but rather in Tempe "twixt sleepe and wake." We can observe the ode unfolding as a self-renewing surmise of fruitfulness: as waking dream or "widening speculation" rather than nature-poem and secularized hymn.

Concerning *surmise*: I have suggested elsewhere its importance for Romantic poetry, how it hovers between factual and fantastic. Its presence is often marked by a "magic casement" effect: as in Wordsworth's "Solitary Reaper," a window opens unexpectedly on a secret or faraway scene.

> No nightingale did ever chaunt
> More welcome notes to weary bands
> Of travellers in some shady haunt,
> Among Arabian sands:

Keats has the interesting habit of interpreting pictures (usually imaginary) as scenes beheld from a magic window of this kind. Yet since the frame of the window is also the frame of the picture, he finds himself on an ambiguous threshold, intimately near yet infinitely removed from the desired place. Most of the odes are a feverish quest to enter the life of a pictured scene, to be totally where the imagination is. In the Autumn ode, however, there is no effort to cross a magic threshold: though its three stanzas are like a composite picture from some Book of Hours, we are placed so exactly at the bourn of the invisible picture window that the frame is not felt, nor the desperate haunting of imagination to get in. There is no precipitous "Already with thee" and no stylized dejection.

Something, perhaps, is lost by this: the sense of dangerous transition, of consciousness opening up, of a frozen power unsealing. But the ode remains resolutely meditative. When important images of transition occur they are fully *composed* and no more vibrant than metrical enjambments: "And sometimes like a gleaner thou dost keep / Steady thy laden head." Or, "Sometimes whoever seeks abroad may find / Thee sitting careless." Strictly construed the "sometimes" goes here both with the seeking and with the finding: it is factored out and made prepositional. This is a framing device which further augments the feeling of surmise, of lighthearted questing. What reverberates throughout, and especially in this image of the gleaner, the most pictorial of the poem, is a light but steady pondering. It is not a pondering, of course, devoid of all tension: "keep / Steady," understood as a performative or "cozening imperative," suggests that the poet is not so much describing as urging the image on, in-feeling it. Let us follow this picture-pondering from verse to verse.

The opening stanza is strongly descriptive, so loaded with told riches, that there seems to be no space for surmise. A desire to fill every rift with Autumn's gold produces as rich a banquet as Porphyro's heap of delicates in "The Eve of St. Agnes." Thesaurus stanzas of this kind are self-delighting in Keats; but they also have a deeper reason. Porphyro knows that Madeline will find reality poorer than her dream and enhances his value by serving himself up this way. The sumptuous ploy is to help him melt into his lady's waking thought. So Autumn's banquet, perhaps, intends to hold the awakening consciousness and allow the dream to linger. Not only the bees are deceived; the dream "Warm days will never cease" is not in them alone; it is already in Autumn, in her "conspiring." On this phrase all the rich, descriptive details depend; they are infinitives not indicatives, so that we remain in the field of mind. "Conspiring with him how to load and bless . . . To bend with apples . . . fill all fruit . . . To swell the gourd." As we move through Autumn's thought to the ripening of that thought, we cease to feel her as an external agent.

Thus, the descriptive fullness of the first stanza turns out to be thought-full as well: its pastoral furniture is a golden surmise, imagination in her most deliberate mood. By moving the point of view inward, Keats makes these riches mental riches, imaginative projects. He does not, at the same time, push the mental horizon to infinity: the mood remains infinitive, looking onto "something evermore about to be."

Once we see that what is being satisfied is empathy or in-feeling, and that to satisfy it Keats (like Autumn) fills outside with more and more inside, the structure of the poem as a progressive surmise becomes clear. In-feeling, in Keats, is always on the point of overidentifying; and even here it demands more than the first stanza's dream of truth. However glowing a prospect Autumn paints, it must still, as it were, come alive. This happens in the second stanza where the drowsy ponderer meets us in person. Now we are in the landscape itself; the harvest is now. The figure of Autumn amid her store is a moving picture, or the dream personified. Yet the two stanzas are perfectly continuous; in-feeling is still being expressed as the filling-up of a space—a figure like Autumn's was needed to plump the poem. Though we approach epiphanic personification in the figure of Autumn, the casualness of "sometimes" "sometimes," together with the easy mood of the opening question, gives us a sense of "widening speculation" and prevents a more than cornucopial view of the goddess.

But the dream is almost shattered at the end of the stanza. The word "oozings" extends itself phonically into "hours by hours," a chime that leads to the idea of transience in "Where are the songs of Spring?" Though immediately reabsorbed, this muted ubi sunt introduces the theme of mutability. Oozings—hours—ubi sunt . . . A single word, or its echoes, might have disenchanted Keats like the turn on "forlorn" in the Nightingale ode. Disenchantment, however, does not occur: there is no reverse epiphany as in "La Belle Dame sans Merci," no waking into emptiness.

We have reached, nevertheless, the airiest of the stanzas. Does a chill wind not brush us, an airiness close to emptiness? Do we not anticipate the "cold hill's side"? Even if the mood of surmise is sustained, it might well be a surmise of death rather than fruitfulness.

Here, at the consummate point of Keats's art, in-feeling achieves its subtlest act. Keats conspires with autumn to fill even the air. Air becomes a granary of sounds, a continuation of the harvest, or *Spätlese*. In this last and softest stanza, the ear of the ear is ripened.

More than a tour de force or finely sustained idea is involved. For at the end of other odes we find an explicit *cry*, which is part of their elegiac envoi. Here that cry is uttered, as it were, by the air itself, and can only be heard by an ear that knows how to glean such sounds. What is heard, to quote the modern poet closest to Keats.

> . . . is not a cry of divine attention,
> Nor the smoke-drift of puffed-out heroes, nor human cry.
> It is the cry of leaves that do not transcend themselves.

In lyric poetry the cry is a sign of subjective feelings breaking through and in the cult-hymn of being possessed by divine power. It signifies in both a transcendence absent from this "final finding of the air." Lyricism, in "To Autumn," frees itself for once of elegy and ecstasy: it is neither a frozen moment of passion nor the inscription that prolongs it.

The Grecian urn's "Beauty is Truth, Truth Beauty" remains an extroverted, lapidary cry. However appropriate its philosophy, its form is barely snatched from a defeat of the imagination. "To Autumn" has no defeat in it. It is the most negative capable of all of Keats's great poems. Even its so-called death-stanza expresses no rush toward death, no clasping of darkness as a bride, or quasi-oriental ecstasy. Its word-consciousness, its mind's weather—all remains Hesperian. As its verses move toward an image of southerly flight (the poem's nearest analogue to transcendence), patterns emerge that delay the poet's "transport to summer." Perception dwells on the border and refuses to overdefine. So "full-grown lambs" rather than "sheep." Add such verbal ponderings or reversing repetitions as "borne aloft . . . hilly bourn," a casual chiastic construction, playing on a mix of semantic and phonetic properties. Or the noun-adjective phrase "treble soft" which becomes an adjective-noun phrase when "treble" is resolved into the northern "triple." And consider the northernisms. The proportion of northern words increases perceptibly as if to pull the poem back from its southerly orientation. There is hardly a romance language phrase: sound-shapes like sallows, swallows, borne, bourn, crickets, croft, predominate. And, finally, the poise of the stanza's ending, on the verge of flight like joy always bidding adieu. How easily, in comparison, Hölderlin turns eastward, and converts wish into visionary transport on the wings of an older rhetoric:

> These my words, when, rapt
> faster than I could have known,
> and far, to where I never
> thought to come, a Genius
> took me from my own house. They glimmered
> in the twilight, as I went,
> the shadowy wood
> and the yearning brooks
> of my country; I knew the fields no more;

> Yet soon, brighter and fresher,
> mysterious
> under the golden smoke
> flowering, rising fast before me
> in the sun's steps
> with a thousand fragrant hills
> Asia dawned
>
> ("Patmos")

Less magnificent, equally magnanimous, "To Autumn" remains a poem "in the northwind sung." Its progress is merely that of repetitions "in a finer tone," of "widening speculation," of "treble soft" surmise. Yet in its Hesperian reach it does not give up but joins a south to itself.

Keats's respect for the sublime poem does not have to be argued. There is his irritation with the "egotistical sublime" of Wordsworth, his admiration for Milton who broke through "the clouds which envelope so deliciously the Elysian field of verse, and committed himself to the Extreme," his anguished attempt to write the *Hyperion*, and the testimony of lesser but affecting verses like those to the "God of the Meridian" in which he foresees madness:

> ...when the soul is fled
> To high above our head,
> Afrighted do we gaze
> After its airy maze,
> As doth a mother wild,
> When her young infant child
> Is in an eagle's claws—
> And is not this the cause
> Of madness?—God of Song,
> Thou bearest me along
> Through sights I scarce can bear

The "bear...bear" pun shows well enough the tension of epic flight. I must now make clear what kind of problem, formal and spiritual, the sublime poem was.

A first difficulty centers on the relation of romance to sublime or epic. The romance mode, for Keats, is now presublime (and so to be "broken through") and now postsublime. Where, as in the first *Hyperion*, Keats wishes to sublimate the sublime he turns with relief to the "golden theme" of Apollo after the Saturnine theme of the first two books. In the *Fall of Hyperion*, however, romance is an Elysium or Pleasure-garden to be transcended. While in "La Belle Dame sans Merci" romance becomes sheer oxymoron, a "golden tongued" nightmare.

It is best to find a view beyond this special dialectic of romance and epic in Keats, all the more so as that is complicated by the dream-truth, or vision-reality split. No formal analysis will disentangle these rich contraries. It can only reduce them to the difference suggested in the *Fall of Hyperion* between "an immortal's sphered words" and the mother-tongue. This is the dichotomy on which Keats's epic voyage foundered: the opposition between Miltonic art-diction and the vernacular. "Life to him [Milton] would be death to me." "English must be kept up." Yet such a distinction is no more satisfying than one in terms of genre. Vernacular romance is perhaps more feasible than vernacular epic—but we get as mixed up as Keats himself when we define each genre in family terms and put romance under mother, epic under father. In the *Fall of Hyperion* Moneta is as patriarchal as she is womanly.

A solution is to consider both romance and epic—or the high-visionary style in general—as belonging to an older, "epiphanic" structuring of consciousness. Against it can be put a nonepiphanic structuring; and if the older type is primarily associated with the East, the modern would be with the West or, at its broadest, Hesperia. It is possible to treat this distinction formally as one between two types of structuring rather than two types of consciousness. Eventually, however, Keats's charge of superstition or obsolescence against the earlier mode will move us into ideology and beyond formalism. A man who says, like Keats, that life to Milton is death to him is concerned with more than formal options.

Epiphanic structure implies, first of all, the possibility of categorical shifts: of crossing into *allo genere*, and even, I suppose, out of ordinary human consciousness into something else. Apotheosis (as at the end of *Hyperion*), metamorphosis, and transformation scenes are type instances of such a crossing. It is accompanied by a doctrine of states, a philosophy of transcendence, and a formulary for the "translation" of states. Epiphanic structure can bear as much sophistication as an author is capable of. Take the sequence, based on *Paradise Lost*, Book VIII, which haunted Keats: "The Imagination may be compared to Adam's Dream: He awoke and found it truth." This refers chiefly to Adam seeing Eve first in dream and, upon waking, in the flesh. Keats will often use it ironically rather than not use it at all. So in the "Eve of St. Agnes" Madeline wakes into Imagination's truth and finds it—how pale, how diminished! She melts the reality—Porphyro— back into her dream in a moment of, presumably, sexual union.

A more complex instance is the dark epiphany in "La Belle Dame sans Merci" where the enchanted knight wakes, as it were, into the arms of the wrong dream and cannot find his way back to the right one. Whereas, in Milton, one cunning enjambment expresses the intensity of the quest springing from imaginative loss,

> She [Eve] disappear'd, and left me dark, I wak'd
> To find her

a moment Keats repeats faintly in the Autumn ode,

> Sometimes whoever seeks abroad may find
> Thee

in "La Belle Dame" there is nothing—no natural food—can satisfy the knight. He starves for his drug, like Keats so often for the heightened consciousness of epiphanic style.

In *Paradise Lost*, Adam's dream prepares him for the truth he is to meet. Truth is conceived of as a fuller, perhaps more difficult, dream; and God seeks to strengthen Adam's visionary powers by engaging him in these dream-corridors. Instead of a single dramatic or traumatic change there is to be a gradual tempering of the mind. This modification of epiphanic structure may have inspired a favorite speculation of Keats, that happiness on earth would be enjoyed hereafter "repeated in a finer tone and so repeated." Miltonic tenderness, by allowing Adam's consciousness to develop, by giving it time for growth, lightens the all-or-nothing (sometimes, all-and-nothing) character of epiphanic vision. Though the end remains transport and deification, the means are based, at least in part, on a respect for natural process.

The naturalization of epiphanic form is less effective in "La Belle Dame" than in this prototypal sequence from Milton. The reason lies perhaps in the genre as much as in Keats himself. Quest-romance is a particularly resistant example of epiphanic form. Though Spenser helps to detumesce it he also throws its archaic lineaments into relief: his faërie remains a montage, a learned if light superposition. The dominant feature of quest-romance (as of fairy-tale) is the ever-present danger of trespass: of stepping all at once or unconsciously into a daemonic field of force. Often the quest is motivated by redeeming such a prior trespass; but even when it starts unburdened it cannot gain its diviner end without the danger of *allo genere* crossings. Keats's knight steps ritually, if unknowingly, into demonry. So also Coleridge's mariner, whose act of trespass is clear but who before it and after crosses also invisible demarcations. From this perspective the exile of Adam and Eve and the wanderings of Odysseus are both the result of a trespass against the divine, or of stepping willy-nilly into a daemonic sphere.

This is not the place to work out the formal variations of quest-romance. But when a poet does succeed in subduing the form, the result is both remarkable and mistakable. In "Strange Fits of Passion" Wordsworth's rider is a becalmed knight from Romance whose rhythm parodies the chivalric gallop and who is always approaching yet never crossing a fatal border. The moon that drops and deflates the dreaming into a mortal thought is a pale metonymy of itself when considered against the backdrop of epiphanic romance. It alone belongs to the sphere of "strange fits"; and while it still divides before and after and even suggests that an imaginative or unconscious trespass has occurred, it cannot be drawn fully into the lunatic symbolism of romance. Keats, I think, did not manage to humanize this form: he feared too much that leaving Romance behind meant being exiled from great poetry. He was unable to "translate" the inherited code either into the Miltonic Extreme or into Wordsworth's fulfillment of Miltonic tenderness.

And yet: did he not humanize epiphanic form in the special case of the ode? Recent scholarship by Kurt Schlüter and others has established the basic form of the ancient cult-hymn as it impinged on European poetry. The easiest division of the form is, as you might expect, into three: invocation, narrative or mythic portion, and renewed invocation. Sappho's "Ode to Aphrodite" is a clear example; so is Shelley's "Ode to the West Wind." Basically, however, the structure consists simply of a series of apostrophes or turns petitioning an absent god or attesting his presence. To the modern reader it may all seem somewhat hysterical: a succession of cries modulated by narrative or reflective interludes.

The sublime or greater or Pindaric ode flourished in the eighteenth century like a turgid weed, all pseudo-epiphany and point, bloat and prickles, feeding off an obsolescent style. Dr. Johnson vilified Gray's Pindaric experiments as "cucumbers." The best that can be said for the genre is that like contemporary opera it became a refuge for visionary themes: an exotic and irrational entertainment which reminded the indulgent consumer of the polite good sense of his society, and sent him back, all afflatus spent, to trifle with the lesser ode. It is not till Collins that a dialogue begins within the genre between its sublime origins and the English ground to which it is transplanted.

A brief notice of this dialogue in Collins's "Ode to Evening" prepares us for Keats. Collins uses all the features characterizing the sublime ode except one. His extended apostrophe suggests the hieratic distance between votary and the invoked power, anticipates at the same time its presence, and leads into a narrative second half describing in greater detail the coming of the divinity and its effect on the poet. This is followed by a renewed invocation which acts as the poem's coda. The one feature conspicuously absent is the epiphany proper. The invoked personification, evening, is a transitional state, a season of the day, whose advent is its presence. By addressing in epiphanic terms a subject intrinsically nonepiphanic, and adjusting his style subtly to it, Collins opens the way to a new, if still uneasy, nature-poetry.

What adjustments of style are there? The movement of the ode is highly mimetic, as Collins, suiting his numbers to the nature of evening, slows and draws out his musings.

> If aught of oaten stop, or pastoral song,
> May hope, chaste Eve, to soothe thy modest ear,
> Like thy own solemn springs
> Thy springs and dying gales
> O nymph reserved, while now...

Instead of hastening some eclipsing power, or leaping into a fuller present, his verse becomes a programmatic accompaniment to the gradual fall of night. The form, in other words, is self-fulfilling: as the processional verse blends with processual nature, and an expanding shadow (a "gradual, dusky veil") is all of relevation there is, the poet's prayer results in what it asks for: "Now teach me, *Maid* compos'd / To breathe some soften'd Strain." This "now" is only in echo that of an ecstatic, annihilative present: it refers to an actual time of day, and perhaps to a belated cultural moment. With this drawn-out "now" nature-poetry is born:

> ...and now with treble soft
> The red-breast whistles from the garden-croft;
> And gathering swallows twitter in the skies.

Collins's "soften'd strain," his conversion of epiphanic style, will find its culminating instance in Keats's poetry of process.

That Collins represents Evening as a god is more than a naturalized archaism. Evening, invoked as the source of a new music, stands for Hesperia, the evening-star land; and what the poet asks for, in these prelusive strains, is a genuinely western verse, an *Abendlandpoesie*. Like Keats's Psyche, Evening is a new goddess: the poetic pantheon of the East contained only Sun and Night, but Evening is peculiar to the Western hemisphere. In the courts of the East, as Coleridge noted in his *Ancient Mariner*, "At one stride comes the dark." The East, in its sudden dawn and sudden darkness, is epiphanic country. But the English climate, in weather or weather of the mind, has a more temperate, even, evening effect. Collins embraces the idea that his native country, or the cultural region to which it belonged, has a style and vision of its own. He shows spirit of place as a felt influence, and gothic eeriness as eariness. That is, he uncovers a new sense for nature by uncovering a new sense: the natural ear. What the sublime ode had attempted by overwhelming the eye—or the "descriptive and allegoric style" which dominates the age—Collins achieves through this finer sense. The eye, as in Wordsworth's "Tintern Abbey," and in the last stanza of "To Autumn," is made quiet by "the power of harmony."

In the "Ode to Evening" the concept of a Hesperian poetry conditions even sensory mimesis or impels it into a new region. It is no accident that the last stanza of "To Autumn" contains an evening ode in small. That

"Evening Ear," which Collins elsewhere attributes to Milton, is, to use a rare Wordsworthian pun, an *organ of vision*: responsive to a particular climate or "spiritual air" (*Endymion*, IV) in which poets feel themselves part of a belated and burdened culture yet find their own relation to the life of things. As the landscape darkens gently, the blind and distant ear notices tones—finer tones—that had escaped a dominant and picture-ridden eye: a weak-eyed bat flits by, curious emblem, and the beetle emerges winding its horn, as if even pastoral had its epic notes. There is still, in Collins, this airy faërie which has often dissolved in Keats—who, however, is never very far from it. What matters is that creatures jargon, like "To Autumn" 's parliament of birds; that the sounds are real sounds, a produce of the air; that the heard is not exclusively divine or human; and that within the sheltering dark of the ear other senses emerge: "I cannot see what flowers are at my feet, / Nor what soft incense hangs upon the bough, / But in embalmed darkness guess each sweet." Here absence is presence, though not by way of mystical or epiphanic reversal. In every temperate zone the air is full of noises.

　　This sensory ideology, if I may call it such, must have affected Keats one early autumn day looking at stubble fields:

> How beautiful the season is now—How fine the Air. A temperate sharpness about it. Really, without joking, chaste weather—Dian skies—I never lik'd stubble fields so much as now—Aye better than the chilly green of the spring. Somehow a stubble plain looks warm—in the same way that some pictures look warm—this struck me so much in my sunday's walk that I composed upon it.

That ideology is in the air is proven by what follows:

> I always somehow associate Chatterton with Autumn. He is the purest writer in the English language. [Chatterton's language is entirely northern.] He has no French idiom, or particles like Chaucer—'tis genuine English idiom in English words. I have given up Hyperion.... English ought to be kept up.

We have already commented on the northernisms in "To Autumn" 's last stanza: even romance language (let alone romance) is gently shunned. Nothing but "home-bred glory."

　　Can we see the gods die in "To Autumn," the epiphanic forms dissolve, as it were, before our eyes? Autumn is, by tradition, the right season for this dissolution, or dis-illusion.

> Let Phoebus lie in umber harvest

Stevens writes in "Notes toward a Supreme Fiction,"

> Let Phoebus slumber and die in autumn umber
> Phoebus is dead, ephebe.

But, in tradition also, a new god treads on the heels of the old, and loss figures forth a stronger presence. In Hesperian poetry, from Collins to Keats to Stevens, this entire absence/presence vacillation does no more than manure the ground of the poem, its "sensible ecstasy."

Consider the invocation "Season of mists and mellow fruitfulness." The odic O is hardly felt though the verses immediately fill one's mouth with rich labials extended in a kind of chiastic middle between "Season" and "sun." Nothing remains of the cultic distance between votary and personified power: we have instead two such powers, autumn and sun, whose closeness is emphasized, while the moment of hailing or petitioning is replaced by a presumptive question ("Who hath not seen thee") suggesting availability rather than remoteness. The most interesting dissolve, however, comes with the grammatical shift, in the opening line, from mythic-genealogical to descriptive-partitive "of," which effectively diffuses autumn into its attributes. Compare "Season of mists and mellow fruitfulness" with the following apostrophes:

> Thou foster-child of silence and slow time.

Here the poet uses clearly and finely a formula which alludes to the high descent of the apostrophized object. In our next example

> Nymph of the downward smile, and side-long glance

the grammatical form is analogous, but the "of" has moved from genealogical toward partitive. The nymph is eminently characterized by these two attributes: they *are* her in this statuesque moment. The opening of "To the Nile":

> Son of the old moon-mountains African
> Stream of the pyramid and crocodile

actually brings mythic-genealogical and partitive-descriptive together. Against this background we see how beautifully dissolved into the ground of description is the mythical formula of "To Autumn" 's first line.

We do, of course, by what appears to be a regressive technique, meet Autumn personified in the second stanza. If the poem approaches a noon-point of stasis—of arrest or centered revelation—it is here. The emergence of myth serves, however, to ripen the pictorial quality of the poem rather than to evoke astonishment. The emphasis is on self-forgetful relaxation (at most on "forget thyself to marble") not on saturnine fixation. No more than in "To Evening" is nature epiphanic: Keats's autumn is not a specter but a spirit, one who steals over the landscape, or "amid her store" swellingly imbues it. The poet's mind is not rapt or astonished and so forced back on itself by a sublime apparition.

It is essential, in fact, to note what happens to mind. In the cult hymn the invocation merges with, or is followed by, the god's *comos*: an enumeration of his acts and attributes. But Keats's first stanza becomes simply the filling up of a form, a golden chain of infinitives hovering between prospect and fulfillment, until every syntactical space is loaded and the poet's mind, like the bees', loses itself in the richness. The stanza, in fact, though full, and with its eleven lines, more than full, is not a grammatical whole but a drunk sentence. The poet's mind, one is tempted to say, has entered the imagined picture so thoroughly that when the apostrophe proper is sprung at the opening of stanza 2, and the grammatical looseness corrected, it simultaneously opens a new speculative movement. And when the generative figure of Autumn appears in the second stanza, it is self-harvesting like the poet's own thoughts. The last stanza, then, leaves us in a "luxury of twilight" rather than dropping us into a void where "no birds sing."

The demise of epiphanic forms in "To Autumn" raises a last question: is not the sequential movement of the whole poem inspired by a progressive idea with Enlightenment roots? There seems to be, on the level of sensation, something that parallels the first *Hyperion*'s progress from heavier to lighter, from Hyperion to Apollo, and from fixed burdens to a softer oppression. Several key phrases in Keats's letters suggest an "enlightenment" of this kind. The poet talks of "widening speculation," of "the regular stepping of Imagination toward a Truth," and of easing the "Burden of the Mystery." Magical moments like the fourth stanza of "Ode on a Grecian Urn":

> Who are these coming to the sacrifice?
> To what green altar, O mysterious priest

are surely related to this lightening. Mystery survives, but in a purged, airy, speculative form. The "overwrought" questions of the ode's beginning, which sought to penetrate or fix a symbol-essence, are purified into surmise and evoke a scene of "wide quietness" rather than bacchic enthusiasm.

There is a progress then; but is it toward a truth? We know what the conclusion to the Grecian Urn ode suggests. "Beauty is Truth, Truth Beauty" is a chiastic phrase, as self-rounding as the urn. No ultimate turn or final step toward a truth occurs. Though there are turns in the poem, they are more musical than epiphanic, and the very notion of "the turn" merges with that of the art-object: Keats turns the urn in his imagination until the urn is its turnings. The poet's speculation is circular.

Keats's rondure, his counterprogression, subverts without rejecting the received idea of "enlightenment." Poetry clearly has its own progress, its own lights. Formalistic or art-centered terms have, therefore, a certain propriety. But they cannot suffice for Keats any more than for Wordsworth, who also seeks to ease the "burthen of the mystery" ("Tintern Abbey," line 39). Consider the profound difference between these poets, who both believe in a dispersion of older—poetical or religious—superstitions. Such qualities as decorum, impersonality, symbolic adequacy are a function mainly of the concenteredness of "To Autumn": the poem turns around one image like a "leaf-fring'd legend." Though Wordsworth's poems may also have a center of this kind (Lucy's death, a peculiar landscape, a remembered scene), it rarely appears as picturesque symbol or image. Wordsworth's kernels are mysteries: charged spiritual places which confront and confuse a mental traveler who circles their enchanted ground—or who, like a police-man, tries to cordon off the disturbance. This too is an important "enlightenment" form, delimiting a romance apparition or sublime feelings—yet how different from Keats! In Wordsworth the spirit must find its own containment, and never quite finds it; those "spots of time" erupt from their hiding-places like the Hebraic God; the structure of his poems expresses various attempts at containment which accrete with difficulty into a personal history ("Tintern Abbey") or an eschatological and cultural one ("Hart-Leap Well"). But Keats's experience is limited from the outset by Greek or picturesque example. What perplexes his imagination is a mysterious picture rather than a mystery.

Keats's formal a priori takes us back to Greece and where, according to Hegel, modern consciousness began. Formal beauty mediates "between the loss of individuality... as in Asia, where spiritual and divine are totally subsumed under a natural form, and infinite subjectivity." Greek character is "individuality conditioned by beauty" and in its respect for divine images modern and free, rather than Asiatic and superstitious. "He [the human being] is the womb that conceived them, he the breast that suckled them, he the spiritual to which their grandeur and purity is owing. Thus he feels himself calm in contemplating them, and not only free in himself, but possessing the consciousness of his freedom."

That Hegel's description can fit Keats makes one cautious about the whole enterprise of dividing consciousness into historically localized phases. All the more so as Hölderlin has his own myth of the Hesperian character, which is said to begin when Homer moderates oriental pathos or "fire from heaven." I make no claim for the historical exactness of either Hegel or Hölderlin. Historical speculation and criticism stand, as Professor Wimsatt has observed, in a highly problematic relationship.

Yet there is something like "Hesperian" freedom in "To Autumn," a poem which becomes—in Hegel's words—the womb for the rebirth of an astral or divine image. Such a divine image is certainly there; we should not exaggerate the absence of poetical superstition in Keats. Though his central figure is picturesque its star quality glimmers through.

Much has been written on Autumn's affinities to Demeter or other harvest deities. The divinity, however, that haunts Keats early and late is Apollo: sun-god, god of song, and "fore-seeing god." The difference between Hyperion and Apollo is, in good part, that the former is now doomed to live under "the burden of the mystery." Hyperion cannot dawn any more; he remains darkling. But Apollo in *Hyperion*, even though that poem breaks off and leaves the young god's metamorphosis incomplete—even though he too must shoulder the mystery—should break forth like the sun to "shape his actions" like "a fore-seeing god." In the Autumn ode the major theme of clairvoyance—at once foreseeing and deep-seeing (deep into the heart or maw of life)—is tempered. Yet it is far from absent.

For Autumn's "conspiring" function is comparable to that of the guardian genius, the *natale comes qui temperat astrum*. An idea of poetic or personal destiny enters, in however veiled a form. The poet who writes this ode stands under the pressure of an omen. As summer passes into autumn (season of the year or human season), his dreaming deepens into foresight:

> When I have fears that I may cease to be
> Before my pen has glean'd my teeming brain,
> Before high-piled books, in charact'ry,
> Hold like rich garners the full-ripen'd grain . . .

> Herr: es ist Zeit. Der Sommer war sehr gross

In fear of early death, and sensing riches his pen might never glean, Keats evokes a figure of genial harvests. Three times he renews his surmise of fruitfulness, three times he grasps the shadow without self-defeating empathy. Even fruitfulness is not a burden in "To Autumn." This, at last, is true impersonality.

HAROLD BLOOM

Keats: Romance Revised

Paul de Man engagingly remarks that "it is one of Keats's most engaging traits that he resists all temptation to see himself as the hero of a tragic adventure." De Man says also of Keats that "he lived almost always oriented toward the future," the pattern of his work being thus "prospective rather than retrospective." These are moving observations, and I honor them. They surmise a Keats whose vision "consists of hopeful preparations, anticipations of future power rather than meditative reflections on past moments of insight or harmony." As does Angus Fletcher, de Man sees Keats as one of the *liminal* visionaries, akin surely to Coleridge, to Hart Crane, perhaps to an aspect of Stevens. De Man points to all those phrases in Keats's poems and letters "that suggest he has reached a threshold, penetrated to the borderline of a new region which he is not yet ready to explore but toward which all his future efforts will be directed." If de Man were wholly right, then Keats ought to be happily free of the Shadow of Milton and of Wordsworth, the composite precursor that both inspired and inhibited him. There can be no more extreme posture of the spirit, for a strong poet, than to take up, perpetually, a prospective stance. I regret taking up a more suspicious or demystifying stance than de Man does, but Keats can charm even the subtlest and most scrupulous of deconstructors. No strong poet, of necessity, is wholly liminal in his vision, and Keats was a very strong poet, greatly gifted in the revisionary arts of misprision. I begin therefore by suggesting that de Man's observation accurately describes one of Keats's prime composite tropes, but also declines

From *Poetry and Repression.* Copyright © 1976 by Yale University Press.

(on de Manian principle, of course) to examine the psychic defenses that inform Keats's liminal trope.

Keats no more resembles Nietzsche's Zarathustra than Nietzsche himself did. I myself, perhaps wrongly, tend to read Zarathustra as a highly deliberate Nietzschean parody of the prospective stance that frequently distinguishes the High Romantic poet. Nietzsche had read and brooded upon Shelley, and also upon that indeliberate parodist, Poe. The contrary to prospective vision, in Blakean rather than Nietzschean terms, is the cycle of the being Blake called Orc, who would like to tear loose from Nature's wheel, but cannot. Nietzsche dreamed an antithetical vision, the Eternal Return of the Same, which is transumptive in stance. But these dialectical resources, whether Blakean or Nietzschean, were not congenial to Keats's genius. He was an experiential or retrospective poet at least as much as he was visionary or prospective, and as a poet who lived fully the life of poetry, and very little life of any other kind, he was compelled to one of the fiercest and most problematic struggles with the Covering Cherub of poetic influence that the language affords us.

My primary text in this discourse will be the second and greater of Keats's *Hyperion* fragments or heroic torsos, *The Fall of Hyperion*. I must remark, before commencing a reading of the poem, that here I cannot agree with de Man at all, for in *The Fall of Hyperion* Keats does yield to the temptation to see himself as the hero of a romance that is in the process of turning into tragedy. By the point at which the fragmentary *The Fall of Hyperion* breaks off, Keats (perhaps despite himself) has become the quest-hero of a tragic adventure.

Certainly he had resisted such a temptation for nearly the whole of his writing-life, consciously opposing himself in this to Byron and to Shelley, and emulating the precursor he shared with them, Wordsworth, who had made an aesthetic and moral choice against tragedy, and who had refused to identify himself with his own isolate selfhood, the Solitary of *The Excursion*. But in *The Fall of Hyperion*, and perhaps only there, Keats did write at least the sketch of a tragic romance, a prophetic sketch in that the poem has vital descendants both direct and indirect. A dance-play like Yeats's savage *A Full Moon in March* is a direct descendant, while Hart Crane's *The Bridge* is an indirect but remarkably close descendant, and so, I begin to suspect, is Stevens's *Esthétique du Mal*.

In reading Keats as having been a revisionist of Romance, I need to commence by revising the way I have read him in the past, for he too has suffered, and from other critics as well as myself, by the kinds of misreading that canon-formation enforces. In the past, I would have given an account of Keats's development somewhat as follows: after the subjectivizing disorders that rhetorically disfigured *Endymion*, Keats returned to the austere program of his own *Sleep and Poetry*, by attempting to write in what he himself disarmingly called "the more naked and Grecian manner" of the first *Hyperion*. But he discovered that his supposedly more objective epic could not be freed of the not-so-naked and not-so-Grecian manner of *Paradise Lost*, and so he broke off, on the polemical plea that, as he put it: "English must be kept up." His rallying cry became the rather transparent self-deception of: "Back to Chatterton!" which of course turned out to mean: "Back to Wordsworth!" Turning to the not un-Wordsworthian Cary translation of the *Purgatorio*, Keats then attempted his own purgatorial vision in *The Fall of Hyperion*, and did not so much break that off as discover, quite suddenly, that he had finished the poem as much as it could be finished. This canonical or Bloomian misreading traced a kind of cycle, in which Keats went from Romantic subjectivism to a kind of "Modernist" reaction against Wordsworthian internalization, only to discover at last that the Wordsworthian mode was the authentic and inescapable one for the would-be strong poet. Though I would still have found a critique of Wordsworthianism in *The Fall of Hyperion*, I would have centered any reading of the poem in the movement of a return to Wordsworth, under whatever cover and with whatever saving difference.

So once I would have thought, but now no more. I don't know if I have submitted to a new control, but I do think my sense of how poems make us read them has undergone a distress in which the reader's soul too is humanized, and made more aware of the necessity of error. Keats could not read Milton or Wordsworth without troping what he read, and we do the same to Keats.

Like Shelley, Keats is a poet of the transumptive mode, which is necessarily both retrospective and prospective, as I have been trying to show. [Previously], I emphasized Shelley's radical development of the prime Western poetic image of transumption, the Merkabah. In tracing the conflict between fire as the prime image of perspectivizing and the chariot as the image of overcoming belatedness, I concluded that Shelley's yielding to the chariot is equivocal, and unwilling. His heart remained in and with the Condition of Fire; the Fire, he insisted, for which all thirst. Keats, as I surmise we will see, gives himself more graciously to the chariot, to the great image of human and poetic continuity. Here is Keats's own early version of the chariot, from *Sleep and Poetry*, the programmatic poem he wrote at the hopeful age of twenty-one. After a passage of cheerfully erotic wish-fulfillments, involving at least three "white-handed nymphs in shady places," Keats addresses himself to higher things:

> And can I ever bid these joys farewell?
> Yes, I must pass them for a nobler life,
> Where I may find the agonies, the strife
> Of human hearts: for lo! I see afar,
> O'er-sailing the blue cragginess, a car

> And steeds with streamy manes—the charioteer
> Looks out upon the winds with glorious fear.

The chariot is the throne-world in motion, but here the throne-world is that of Apollo, or rather of the Apollo of Collins, the Apollo of Sensibility, and not the High Romantic Apollo of Nietzsche. Keats's oxymoron of "glorious fear" suggests Collins's use of fear as a psychic defense and rhetorical trope, of "fear" as the repression of the daemonic force of a belated creativity that needs to forget that it knows itself as a belatedness. "Glorious fear," in Keats or Collins, therefore means a creative repression, as here in Collins's *Ode to Fear*:

> Dark power, with shuddering meek submitted thought,
> Be mine to read the visions old,
> Which thy awakening bards have told . . .

We associate Shelley with rhetorical speed and glancing movement, while Keats, like Collins, is deliberately slow-paced, at times approaching a stasis. The chariot or throne-in-motion is therefore less congenial to Keats than a stationary throne-world, and so his prime transumptive image returns us to the source of Ezekiel's Merkabah in the throne-vision of Isaiah. Keats's version of the Hekhaloth or heavenly halls has been too little admired, or studied. Here is Book I, lines 176–200, of the first *Hyperion*:

> His palace bright
> Bastioned with pyramids of glowing gold,
> And touched with shade of bronzèd obelisks,
> Glared a blood-red through all its thousand courts,
> Arches, and domes, and fiery galleries;
> And all its curtains of Aurorian clouds
> Flushed angerly: while sometimes eagle's wings,
> Unseen before by Gods or wondering men,
> Darkened the place; and neighing steeds were heard,
> Not heard before by Gods or wondering men.
> Also, when he would taste the spicy wreaths
> Of incense, breathed aloft from sacred hills,
> Instead of sweets, his ample palate took
> Savour of poisonous brass and metal sick:
> And so, when harboured in the sleepy west,
> After the full completion of fair day,—
> For rest divine upon exalted couch
> And slumber in the arms of melody,
> He paced away the pleasant hours of ease
> With stride colossal, on from hall to hall;
> While far within each aisle and deep recess,
> His wingèd minions in close clusters stood,

Amazed and full of fear; like anxious men
Who on wide plains gather in panting troops,
When earthquakes jar their battlements and towers.

Partly, Keats is writing in the mode of Walter Savage Landor here, a
mode of marmoreal reverie, but partly he evokes (consciously, I think) the
omen-ridden world of Shakespeare's Roman tragedies, particularly *Julius
Caesar*. But these surface similarities or allusions induce no anxieties in
Keats, and so do little to determine the tropes and images of the first
Hyperion. The true precursor-text is the vision of Heaven in *Paradise Lost*, a
Heaven in which the impending Fall of Satan and his Host is scarcely a
major disturbance, in which the actual War between the faithful and the
rebels is at most a minor annoyance for God, the smashing of a few Divine
breakfast dishes. The passage that I have just quoted from *Hyperion* is a
misprision of the Miltonic Heaven, but it is not itself a Miltonic kind of
misprision, in that it is not transumptive; that is, it does not project the
Miltonic Heaven into belatedness, while establishing instead its own earliness. It fails to do to Milton's Heaven what Milton did to the Olympus of
Homer, and this failure is at the heart or one might say nerve of its powerful
uneasiness, an uneasiness that has a thematic function, certainly, but that
transcends even thematic necessity. The tropes of this passage (lines 176–
200) are all tropes of representation, and yet they over-represent.

Let me return to, and now adumbrate, a distinction I ventured in *A
Map of Misreading*, between ratios (tropes, defenses, images) of limitation
and ratios of representation. I said there that "limitations turn away from a
lost or mourned object towards either the substitute or the mourning
subject, while representations turn back towards restoring the powers that
desired and possessed the object. Representation points to a lack, just as
limitation does, but in a way that *re-finds* what could fill the lack. Or, more
simply: tropes of limitation also represent, of course, but they tend to limit
the demands placed upon language by pointing to a lack both in language
and the self, so that limitation really means recognition in this context.
Tropes of representation also acknowledge a limit, point to a lack, but they
tend to strengthen both language and the self."

I quote this gnomic passage because I am now ready to unpack it, to
illustrate it by the passage of *Hyperion* under consideration and, I hope, to
illuminate Keats's lines by the application of my distinction. But I want to
return my distinction to its Kabbalistic source, in order to be reminded that
"limitation" and "representation" are highly dialectical terms in the context
of poetic interpretation. The Lurianic *zimzum* is not so much a contraction
or a withdrawal as it is a concentration upon a point, a kind of intensifica-
tion of God as he takes a step inside himself. A poetic image of limitation

tends to cluster in three areas: presence and absence, fullness and emptiness, insideness and outsideness. In the dialectic of rhetorical irony or of
defensive reaction-formation, absence tends to dominate over presence, yet
this is more a pointing to an absence or a lack, in language or the self, than
it is itself a state of absence. Similarly, the metonymic reductiveness from
images of fullness to those of emptiness, these defensive undoings, regres-
sions, and isolations indicate more a *recognition* of emptiness, whether of the
empty word or the empty self, than they actually mean an emptiness itself.
Most crucially, in the sublimating perspectivism of metaphorical images,
though the emphasis in poems tends most often to be upon the outsideness
of objects, sharply distinguished from the inwardness of subjective consciousness, the ratio or trope does not so much limit meaning to the aching
sense of a loss of inwardness, but rather concentrates attention upon the
process of perspectivizing itself. The Lurianic *zimzum*, as a master, composite ratio or trope of limitation, betrays in its most problematic kinds of
meaning its usefulness as a paradigm for all tropes of limitation. *Zimzum* is
the ultimate *askesis* because it is God's own *askesis*, His self-truncation, but
paradoxically it strengthens rather than weakens God, by concentrating
Him, and by making Creation possible. The great Renaissance commonplace, most beautifully phrased by Tasso and by Sidney, that only the poet
truly merited the term of Creator, as God did, took on a special force in the
context of Lurianic Kabbalah, which is I think why figures like Bruno and
Pico were so enraptured by Kabbalah.

But this digression has gone out and away, apparently, from the
passage of Keats's *Hyperion* in question, for there I said we meet only tropes
of representation, even of overrepresentation, which I think is largely true of
the first *Hyperion* as a poem, and is another indication of why the earlier
Hyperion is so much less moving and magnificent than its replacement in
The Fall of Hyperion. Though tropes of representation also acknowledge
limits, and point to lacks, primarily they tend to strengthen both language
and the self. Can we not say of the first *Hyperion*, and not just of its single
passage under discussion, that the poem's language tries to be stronger than
the poem's language can sustain being, and also that Keats's own poetic self
is being put under too strong a burden throughout, both as the impersonal
narrator and as the Apollo of the fragmentary third book? Too much is
being refound, and nearly all at once, throughout the first *Hyperion*, and
the poem as a whole, at least as it stands, implies and even exemplifies too
sharp a turning-back towards restoring our mutilated human powers,
powers for not only desiring a totality, but even for hoping to possess the
object of such desire. The function of images or tropes of limitation is to
turn us away from the lost or mourned object, and so to bring us back to
either a sublimated substitute for the object or, more crucially, a reconsider-

ation of ourselves as mourning subjects. In the first *Hyperion*, Keats took up too directly the burden of synecdoches, Sublime hyperboles, and—as we will see—transumptive or metaleptic reversals of tradition. To recognize himself again, Keats had to write *The Fall of Hyperion* and his five great odes, and both the *Fall* and the Odes do follow the structure or pattern of ratios that Wordsworth and most strong post-Wordsworthian poets have followed.

I return, at last, to lines 176–200 of Book I of *Hyperion*, to demonstrate some of these conclusions, after which I will proceed to the main business of this discourse, which is to give a full antithetical reading of *The Fall of Hyperion*, and by it come back full circle to the starting point of my dissent from de Man, which was my insistence that Keats was as much a retrospective as a prospective poet, and also that in his last major work he was compelled, despite himself, to see himself as a hero of quest-romance on the very threshold of becoming a tragic hero. It was a threshold that he did not cross, in poetry or in life, and I hope to surmise before I end this chapter why he would (or could) not cross it in the poem.

When we first confront Hyperion in the earlier poem, he is remarkably balanced between Sublime and Grotesque representation, a balance that, I hasten to add, belongs to Keats's art alone, and not to Hyperion himself, for Hyperion is suffering what we tend to call a failure of nerve, or even a nervous breakdown. At this point Hyperion as Sun God reminds us too well that Freud's formulation of the defense of repression centers it in the psychic area of hysteria. We see and hear a Sublime being, but we are aware, all too uneasily, that this hyperbolical sublimity is founded upon a really fierce repression:

> Blazing Hyperion on his orbèd fire
> Still sat, still snuffed the incense, teeming up
> From man to the sun's God; yet unsecure:
> For as among us mortals omens drear
> Fright and perplex, so also shuddered he—
> Not at dog's howl, or gloom-bird's hated screech,
> Or the familiar visiting of one
> Upon the first toll of his passing-bell,
> Or prophesyings of the midnight lamp;
> But horrors, portioned to a giant nerve,
> Oft made Hyperion ache.
>
> (166–76)

A God who shudders at divinations is in the process of ceasing to be a God, and too nervous a God is a grotesque God. The meaning of Hyperion's repression here rises from its interplay with the grand repressive God of Book III of *Paradise Lost*. From the first moment we see him, Milton's God, unlike Milton's Satan, has no relation whatsoever to the stance and condition of being a poet. From our first encounter with him, Keats's Hyperion is a touch closer to Milton's Satan than Keats would care for him to have been, since like Satan Hyperion is not so much a God in dread of losing his kingdom as he is a poet in dread of losing his poetic powers or mortal godhead. An obsession with divination, a fear of futurity, is the mark of Hyperion, of Satan, and of Blake's Urizen, and its human meaning is the peculiar poetic property not so much of Milton as of Wordsworth, a truth that Keats knew perhaps better than we can know it.

I come now to the particular passage of the first *Hyperion* that I have been circling in upon, the Hekhaloth or heavenly halls of the nervous Hyperion, in the Sublime pathos that will be almost the last of his glory. Here I will want to start with a formula that sums up the revisionary element in lines 176–200: Keats gives us *an earliness that works as a lateness*, almost the reverse of the Miltonic scheme of transumptive allusion. Milton knowingly sacrifices the living present, the moment of his empirical being as he writes, in order to achieve an ontological earliness that triumphs over almost the entire tradition that produced him, and makes us see that tradition as being belated in contrast to him. I do not think that Keats, any more than Milton or Wordsworth, ever sought that all-but-impossible union between the ontological and empirical self, *in a poem*, that became the peculiarly American tradition of Romantic poetry, from Emerson and Whitman on to Hart Crane and A. R. Ammons. But, in the first *Hyperion*, Keats is not yet the master of transumptive allusion that, following Milton, he was to become. We can date the transition to Keats's maturity as a poet very precisely, since it was by April 1819 that he gave up the first *Hyperion* for good, and it was during the month from April 20 to May 20, that he fully found himself in the writing of the *Ode to Psyche*.

Let us examine Hyperion's palace. Its characteristic imagery is of height and depth, but we may be reminded by it of Blake's comment upon Dante: "In equivocal worlds up & down is equivocal." Hyperion is still sitting exalted, but he acts like ourselves, beings *beneath* the sun. His Shakespearean palace, at once Roman and exotically Eastern, is both "glowing" and "touched with shade," the light also showing an equivocal height and depth. The images of what ought to be earliness crowd upon us: a rising sun; clouds accompanying Aurora, goddess of the dawn; eagles never seen before, and horses never heard before, whether by Gods or men. But all these have to be taken on the lateness of "the sleepy west," of incense turned to "savour of poisonous brass." The Sun God, moving through his domain, is imaged lastly by his angelic attendants or minor Titans, who are waiting for the final lateness of an apocalyptic earthquake. Keats has achieved a surprising immediacy here, but at a triple cost: the only future is a final fall, or utter projection; there is no past surviving into the present, except for a grotesque parody of the Sublime; and the present is introjected as a pure anxiety. I suggest that a full-scale reading of the first *Hyperion* would show that this passage is a part standing for the whole of the fragment. There are essentially only two ratios in the first *Hyperion*, and they are a *kenosis* and a *daemonization*, in uneasy alternation. The fragment vacillates between a defensive isolation of Sublime tradition, through met-onymic reduction, and a powerful repression of the Sublime that fails to make the passage from hyperbole to a metaleptic reversal, that is to say from a perpetually mounting force of still greater repression to a stance finally the poet's own.

In contrast, I turn at last to *The Fall of Hyperion*, which is at once Keats's revision of romance and also his acceptance of the necessity of internalizing romance. This supposed fragment is an entire poem, showing the total structure of misprision, the complete patterning of images that Romantic or belated poetry demands. It is not accidental that, of all the Great Odes, the *Ode to Psyche* most resembles *The Fall of Hyperion*, for it was in the *Ode to Psyche* that Keats, with high good humor, came to terms with his own belatedness. As I have sketched an antithetical reading of the *Ode to Psyche* in *A Map of Misreading*, I will leap over that poem here and take its pattern of misprision as a prelude to the richer working-out of the same pattern in *The Fall of Hyperion*.

The fundamental principle of an antithetical or Kabbalistic criticism is that, in poetic texts, tropes are best understood as psychic defenses, because they *act as defenses*, against the tropes of anteriority, against the poems of the precursors. Similarly, in poetic texts, the poet's (or his surrogate's) psychic defenses are best understood as tropes, for they trope or turn against anterior defenses, against previous or outworn postures of the spirit. I shall illustrate this principle by contrasting the opening lines of *The Fall of Hyperion* to part of the opening passage of Wordsworth's *The Excursion*, Book I, lines 77 ff., that describes the Wanderer:

> Oh! many are the Poets that are sown
> By Nature: men endowed with highest gifts,
> The vision and the faculty divine;
> Yet wanting the accomplishment of verse
>
> Nor having e'er, as life advanced, been led
> By circumstances to take unto the height
> The measure of themselves, these favoured Beings,
> All but a scattered few, live out their time,
> Husbanding that which they possess within,
> And go to the grave, unthought of . . .

The first verse-paragraph of *The Fall of Hyperion* may be thought of as a *clinamen* away from this passage of Wordsworth, among others, one of which might be *The Excursion*, Book IV, lines 1275 ff., yet another panegyric in praise of (let it be admitted) that egregious bore, the Wanderer or the censorious Wordsworthian superego:

> Here closed the Sage that eloquent harangue,
> Poured forth with fervour in continuous stream,
> Such as, remote, 'mid savage wilderness,
> An Indian Chief discharges from his breast
> Into the hearing of assembled tribes,
> In open circle seated round, and hushed
> As the unbreathing air, when not a leaf
> Stirs in the mighty woods.—So did he speak:
> The words he uttered shall not pass away
> Dispersed like music that the wind takes up
> By snatches, and lets fall, to be forgotten . . .

Behind both Wordsworthian passages is an anxiety of Wordsworth's, that the part of his mind represented by the Wanderer may be inimical to poetry, as opposed to the more dangerous part represented by the Solitary, who in Shelley and in the Keats of *Endymion* becomes a figure nearly identical with poetry itself. I think we have underestimated Keats's savagery in *The Fall of Hyperion*, and that he begins the poem with a very bitter rhetorical irony that is his psyche's reaction-formation to this Wordsworthian anxiety:

> Fanatics have their dreams, wherewith they weave
> A paradise for a sect; the savage too
> From forth the loftiest fashion of his sleep
> Guesses at Heaven; pity these have not
> Traced upon vellum or wild Indian leaf
> The shadows of melodious utterance.
> But bare of laurel they live, dream, and die;
> For Poesy alone can tell her dreams,
> With the fine spell of words alone can save
> Imagination from the sable charm
> And dumb enchantment. Who alive can say,
> Thou art no Poet—mayst not tell thy dreams?
> Since every man whose soul is not a clod
> Hath visions, and would speak, if he had loved,
> And been well nurtured in his mother tongue.
> Whether the dream now purposed to rehearse
> Be poet's or fanatic's will be known
> When this warm scribe my hand is in the grave.
> (1–18)

What is present, and what is absent in these lines, and why does

Keats commence his poem with them? "Fanatics" here mean believing Christians, and so "dreams" here mean religious conceptualizations of a heavenly paradise, or else yet more "primitive" mythologies of paradise. Keats's distinction is between dreams and the telling of dreams, which he defines as poetry. Keats's irony, the *clinamen* directed against Wordsworth, is that fanatic and savage alike are present only as dreamers, but absent as poets, and by Keats's allusive implication Wordsworth's Wanderer, who is all but one with the poet writing most of *The Excursion*, is at once fanatic and savage, a complex dreamer but not a poet. But there is a deeper irony here, though it is still a figuration, still a saying of one thing while meaning another. Keats's concern is purgatorial and self-directed; is *he* present only as dreamer, and absent as poet? He is to rehearse a dream for us, but is he poet or fanatic? Can he tell his dream, which must mean something beyond a rehearsal, or will *The Fall of Hyperion* fail even as *Hyperion* failed? As he says himself, the answer came after he was in the grave, and never more greatly than from this poem. But I need to digress here, as few poems open more profoundly than this does, or confront a reader with so problematic a distinction.

The problem of the status and significance of poetry must be resolved at last in the area where our understanding of the following will meet: dreaming, and the telling of dreams in poetry, and the analogy: sex, and the telling of sex in love. The dialectic of Romantic love, which involves dream and identity, is the core problem. In *The Fall of Hyperion*, Keats moves himself and Moneta from one state of Identity to another state, still of Identity, but involving a self less insistent and more given to the sympathetic imagination. The first state is that of the dream, the second that of the dream's telling.

Geza Roheim, the most interesting speculative mind to arise on the Freudian Left, thought that there was only one basic dream, and that all we needed to understand, finally, was our motive for telling it. Wittgenstein in effect says that the dream and the motive alike cannot be spoken of; for him there is only the telling of dreams. To Freud, it does not matter whether the telling is "accurate" or not, just as it does not matter that the therapeutic image is intruded into the patient's consciousness by the analyst. But it matters to a poet that he get his "dream" right, and matters even more that he draw inevitable images *out of* the consciousness of his proper readers, whether in his own time or afterwards. It is because *pleasure* is legitimately one of his criteria, that the poet has his advantage. Perhaps the Stevensian criteria for poetry as the Supreme Fiction can be modified, to be more active: it must abstract, or withdraw perception from belatedness to earliness; it must *cause* change; it must *create* pleasure; it must humanize; all of these appropriate criteria also, surely, for the other Supreme Fiction— Romantic Love.

Is there an analogy between the strong poet's desire for priority and the motives or necessity for *telling*, whether of dreams in poetry or sexuality in love? We border on the realm of solipsism again; priority perhaps means not being first, but being alone, and is the demonic form of the apocalyptic impulse to be integrated again. "I sure should see / Other men here," Keats says to Moneta, and then adds: "But I am here alone." Yet he has not come to tell her his dreams, but to listen to hers, or rather to hear her study the nostalgias. I will return to this stance of faithful listening to the Muse when it comes to dominate the poem, but for now I return to the poem's opening, this time to map it through to the end.

Let us call the opening verse-paragraph, with its reverberations directed against Wordsworth's Wanderer, Keats's poetic reaction-formation against the anxiety of Wordsworthian presence, a conscious *illusio* that knows at once that Keats is an elected poet, but also that in this poem of trial he will not be free to tell his deepest dreams. The answering restitution or representation is in the noble synecdoche of the next, long verse-paragraph, lines 19–80, where Keats antithetically completes both Book V of *Paradise Lost* and his own *Ode to Psyche*. Notice that there is no entrance into this movement of the poem except for the abrupt "Methought I stood," and it is this unmerited and unexplained re-entry into the earthly paradise which is the only dream that Keats will tell in this poem. The recall of lines 60–63 of the *Ode to Psyche* establishes the new poem's largest difference from earlier Keats; the "wreathed trellis of a working brain," there, has been externalized, here, just as the Miltonic dream of Angels and humans feasting together is seen here as belonging to a naturalistic and recent past. Keats stands in a microcosm of the poet's paradise, drinks the honey of Eden, and enters what would be a dream-within-a-dream if it were not so insistently and persuasively a vision of Instruction. When he wakes from his swoon, he is in a poet's purgatory, a ruined sanctuary of every dead faith, and defensively he is turned dangerously against himself, without as yet overtly knowing it.

To stand before the purgatorial stairs is to stand in the realm of displacements, where the center of a dream lances off into indirect byways, into reductions and emptyings-out of things into aspects of things. Rhetorically this is the realm of metonymy, an object-world where there are no resemblances but only contiguities. In lines 81–181 of *The Fall of Hyperion* Keats confronts his Muse in a state of heightened awareness, but also in a state of reified vulnerability. The Keatsian *kenosis* is neither a Wordsworthian regression nor a Shelleyan undoing, but rather resembles Stevens, Keats's descendant, in being a radical isolation. The passage begins just after a repetition of the *Ode to Psyche*'s reduction of dead religion to a metonymic catalog, and continues in a curious tone of the cataloger of contiguities, who cannot summon haste or urgency even to ward off his own destruction until the last possible moment. I will concentrate in this movement upon one moment only, where Keats nearly undoes himself. Moneta has just spoken, with the bitter eloquence that marks her, not so much warning the poet as harshly proclaiming the quick death she confidently expects for him. The purgatorial steps, she says, are immortal, but Keats is only so much dust and sand, a mass of displacements. The poet who had preached disinterestedness is at first so disinterested that he almost fails to move in time. Characteristically, he is roused only by hearing his own involuntary shriek, a rousing or being stung that sets him moving:

> I heard, I looked: two senses both at once,
> So fine, so subtle, felt the tyranny
> Of that fierce threat and the hard task proposed.
> Prodigious seemed the toil; the leaves were yet
> Burning—when suddenly a palsied chill
> Struck from the pavèd level up my limbs,
> And was ascending quick to put cold grasp
> Upon those streams that pulse beside the throat:
> I shrieked, and the sharp anguish of my shriek
> Stung my own ears—I strove hard to escape
> The numbness; strove to gain the lowest step.
> Slow, heavy, deadly was my pace: the cold
> Grew stifling, suffocating, at the heart;
> And when I clasped my hands I felt them not.
> One minute before death, my iced foot touched
> The lowest stair; and as it touched, life seemed
> To pour in at the toes...

This is, at the least, a strong revision of a romance commonplace; the quester's ordeal of recognition, which is not so much a crisis of self-recognition as it is the agony of being brought to what Yeats called "the place of the Daemon." Keats describes in himself a suffering that is at the threshold of strength, even a pragmatic weakness that becomes a poetic power. This is a quester so detached that he broods first on the fineness and subtlety of his own hearing and seeing, before he bothers to consider the danger he confronts. It is as though various reductions of himself—hearing, sight, chilled limbs, tubercular symptoms—were contiguous with the emblems of danger—the harsh voice of the seeress, the burning leaves, the stairs—but so displaced from a universe of resemblances that the contiguity assumed a solitary emphasis as a characteristic. But why does Keats, as a poet, so empty himself out here? Why does he station himself so deliberately, as though he were one more falsely reified entity in a world of such entities, so that the prophetess Moneta becomes yet another such, and so a kind of false prophetess? Freud tells us that the dream world necessarily involves displacement, which rhetorically becomes the mode of metonymy, of so troping or turning from the literal that every complex thing is replaced by a simple, salient aspect of that thing. Keats enters his own poem in the self-proclaimed role as poet, indeed as *the* poet of his own time. Why should he have to undergo such an emptying-out of the poetic self in what is, after all, his annunciation as a strong poet?

I suggest that Keats, a startlingly clear intellect, had a proleptic understanding that there is no breakthrough to poetic strength without a double distortion, a distortion of the precursors and so of tradition, and a self-distortion in compensation. There is no growth into poetic strength without a radical act of interpretation that is always a distortion or misprision and, more subtly, without the necessity of so stationing the poet's ontological self that it too is held up to an interpretation that necessarily will also be distortion or misprision. Keats differs only in degree from previous strong poets by his *acceptance* of these necessities. The prime function of Moneta in the poem is to *misinterpret* Keats, but by so misinterpreting she canonizes him, in a dialectical reversal of her attitude that I now would say does not leave her at the end misunderstanding him any less radically than she misunderstands him when first he stands before her purgatorial stairs. As the Muse, Moneta presides over the canon of poetry and mythology and dead religion, but the canon is a grand ruin, as the poem makes clear. The great sanctuary of Saturn is a wreck, and to be accepted by Moneta as the properly qualified quester is to join an enterprise of disaster. By courteously troping or turning the harsh Muse into accepting him, Keats wins a dubious blessing, as he well knows. It is as though romance is poised already on the verge of what it will become in Tennyson's *The Holy Grail*, where Percivale's quest will destroy everything it touches, or in Browning's *Childe Roland to the Dark Tower Came*, where just the quester's glance will be enough to deform and break all things it views.

We have reached that point in *The Fall of Hyperion* where Keats, mounting up into the shrine of Moneta, mounts up into the Sublime, through the characteristic, paradoxical defense of repression, and by the trope of hyperbole, a trope of excess, of the violent overthrow. A theoretical digression opens before me, in which I hope to clarify not only the poem, but my own antithetical theory of poetry, or rather of the antithetical element in post-Enlightenment poetry.

Richard Wollheim, in his book *On Art and the Mind*, reminds us that Freud knew his favorite models differed in their own purposes from the purposes of art. Freud's models were the dream, the neurotic symptom, the tendentious joke, and all of these have a directness and an immediacy that art fortunately does not have and does not seek. A poem, as Freud well knew, was not a dream, nor a joke, nor a symptom. But Freud, as a humanistic scientist, and Wollheim, as an analytical philosopher, do not know that a poem *is* a kind of error, a beautiful mistake or open lie, that does have the function of, somehow, *telling a dream*. Wollheim, following and expounding Freud, says that a poem does not avail itself of a drop in consciousness or attention in order to become the sudden vehicle of buried desires. But here I think Wollheim is not close enough to what poems actually do, perhaps because he is more interested in the visual arts and less in poetry. Poems, I would insist, indeed do just the reverse of what Wollheim says they don't do, but as this is a dialectical reversal it too is frequently reversed, and so poems do refute Wollheim, not in theory but in the ways they behave. It is by the mode of sublimity that poems suddenly do become the vehicle of buried desires, by violent heightenings of consciousness or attention. But these heightenings can drop away just as suddenly, and abandon us to the consequences of repression, a process rhetorically manifested through the substitution of the trope of litotes for that of hyperbole, by a turning to an underthrow of language that plunges us from the Sublime down into its dialectical brother, the Grotesque.

I would say then that Wollheim, following Freud, is only partly right, because Freud was only partly right, about poetry. Poetic meaning, or the absence of it, exists in the psychic and linguistic gap that separates repression from sublimation. It is true that art, for Freud, does not link up directly with wish and impulse expressing themselves in neurosis, but it does link up, for Freud, and I think in actuality, with defense, and psychic defense need not be or become neurotic, though sorrowfully it usually is or does. Wollheim wisely says that when you abandon the false and non-Freudian equation, neurosis = art, you lose all justification for thinking of art as showing a single or unitary motivation, since except for the relative inflexibility of a neurosis there is no single, unchanging, constant form that our characters or temperaments assume, but rather endless vicissitudes of impulse and feeling, constant formings and re-formings of fantasy, and while there *are* patterns in these, they are as flexible as those of art. I accept Wollheim's formulation of this principle, but with a vital, antithetical proviso—these patterns in feeling and fantasy are frequently defensive without being neurotic, and there are patterns in poetic imagery, rhetoric, and stance that are also defensive, without being neurotic. Wollheim says that art for Freud was constructive as well as expressive, and I would add that what poetry constructs can be a healthy defense against the real dangers of both the inner and the outer life.

Wollheim usefully adds that there is a gap in Freud's account of art, a gap that I think a more antithetical criticism of poetry can help to fill. Freud's vision or poem of the mind developed (as Wollheim indicates) through three stages: first, one in which the unconscious was identified with repression; second, one in which the unconscious was seen as the primary process of mental functioning; third, one in which the unconscious attained a function that went beyond defense, and beyond the ongoing functions of the mind. In this third and final stage, Freud's vision is surprisingly close to Blake's, for the unconscious plays its part as what Blake called the Devourer, binding energy and so building up the ego, the role Blake assigned to Urizen, so that in Freud's final stage the unconscious has turned potentially reasonable. The defenses of projection and introjection are seen by Freud as capable of being transformed beyond defense into a healthful, constructive, ongoing process of *identification*, a Freudian vision in which he again followed the poets, as I have been trying to show, with my emphasis upon schemes of transumption as the characteristic post-Miltonic poetic mode for successfully concluding poems. Wollheim remarks: "In a number of celebrated passages Freud equated art with recovery or reparation on the path back to reality. But nowhere did he indicate the mechanism by which this came about. By the time he found himself theoretically in a position to do so, the necessary resources of leisure and energy were, we must believe, no longer available to him."

It is in the absence of this third-stage Freudian model that I have proposed a Kabbalistic model or paradigm for the image-patterning, for the movement of tropes and defenses towards the strengthening of the poetic ego, that I think is characteristic of the major poets of the last several centuries. But Keats in particular, and in *The Fall of Hyperion* more than anywhere else, gives us yet another critical reason for following Gnostic or Kabbalistic paradigms of belatedness rather than hypothesizing what a mature Freudian psychoesthetics might have become. Most students of Freud would agree that for him the dream and/or the unconscious are at once three things—a representation, a staged scene, and a distortion. But a poem is all three at once also, and we can distinguish between a poem and a dream or unconscious process simply by remarking that the dream or unconscious process is overdetermined in its *meanings*, since we are discovering, if I am right, that belated poems suffer an increasing overdetermination in *language*, but an increasing *under-determination in meaning*. The dream or the symptom has a redundancy of meaning, but the Wordsworthian or modern poem has an apparent dearth of meaning, which paradoxically is its peculiar strength, and its demand upon, and challenge to, the interpretative powers of the reader.

I return to Keats confronting Moneta. Poetic images are not just condensations or displacements of signs, which would make all poetic images either metaphors or metonymies, and hence all *images-of-limitation*. Poetic images, whether as synecdoches, hyperboles, or transumptions, also transform signs, whether by antithetical completion, by heightening, or by the final illusion of making the sign appear to be earlier than it actually is.

But whatever the images of a dream may try to be, they *do* tend to be only images of limitation, and so the dream-tropes are irony, metonymy, metaphor, or in Freudian language: distortion, displacement, condensation. To understand a dream, the dreamer must tell it as a text, which means that he must translate or interpret it into either the language of Freudian reduction, or into the restituting language of poetry, as Keats does. In the scene we have now reached, with Keats facing Moneta after ascending the purgatorial stairs, the language joins the issue for us, between the Freudian, reductive view of repression, and the poetic or Sublime translation or interpretation of repression.

According to Freud, repression is a *failure in translation,* and since I would insist that a strong poem is a triumph of repression, and *not* of sublimation, then I would acknowledge that there must be *some* failure in translation or interpretation in order for a dream to become a poem, which is another way of stating the necessity of *misreading,* if strong poems are to be written or indeed if they are to be read. Just as no dream has a meaning except in relation to other dreams, so that in some clear sense the meaning of a dream can be only another dream, so also poems behave in relation to other poems, as my theory hypothesizes. I want now to break back into Keats's text, at line 134, by venturing this new antithetical formula: *Within a poem the Sublime can only result when translation fails, and so when misprision is heightened, through hyperbole, to a daemonic climax.* The great climax of *The Fall of Hyperion* will be seen to be a revision of the Wordsworthian version of romance, a revision dependent upon an even greater repression than Wordsworth had to accomplish.

The dialogue between Keats and Moneta concerns the problematic of poetic identity, which is an extreme form of the idea of an autonomous ego. Keats, in his speculation upon identity, is part of a very complex nineteenth-century questioning of the notion of a single, separate self, a questioning that culminated in the analytics of Nietzsche, Marx, and Freud, but which may be stronger in the poets even than it was in the great speculators. Is the poetic identity or autonomous ego only a reification? Emerson, who identified the power of poetry with what he called unfixing and clapping wings to solid nature, certainly rejects any notion of a fixed poetic identity or of a single, confined human ego. Nietzsche, on more language-centered grounds, did the same in denying what he called the unnecessary hypothesis of the human subject. There are insights in Keats that may be more subtle than all but a few in nineteenth-century traditions, and these insights tend to cluster around the image of the sole self or poetic identity as a negation of the human. In *Endymion,* Keats had celebrated love and friendship for their work in destroying the autonomy of the self, and had called "crude and sore / The journey homeward to habitual self." But Keats, I think, protested too much his zeal to overcome self-concern, and I think also that Keats has deceived his critics into literalizing his figuration of destroying the self. I am very startled when a critic as demystifying and demystified as Paul de Man says of Keats: "He almost succeeds in eliminating himself from his poetry altogether," or again that "the only threat that Keats seems to experience subjectively is that of self-confrontation." I would venture the paradox that Shelley, who so overtly dramatizes himself in his poetry, is nevertheless far more authentically selfless than Keats in poetry, as he was in life. Keats's speculations on selfhood and identity are not so much deceptive or even self-deceiving as they are evidences of a remarkable repression of anxiety, and also of a will-to-poetic power, and simply cannot be read and accepted at anything near face value.

Shall we not call Moneta the Muse of repression? Criticism has not explained, nor even attempted to explain, her initial hostility to Keats. It is more than haste that Keats represses as he approaches her altar; it is the highest kind of poetic ambition, which is the dream of an active divination, of the poet becoming a god. All through Keats's poetry, critics rightly have seen different aspects of the same situation recur: a mortal, human male quester-poet confronts an immortal, divine, female Muse-principle, and almost always in a context in which the quester-poet is threatened by death, a death marked by privation, particularly by the cold. But Moneta paradoxically is at once the most ultimately benign and the most immediately hostile of these Muses. Keats asks her the wholly modest question, "What am I that should so be saved from death?" And she snaps that all he has done is "dated on" his doom. When Keats says that he is "encouraged by the sooth voice of the shade," he does *not* mean "consoling" but "truthful," for while he is as courteous as she is abrupt, the truth is that he is now as harsh as she is, because it is harsh to confront truth so directly, or at least what one takes to be truth. What could be harsher, or more apparently un-Keatsian, than the shocking hyperbole that Keats allows himself here?

> Then shouted I
> Spite of myself, and with a Pythia's spleen,
> 'Apollo! faded! O far flown Apollo!
> Where is thy misty pestilence to creep
> Into the dwellings, through the door crannies
> Of all mock lyrists, large self worshippers
> And careless Hectorers in proud bad verse.
> Though I breathe death with them it will be life
> To see them sprawl before me into graves....'
> (202–10)

These are not the accents of a poet who has eliminated himself from his own poetry, or for whom self-confrontation is the only subjective threat. What is audible here is spleen all right, and I am afraid that this rancor, from our perspective, is precisely the "good will" on Keats's part that Moneta praises and reciprocates. Keats has done something audacious and only dubiously successful; he purports to speak for Apollo, and to have Moneta speak for all the dead gods of poetry. It is from *that* undemonstrable perspective that Keats so cruelly condemns Shelley, Wordsworth, and Byron, and so it is by being as cruel as Moneta, but towards *other poets*, that Keats has found acceptance by her.

There is no reason to condemn the prevalent critical idolatry of Keats, which as I have remarked elsewhere is a rather benign literary malady. But I do think that such idolatry has blinded us from seeing just what is happening in *The Fall of Hyperion*, and perhaps also in *Lamia*. We have overcanonized Keats, and so we do not read him as he is, with all his literary anxieties and all his high and deep repression plain upon him. From the hyperbolical Sublime of Pythian spleen that he shares with Moneta, Keats attempts the great description of Moneta's face in lines 256–81, which may be the most remarkable extended metaphor in his poetry. I will not analyze it here, except to observe that it fails grandly just as all High Romantic inside/outside metaphors fail, because in attempting to overcome a subject-object dualism it instead extends such dualism. Yet the passage is terribly moving because it persuades us that Keats at last has fulfilled his quest, and has seen what he always wanted to see. He has revised romance, even his own kind of romance, by reconciling and almost integrating the quester and the object of quest. He is no knight-at-arms pining for a Belle Dame, not even the quester after the Melancholy whose "soul shall taste the sadness of her might, / And be among her cloudy trophies hung." Yet his Muse suffers "an immortal sickness which kills not," and is so oxymoronically described that we are bewildered by the shifts-in-perspective that Keats himself cannot control. "Death is the mother of beauty" in Keats's disciple, Stevens, because nothing can be beautiful that does not change, and the final form of change is death. But Keats defies this obvious wisdom, since the "immortal sickness" works a constant change that does not end with death, however unhappy. Earlier in the poem, Keats has referred to his own oxymoronic sickness as being "not ignoble," and we can surmise therefore that Moneta's "immortal sickness" is the fearful repression that results in the poetry of the Sublime, which is Keats's own, overt "illness."

What remains in *The Fall of Hyperion* are traces of a scheme of transumption that Keats sketches without fully working it through. It emerges in two passages of belatedness reversed into earliness:

> ...whereon there grew
> A power within me of enormous ken
> To see as a god sees, and take the depth
> Of things as nimbly as the outward eye
>   Can size and shape pervade...

> —Now in clear light I stood,
> Relieved from the dusk vale. Mnemosyne
> Was sitting on a square-edged polished stone,
> That in its lucid depth reflected pure
> Her priestess-garments.—My quick eyes ran on.

The second of these passages seems to allude to an image in Cary's translation of the *Purgatorio* 9:85–87: "The lowest stair was marble white, so smooth / And polish'd, that therein my mirror'd form / Distinct I saw." As we would expect in the trope of metalepsis, Keats tropes upon his own earlier trope (and Dante's) of the purgatorial stairs. What earlier menaced Keats, the cold stairs that nearly killed him, is now a further means to vision as Keats projects the past, introjects the future, and stands knowingly in a moment that is no moment, a negation of present time. But a transumptive stance, whether in Milton or in Keats, is not simply a prospective one. Its emphasis is not upon a time-to-be, but on the loss-of-being that takes place in present experience.

What then would an antithetical as opposed to a canonical reading of *The Fall of Hyperion* be? All canonical readings (my own earlier one included) have *naturalized* the poem; an antithetical reading would abstract the poem from the irrelevant context of nature, in every sense of "nature." Poems are not "things" and have little to do with a world of "things," but I am not endorsing either the Stevensian notion that "poetry is the subject of the poem." There is no subject *of* the poem or *in* the poem, nor can we make the poem into its own subject. There is a dearth of meaning in a strong poem, a dearth so great that, as Emerson says, the strong poem forces us to invent if we are to read well, or as I would say, if we are to make our misreading stronger and more necessary than other misreadings. *The Fall of Hyperion* is a very strong poem because it impels every reader to return upon his or her own enterprise as a reader. That is the challenge Keats gives us: his stance in relation to Moneta, which means to tradition, which means in turn to the composite precursor, becomes the inevitable paradigm for our stance as readers in relation to his text.

Let me return to the question of a dearth-in-meaning, and elaborate upon it. Only a strong poet can make a dearth-in-meaning, a *zimzum* or limitation that compels subsequent substitution and the *tikkun* or restitution of poetic representation. Any poetaster or academic impostor can write a poem for us that oozes a plenitude of "meaning," an endless amplitude of significances. This late in tradition, we all come to one another smothered in and by meaning; we die daily, facing one another, of our endlessly mutual interpretations and self-interpretations. We deceive ourselves, or are deceived, into thinking that if only we could be interpreted rightly, or interpret others rightly, then all would yet be well. But by now—after Nietzsche, Marx, Freud, and all their followers and revisionists—surely we secretly—all of us—know better. We know that we must be misinterpreted in order to bear living, just as we know we must misinterpret others if they are to stay alive, in more than the merely minimal sense. The necessity of misreading one another is the other daily necessity that accompanies sleep and food, or that is as pervasive as light and air. There is no paradox in what I am saying; I but remind myself of an obvious truth, of *Ananke*, or what Emerson called the Beautiful Necessity.

Keats, revising his lifelong obsession with romance, confronts Moneta as the final form of romance, and sees in her more-than-tragic face the Beautiful Necessity. Of what? Of a mode of repetition in self-destroyings, I think, and a repetition also in the redefinition of romance. I conclude then by asking two questions, both of them in the antithetical context of *The Fall of Hyperion*: what is romance? and what is the repetition of romance?

Freud once described repression as being only a middle stage between a mere, reflex-like defense and what he called an *Urteilsverwerfung* or moral judgment of condemnation. There may be a connection between this description, as Anthony Wilden suggests in his *System and Structure*, and Freud's very difficult essay on "negation," with its much-disputed key sentence: "Through the mediation of the symbol of negation, thought frees itself from the consequences of repression and enriches itself with a content necessary for its accomplishment." Thus freed by negation from the reign of the pleasure principle, thought (according to Freud) is able to attain the more fixed or devouring forms of the reality principle or, as Freud says elsewhere, thought at last is enabled to free itself from its sexual past. I would transpose Freud's formula of negation into the realm of poetry, and specifically into the context of *The Fall of Hyperion*, by suggesting that, in Keats's poem, Moneta, as what Freud calls the symbol of negation, mediates for Keats not so as to free his thought from the consequences of repression but so as to show him that his thought cannot be so liberated, if it is to remain *poetic* thought. When she has shown Keats this, then it is his heroism that permits him to accept such dark wisdom. Romance, as Keats teaches us to understand it, cannot break out of the domain of the pleasure principle even though that means, as Keats knows, that romance must accept the vision of an endless entropy as its fate.

If this is Keatsian or revised romance, then what is the repetition of romance, which is the actual mode of *The Fall of Hyperion* from its first until its final vision of Hyperion: "On he flared"? Though Kierkegaard joked that the dialectic of repetition is easy, he employed his customary rhetorical irony in so joking. At the center of his idea of repetition is the problem of continuity for the individual, a problem that he believed could be solved only by first arriving at a decision, and then by continually renewing it. The best analogue he could find for his vision was the Christian idea of marriage, which he exalted, but pathetically recoiled from personally. Only Christian marriage could give the daily bread that could undergo the severities of repetition, and so finally repetition became meaningless without the perpetual and difficult possibility of *becoming* a Christian.

In Keats, the repetition of romance becomes the perpetual and difficult possibility of *becoming* a strong poet. When Keats persuaded himself that he had mastered such repetition, *as a principle*, then *The Fall of Hyperion* broke off, being as finished a poem as a strong poem can be. Keats had reached the outer threshold of romance, and declined to cross over it into the realm of tragedy. Poised there, on the threshold, his stance is more retrospective than he could have wanted it to be, but there he remains still, in a stance uniquely heroic, in despite of itself.

PAUL SHERWIN

Dying into Life:
Keats's Struggle with
Milton in "Hyperion"

One of the most famous Romantic characterizations of Milton is Wordsworth's in the sonnet "London, 1802":

> Thy soul was like a Star, and dwelt apart:
> Thou hadst a voice whose sound was like the sea:
> Pure as the naked heavens, majestic, free.

The lines illumine Keats's "Bright Star" sonnet, which distinguishes two kinds of steadfastness and, by implication, two contrary poetic standpoints. The star of the octave, "in lone splendour hung aloft the night," is an emblem of the Miltonic visionary, the sublimely self-sufficient artist who "abstracts" himself from nature and common humanity. In the sestet there is a descent from the skies, a humanizing degradation of the bright star's regal solitude. What the star watches from its eminence far above "all breathing human passion," Keats immerses himself in. Pledging himself to a sea of erotic desire, he becomes the "human shores" that are embraced by the "moving waters" of natural process. That watery embrace, Keats knows, is the prelude to a wintry shroud, and so he must pray for a steadfast commitment to a process that is at once self-renewing and self-obliterating.

The sonnet's stark opposition is paralleled in the letters by what may

From *PMLA* (May 1978). Copyright © 1978 by the Modern Language Association of America.

seem Keats's ultimate judgment on Milton: "Life to him would be death to me." In Keats's greatest poetry, beginning with the "Ode to Psyche," Milton serves as an antimuse, less a "Covering Cherub" or traumatizing daemon than an antiphonal voice to be engaged in dialogue. Against Miltonic abstracted vision, which Keats fears may blast our natural faculties, and Milton's vatic estimation of the poet's role, which he suspects is self-inflating false surmise, he marshals his own comparatively unarmed vision.

The "Ode to a Nightingale," for example, is written in such a way as to dramatize Keats's differences from Milton. In stanza 5 Keats initiates a dialogue with "Lycidas" that recalls Milton's parodistic manipulation of tradition, except that, while Milton characteristically overpowers the past, Keats is willing to make do with less. The dialogue culminates in stanza 7, where the stunningly assertive peripety of "Lycidas" ("Look homeward Angel now, and melt with ruth: / And, O ye Dolphins, waft the hapless youth") is subdued to meditative surmise: the bird's immortal song, perhaps, "found a path / Through the sad heart of Ruth, when, sick for home, / She stood in tears amid the alien corn." Milton advances from "melt with ruth" to "weep no more," drying his own melodious tear. Keats, however, passes from Ruth to a forlorn prospect of those perilous seas that Milton abandons for his vision of the heavenly host and that he subsequently entrusts to Lycidas' guardianship. Sick for home, Milton looks homeward. At the very moment that the sun drops into the western bay, Milton himself is "mounted high," emerging as a new and greater sun: "at last he rose" to commence his prophetic exploits of raising a mortal to the skies. At the end of his poem Keats is alienated from his own visionary experience: the nightingale's song is "buried deep / In the next valley-glades." With nothing other than a natural homecoming to look forward to, Keats finds the proper emblem of his mode of being in the arresting image of Ruth, an alien doomed to perpetual homelessness.

Recognizing the dialogical element of the "Ode to a Nightingale" enriches one's understanding of the poem. Whether one conceives the ode, à la Bloom, as psychic battlefield or as playground probably reveals more about the interpreter's rhetorical strategy than about the poem itself. That is a measure of its strength. "Bright Star," however, demands to be read more as defensive warfare than as manipulative game. Here too Keats focuses on the distance between himself and Milton, but the distance is achieved at a terrible cost. Magnifying and distorting Milton's genius, Keats gives to his evocation of the star's splendor what is strongest in his own sensibility. To himself he gives a strained, uneasy rhetoric and a final "swoon to death," which wavers embarrassingly between anguishing and languishing. Keats's self-definition in reference to Milton, or the Miltonic, has driven him to an unnecessarily constrictive opposing standpoint, a modest counterassertiveness that renounces more than it redresses. Perhaps he cannot be where Milton is, but there is no need for Keats to shrink into less than he can be. Although a psychoesthetic reading of the "Ode to a Nightingale" can uncover a similar process of distortion and diminishment, the poem surmounts such reduction: Milton's life need not be Keats's death.

That Keats knew his distance from Milton is owing not only to temperamental but to temporal difference: the voice of an alien age, Milton's poetry had become a fixed star in the constellation of English literature, so monumental that it could not speak directly to a modern consciousness. That Keats should want or need to augment that distance indicates that for him Milton was a dangerous center of power, at once cherished and dreaded. Milton first becomes this ambivalent daemonic presence in *Hyperion*, the poem in which, as Bate remarks, "the powerful influence of Milton suddenly lifted Keats to the high plateau on which he henceforth proceeded." In terms of psychogenesis, *Hyperion* reverses the direction of "Bright Star." Keats's point of departure is the feverish press of his brother Tom's illness, a "hateful siege of contraries" that is assuaged by a "plunge into abstract images." Yet "those abstractions which are my only life" are also termed a "feverous relief." The press of mortal illness yields to, or merges with, the anxious press of Milton's influence, "an awful warmth about my heart like a load of Immortality."

Entering the threatening ancestral space of Miltonic epic and sublime fable, Keats endeavors to occupy and master it, making it his own by subduing the phantom he raises. To read *Hyperion* as "mental fight," as Keats's dubious battle with Milton's overshadowing presence, may seem a dubious interpretive approach. Is it not, at its best, a poem that has succeeded in sublimating the sublime, a poem so thoroughly objectified as to assume the coolness of monumental sculpture? If Keats revives the ancient theme of war in heaven, he shuns the presentation of actual combat. Nevertheless, *Hyperion* is a poem of revisionary strife. The celebrated objectivity of Books I and II, while on one level a purgation of Miltonic palpable design and self-dramatization, also masks an assault upon Milton that is as vehemently subjective, if not as profound, as the revisionism of Blake. Whereas Blake is the Juvenal among Milton's revisionists, Keats is the Horace, preferring gestures of submission to threat gestures, perhaps because he is more fearful of both his antagonist and himself and must therefore exercise greater rational control. The problem for Keats in *Hyperion* is that he cannot adequately control Milton or his own movements. He begins the poem with the intention of putting Milton in his place, both historically and spiritually. Milton, however, is a portion of the past that will not maintain its place. He returns "uncannily" to bewilder Keats's sense of time and self, subverting Keats as powerfully as Keats subverts him. Not only is this mutual subversion the chief source of the poem's vitality, but it immeasurably deepens Keats's understanding of his situation as a poet, preparing him for the achievements that are to be built on the ruins of *Hyperion*.

The origins of Keats's design for *Hyperion* can be traced to his brooding over the abyss of Milton and the abyss of Wordsworth in the "Grand March of Intellect" letter. "When the Mind is in its infancy," he states, "a Bias is in reality a Bias, but when we have acquired more strength, a Bias becomes no Bias." Milton and Wordsworth represent distinct imaginative biases, but Keats is hoping to comprehend them within an angle of vision so wide that bias is eliminated. Although he recognizes that Wordsworth has surpassed Milton in understanding the human heart and mind, he attributes Wordsworth's superiority to a more enlightened age rather than to superior genius. Time, according to Keats's progressivist trope, befriends the weaker moderns. Yet there is a problem. The negative burden of the letter centers upon the potentially irremediable loss of poetic strength purchased by Wordsworth's advancement of knowledge, the fear that it is time, or its disenchanting insights, that has sapped the genius of the moderns. He wonders "whether Wordsworth has in truth epic passion, and martyrs himself to the human heart." *Hyperion* may be viewed as an apotropaic work aimed at warding off this depletion anxiety. Keats sets out to subsume his two most troublesome precursors by combining the strengths of both, the profundity of Wordsworthian human understanding and the amplitude of Miltonic mythological epic, the "large utterance of the early Gods" (*Hyperion* 1.51). His great hope is that historical and personal progress will coincide in his achievement, that the forward momentum of the grand march of intellect will simultaneously thrust him away from his precursors and direct him to the fulfillment of his individual destiny.

That *Hyperion* is a "progress" poem is evident. This theme is most fully articulated in the Titan Oceanus' speech, the theoretical core of the poem:

> As Heaven and Earth are fairer, fairer far
> Than Chaos and blank Darkness, though once chiefs;
> And as we show beyond that Heaven and Earth
> In form and shape compact and beautiful,
> In will, in action free, companionship,
> And thousand other signs of purer life;
> So on our heels a fresh perfection treads,
> A power more strong in beauty, born of us
> And fated to excel us, as we pass
> In glory that old Darkness. . . .
>
> (II.206–15)

More specifically, *Hyperion* is a poem about the progress of poetry, a major Enlightenment theme. Its chief concern is Apollo's coming of age, his mastery of the sun and his own poethood, and its fundamental cosmic law is that "first in beauty should be first in might" (II.229). Progress or renewal here is effected via the displacement of an older generation by a younger, who are always more beautiful than their ancestors. Oceanus' lines on the young god of the sea who is his dispossessor reveals the manner in which Keats wants this transfer of power to take place:

> ...Have ye seen his face?
> Have ye beheld his chariot foam'd along
> By noble winged creatures he hath made?
> I saw him on the calmed waters scud,
> With such a glow of beauty in his eyes,
> That it enforc'd me to bid sad farewell
> To all my empire:...
>
> (II.233–39)

Oceanus abdicates his realm when he beholds one who can fashion more "noble winged creatures"—that is, finer poems—than he can. His action is curious, but his reaction is even more so, for although he has no reason to exult, this is the only occasion in his speech when his rhetoric becomes impassioned. The passage becomes more telling if we recognize that the excitement of the Titan's esthetic response is in fact Keats's own as he glories in the foretaste of a "power for making" that will enable him to dispossess his precursors.

In order to realize his desire Keats must first transcend the stage of poetic consciousness represented by the Titans. Their situation, of course, is largely derived from that of the fallen angels in the first two books of *Paradise Lost*, but they are more radically "Miltonic" than that. Unlike the Satanic host, but like Milton himself in Keats's view, the massive yet crude Titans are the victims of evolutionary progression. Gods of the "infant world" (I.26), they correspond to Milton as he is characterized in the grand-march-of-intellect letter: "From the Paradise Lost and the other works of Milton, I hope it is not too presuming...to say, his Philosophy, human and divine, may be tolerably understood by one not much advanced in years." Displacement of the Miltonic Titans is as natural as the passage from youth to maturity or—to borrow a favorite metaphor of the progress myth—as the westering passage of the sun across the heavens. In *Hyperion* Keats preserves the traditional geographical direction of the progress poem but foreshortens it, delineating a westward movement from the Asiatic Titans to the purer gods of Hellas. Milton's devils are similarly often portrayed as Oriental powers; yet there is again a parallel to Milton himself, a Hebraic avatar of that "eastern voice of solemn mood" Keats refers to in his brief account of poetic progress in *Endymion.*

A further index of Keats's intentions is his description of Hyperion at his final appearance in the poem as he stands majestically above the disconsolate Titans:

> Regal his shape majestic, a vast shade
> In midst of his own brightness, like the bulk
> Of Memnon's image at the set of sun
> To one who travels from the dusking East:
>   (II.372–75)

Keats seems to be directly responding to his friend Hazlitt. Contemplating the general decline of poetry since Milton's time, in his *Lectures on the English Poets,* Hazlitt says of the great masters of the past: "These giant-sons of genius stand indeed upon the earth, but they tower above their fellows; and the long line of their successors, in different ages, does not interpose any object to obstruct their view, or lessen their brightness." Keats counters this rich gloom with the proposal that the *genii* of the past are self-eclipsing. His own dazzling god of the meridian will supplant that giant brood as effortlessly as Milton's babe routs the hapless pagan oracles in the "Nativity Ode."

But unlike Milton, who, despite some nostalgic misgivings, remains an audaciously confident displacer or redeemer of all imaginative traditions whatsoever (including Christianity), Keats is not at all self-assured when he sets out to transcend the Titanic powers in Book III of *Hyperion.* Waylaid in the dark passages between youth and maturity, he cannot transfer the torch of poetic consciousness from the ancestral sun god who is setting to the new god who is waiting to dawn. What, then, perplexes Keats's program? Perhaps, as has frequently been argued, he cannot proceed because he has given too much of his sympathy to the Titans. Many, too, have felt that for similar reasons there is a falling-off in *Paradise Lost* after the richness of its first two books; but Milton is able to continue in spite of his achievement, indeed to build upon it, because he possesses a vision large enough to counter, if not wholly displace, his portrait of hell. Keats, however, has only his surmises about progress to guide him, and his predicament stems from the nature of the progress myth itself.

His dilemma is an evolutionary one, the same that confronts any authentic historiography or psychology of personal growth. He must decide whether change is to come by gradual adaptation or by mutation. Is the progression a chain of causal enlinkedness, a continuum marked out by an interpenetrating series of graduated stages, or does transition between stages necessitate abrupt, fortuitous leaps? Although Keats's firmly naturalistic sensibility and his desire to extend the achievement of the past ally him with the former position, it would seem that he would have to embrace the latter, given his catastrophic myth of war in heaven and his need to assert his authority vis-à-vis the past.

In *Hyperion* Keats's myth of progress occupies a middle (or muddled) position between these options, affording him a precariously discontinuous continuity with the world of natural process and poetic tradition. So far as the literary past is concerned, the issues are how much of the old the new must absorb to progress beyond it and how much alike the lineaments of the old and new will be once that progress is achieved. In the first two books, where he respects, however guardedly, his continuity with Milton, Keats writes self-consciously, yet powerfully, against the grain. But in Book III, when he needs to assert himself, the voice we hear, full of inner haltings, is that of *Endymion*, indicating that he has not progressed at all. Despite Keats's intentions, *Hyperion* is an unmoving sequence of liminal moments; it is a poem eager for crossing that remains a passenger, a prisoner of the passage.

Milton's preemptive presence helps to explain Keats's unsuccessful passage. There is, of course, the matter of his reliance on Milton's stylistic mannerisms, the primary scandal according to Keats. At least equally oppressive is his strict adherence to the formal design of *Paradise Lost*, which he regarded as "Apollonian." In addition to inhibiting his invention, this dependence impels him to betray his poem's fundamental truth. Keats wishes to tell a story of progress, but, in opposing hell and heaven in the opening books of *Paradise Lost*, Milton intends to define the locus of choices available to the inhabitants of our pendant world—man being the dramatic fact of Milton's poem, hell and heaven its logical necessities. Why should Keats follow him, polarizing the darkening world of the Titans and the dawning world projected in Book III? His puzzlingly hasty account of Apollo's development may simply be a not so finely toned repetition of the invocation to light in Book III of *Paradise Lost*. What makes Keats's repetition of the Miltonic pattern disastrous is that it all but eliminates the human middle ground of *Paradise Lost*, the only realm in which genuine progress can occur.

Willfully entering and yet unwillingly constricted by Milton's epic universe, Keats suffers what Paul de Man, following Binswanger, calls "harassed confinement." To remedy his situation he must establish his most advantageous relationship to Milton, affirming his own truth as opposed to Milton's error and thereby overcoming Milton's authority even if he cannot undo Milton's priority. The distance from Milton, an experiential fact that Milton's eighteenth-century epigones felt as an anguished separation, must widen, for Keats, into a generative void. Representation recognizes a void and hopelessly tries to fill it; misrepresentation claims it as the space of free creation. At its most benign, Keats's project is re-creative, not only of himself but of Milton as well, since Milton's poetry is liberated by Keats's revisionary labor. Misrepresentation, however, also soothes an absence. In *Hyperion* Keats revises *Paradise Lost* in such a way as to void it of presence, to limit its demands, but those demands keep pressing back, and as a consequence Keats's own presence is severely limited. The void is at least as much in Keats as in Milton. It is not so much that Keats's consciousness willingly dissolves into the impersonality of the first two books, and even less that it has merged with the object of its desire, as that it is hiding there, unable to emerge in its own right, falling back on Milton so as not to lose itself utterly in its own void.

The continuous transfigurative thrust of *Hyperion* is to shrink Milton's cosmos to a manageable size in order that it may be mastered. Mnemosyne, the muse of Keats's heliocentric universe, is the bearer of the cumulative report of historical memory, but Milton's theocentric universe demands a muse whose voice is unmediated by time or place. Milton ventures a takeover of all time and all space, both beginnings and endings, and although he experiences a horror of the abyss in his explorations of hell and chaos, he cannot fall except within the purview of an omnipotent and merciful God. In *Hyperion* there is only a dim sense of "beauteous life / Diffus'd unseen throughout eternal space" (1.317–18), a mysterious force whose ways cannot be justified, and if one is defeated by natural process, there is no reason to suppose that this loss will be redeemed beyond time and space as we know them. The upper spatial bound of *Hyperion*'s universe is that of the shadowy Coelus, regent of what Milton scornfully calls "the middle air," the Olympians' highest heaven (*PL* 1.516). Curtailing Milton's expansiveness, Keats also refuses, despite Miltonic precedent, to follow Hyperion through the void when he plunges to earth at the close of Book 1. There is, in fact, no movement or action on a grand scale in *Hyperion*, only static moments of reflection or passion. An epic less Miltonic in spirit would be difficult to imagine.

The epic poet traditionally soars, but the gravity of Books 1 and 11 of *Hyperion* precludes the possibility of flight. Behind Keats's methodical ponderousness is a temperament resolutely at odds with Milton's. Although espousing an ethical doctrine of patience in *Paradise Lost*, Milton continually displays an impatience with whatever checks the spirit's flight, whether the recalcitrance of familiar nature or the "slow-pac't evil" of fallen human time. He journeys forward and back through space and time, unwilling to be constrained by a horizontal narrative progression. His similes, for example, tend to be vertical explosions that serve less to retard the text than to suspend it, inviting us to dream of other imaginative worlds. The focus of one of Keats's similes, probably the finest in *Hyperion*, is "dreaming" oaks (1.72–79). The passage, however, does not turn in upon itself; magnifying its immediate subject rather than our consciousness, it represents neither a shift in tone nor even a true shift in subject (the reference to oaks is in keeping with the Druidic imagery applied elsewhere to the Titans, and the landscape evoked is consonant with the theme of their naturalization). Keats's treatment of the epic simile is symptomatic of the manner of the first two books. Their most distinctive characteristic is a slow, undeviating "march of passion and endeavour" (*Letters*, I, 207), an insistent linearity that verges on punctuality.

"Whose head," Keats writes, "is not dizzy at the possible speculations of Satan in the serpent prison?... No passage of poetry can give a greater pain of suffocation." Yet, though Milton has Satan express humiliation at being reduced to so mean a stratagem, he never attempts to induce the effect Keats describes. Keats is lavish in his praise of Milton's talent for "stationing," what Bate terms "the dynamic caught momentarily in repose," but the restless vitalism of material and spiritual forms in Milton allow for nothing comparable to the smothering up of energy in the opening tableau of *Hyperion*:

> Deep in the shady sadness of a vale
> Far sunken from the healthy breath of morn,
> Far from the fiery noon, and eve's one star,
> Sat gray-hair'd Saturn, quiet as a stone,
> Still as the silence round about his lair;
> Forest on forest hung about his head
> Like cloud on cloud. No stir of air was there,
> Not so much life as on a summer's day
> Robs not one light seed from the feather'd grass,
> But where the dead leaf fell, there did it rest.
> A stream went voiceless by, still deadened more
> By reason of his fallen divinity
> Spreading a shade: the Naiad 'mid her reeds
> Press'd her cold finger closer to her lips.
>
> (I.1–14)

There is a surprising echo of *Paradise Lost* here. The movement from morn to noon to eve in lines 2–3 and the use of "summer's day" in line 8 and "fell" in line 10 recall Milton's account of Mulciber's fabled fall from heaven:

> ... from Morn
> To Noon he fell, from Noon to dewy Eve,
> A Summer's day; and with the setting Sun
> Dropt from the Zenith like a falling Star,
> On *Lemnos* th'*Ægæan* Isle:
>
> (I.742–46)

As Hartman argues, Milton counterpoints his treatment of Satan's minions, adopting a rhythm reminiscent of the Book of Genesis in order to suggest the ease of divine creativity. Keats, however, tropes against his source, transforming the free fall of Milton's breathing space into a saturnine fixation so intense that, as Thea says, "unbelief has not a space to breathe" (I.67). It can be argued that Keats is pressed down by the burden of Milton's influence—his "divinity / Spreading a shade"—but he is also choosing to submit to realities beyond his control: the suggestion, throughout Books I and II, is that the patience he exhibits is what both we and the Titans are most in need of, as he makes us suffer, along with them, the unremitting pressure of existence within the spatial and temporal confines of our natural condition.

While exaggerating Milton's propensity for physical stationing, Keats voids his poem of Milton's great intellectual fixation: his doctrine of a heaven and hell in which all intelligent beings will eventually be stationed according to God's judgment. Good and evil "abhor to join" (*PL* XI.686) is the principle upon which Milton's visionary cosmos is founded; yet Keats's marginal notes on *Paradise Lost* underscore the likenesses between Milton's heavenly and infernal regions. "Hell is finer than this" is his telling remark beside a passage describing the bliss of heaven. For it is in the portrait of hell—with its "darkness visible," its fiery darkness, where "the parching air / Burns froze, and cold performs th' effect of fire," and its desperate union of melancholy and magnificence—that Milton captures with greatest intensity those warring natural contraries that, although often modulated into a "sweet unrest" ("Bright Star"), are the basis of Keats's human reality.

It may be inferred, then, that the humanizing aim of Keats's revisionism is to preserve the element of dynamic contrariety in his precursor while purging the moral dualism—the cloven fiction of good and ill—that fetters Milton's genius. Yet, in recoiling from what he saw as disastrous finalities in Milton, Keats turns to an esthetic order that is ultimately more static and constrictive than Milton's ethical order. Despite his belief that good and evil abhor to join, Milton knows that *in our world* they are cunningly intervolved; and although the two never enter into the synthesizing dynamics of a dialectic, the obligatory task of culling and sorting them out is an ongoing, heroic labor of self-creation. There can be no self-development of this kind in the deterministic universe of *Hyperion*. To exist here is to confront, not spiritual options, but the fated conditions of fortune and misfortune: all that remains for the fortunate (more beautiful) is to fulfill the law of their being, while the unfortunate (less beautiful) must either suffer the bewildering fact of their doom or, like Oceanus, will to become a sod. Indeed, it is not Apollo, less choosing than chosen, and certainly not the unwieldy giant Hyperion, but Time that is the true hero of *Hyperion*. For it is the grand

march of esthetic progress, a fond hope hardened into necessitarian doctrine, that assumes the burdens of choice and change, releasing the
newcomer from the agonizing labor of displacing his ancestors and of
making his destiny his choice. The final irony here is that Keats *is* fated,
although not in the way he wishes to be, and that it is the vicissitudes of
time that subvert his spatial metaphor of progress.

Thus far I have been concerned largely with what Keats purges and
preserves in Milton, or preserves so as to purge. Still to be considered is his
most obvious and puzzling debt to *Paradise Lost,* his retention of its
mythological superstructure. Is there not something anomalous about a
stridently modernist "progress" poem that uses regressive machinery to
express its vision? The grand-march-of-intellect letter suggests that the great
modern theme is necessarily "the Mind of Man," its quest for self-realization
in a world such as ours; yet how can Keats do justice to this subject if he
refuses to exile the outmoded gods of tradition? *Hyperion* is a poem in which
two generations of immortals are heading in opposite directions: the Titans
are being humanized, and the Olympian Apollo is passing from humanity
into divinity. Keats's design is such that he inevitably sympathizes with the
Titans and, one can surmise, would inevitably have been estranged from the
deified Apollo, who embodies his aspirations. Surely he could have avoided
many difficulties by dispensing with surrogates and telling the story of John
Keats's emergence, or attempted emergence, as a poet.

There are manifold reasons why he did not, and I can only suggest a
few of them here. He is drawn, nostalgically, to the old sublime mythologies,
unwilling to sacrifice their amplitude and charm to the modern spirit of
reflection. More important, he turns to them because he is uncertain of his
way; lost in himself, he needs some authoritative or authenticating principle
to hold on to. The mysteries pressing upon him are the uses of this world,
historical change, vocation, identity—all of them elusive, all virtualities that
can be inexhaustibly represented but never understood in themselves. He is
concerned, moreover, with their relationships—the world's role in the
formation of identity, the link between personal and historical development,
the modern poet's stance in relation to his precursors—and in the letters,
one sees his speculations taking shape through the agency of such genetic
myths as the "Grand March of Intellect" and the "Vale of Soul-making."
Sequential, hierarchic narrative organizes Keats's inner life, giving it substance and direction. The visionariness of myth allows his speculations to
assume palpable form, and its structures provide an emergency bridge
between speculation and speculation. Yet, in addition to mediating potential discontinuities in thought, myth serves as a vehicle to guide him
beyond, or protect him from, his thoughts. Turned reflectively upon himself
and weighing his own endowment against the accumulated wealth of

tradition, Keats is treading on dangerous ground, spiritually as well as intellectually. He requires a certain measure of distance from his thoughts, which is just what the cosmic myth of *Hyperion* promises to afford.

The complicating factor is that Keats remains a self-conscious modern despite his embrace of old-style myth. Insofar as he shares the impulses of the past but not the substance to which they were attached, he is conscious, always, of standing over a void, and—unless he is to be a vacuous archaist— he must allegorize or internalize his myth to an extent that Milton need not have done. New-style Romantic myth, then, is a device of art rather than an object or outgrowth of belief, differing most dramatically from traditional myth in that it is turned principally toward art, the reservoir of forms and psychic energies from which it draws its being. Keats's inspiriting recognition in the "Ode to Psyche" is that he can see what is not palpably present in the great writers of tradition, the inner light that survives their outmoded forms:

> O brightest! though too late for antique vows,
>   Too, too late for the fond believing lyre,
> When holy were the haunted forest boughs,
>   Holy the air, the water, and the fire;
> Yet even in these days so far retir'd
>   From happy pieties, thy lucent fans,
>   Fluttering among the faint Olympians,
> I see, and sing, by my own eyes inspir'd.

In *Hyperion*, a confrontation with Milton on Milton's own ground of sublime fable, Keats wrestles both with Milton's forms and with his inwardness, extroverting the former and submerging the latter. Since Keats is not yet ready to proclaim his own truth, or perhaps not yet sure what it is, his poem is less an elaboration of his own vision than a systematic dismemberment of Milton's.

Launching his argument in *Paradise Lost*, Milton tells us that Satan lay vanquished on hell's burning marl for nine days and nights after his fall, but he presents only the headlong rush of his descent (the ultimate mythic version of the birth wound) and his violent stirrings into wakefulness. At the outset of *Hyperion* we encounter another leader of a band of fallen celestial powers; Keats, however, overlooks Saturn's actual descent, presenting only its paralyzing aftershock. Frozen into nature and bound to an aching present, Saturn has little of Milton's Satan in him, despite the many superficial resemblances between them. The Satan of Books I and II is never so humanly pathetic, and never for a moment does he lose consciousness of his own strong identity, as Saturn does. Instead, Keats models his hoary Saturn chiefly on Milton's God, imagining an enthroned Jehovah's reaction to being cast from his starry fortress. A fallen Satan can feed his guilt with prophecies of vengeance, but a fallen Jehovah, remembering that once "Fate seem'd strangled in [his] nervous grasp," might well become "smother'd up" like Saturn. A baffled sky god reduced to the status of a chthonic deity, he is powerless to act upon his vague longing to destroy the universe and fashion a new one in its stead.

There is as well a likeness between Saturn and Milton, the visionary who wakens from his dreams of heaven to discover himself famished on the cold hillside but also, and more important in this context, a giant of the imagination fallen out of the literary canon. If one listens carefully to Oceanus' address to Saturn, one can hear Keats's ghostly confabulation with his poetic father:

> . . . thou
> Hast sifted well the atom-universe;
> But for this reason, that thou art the King,
> And only blind from sheer supremacy,
> One avenue was shaded from thine eyes,
> Through which I wandered to eternal truth.
> And first, as thou wast not the first of powers,
> So art thou not the last; it cannot be:
> Thou art not the beginning nor the end.
>
> (II.182–90)

"Standing aloof in giant ignorance," Milton could not see what Keats sees. According to the grand-march-of-intellect letter, Milton was blinded by a naïve religious dogma. With the advent of a more enlightened age, Milton's celestial Urania would avail him no more than Saturn's outmoded bible ("that old spirit-leaved book / Which starry Uranus with finger bright / Sav'd from the shores of darkness" [II.133–35]) can teach him what has become of his former power. Yet "aye on the shores of darkness there is light" ("To Homer"): Saturn's darkness is Oceanus' light, even as Keats's perception of Milton's blind spot guides him to the "eternal truth" that is his own salvation, the doctrine of progress that enables his "youngling arm" to topple the edifice of Miltonic epic.

In my earlier consideration of why Keats retains the old mythological machinery I omitted one explanation I find increasingly persuasive. What better means is there to "violate" the "slumbrous solitude" of the ancients (I.69), to stage a meeting between the living and the mighty dead? This confrontation is founded upon a lie against time, a literalization of the poets' claim to immortality. Yet, in accordance with Keats's wishes, it is an unequal confrontation; for although the dead live again in *Hyperion*, they are shorn of their power. Their loss of creative power is, of course, no lie: fixed in the past, the dead are a "mammoth-brood" (I.164) that cannot evolve in consciousness, and if Saturn cannot fabricate another universe, neither can

Milton write any new poems. But when Saturn laments that he is "buried from all godlike exercise / Of influence" (I.107–08), Keats lies against the real immortality of the dead.

That Keats's progress trope is a trope, a necessary lie, is evidenced by the psychic and temporal displacements of his allegory. Who, if not Keats—"cowering under the Wings of great Poets"—is overshadowed, at once pressed down and withdrawn, at the outset of the poem? Keats endeavors to empty the air of Milton's majesty and to render him voiceless, yet when his own voice surfaces *as* voice it is a "feeble tongue" (I.49). Throughout *Hyperion* it is Keats's identity that is bewildered, and the desperate cry of Saturn/Milton,

> ...But cannot I create?
> Cannot I form? Cannot I fashion forth
> Another world, another universe,
> To overbear and crumble this to naught?
> Where is another chaos? Where?...
>
> (I.141–45)

is an index of Keats's suppressed anguish over his inability to destroy Milton's epic universe or to discover a fresh space within it for himself. The fallen divinities of *Hyperion* lament their own ghostliness as the shadows of a former splendor.

Keats's unconscious "preposterous" trope, a fascinating instance of the perverse ingenuity of dissociated thinking, is clearest in the Milton-inspired debate of Book II, where the impotence and anxiety of the moderns are projected onto the ancients. The influx of the Olympians' surpassing beauty has frozen the Titans into fantastic shapes of woe. Saturn and Enceladus, vacillators between rage and pathetic grief, and Clymene, the inarticulate victim of esthetic experience, are three exemplars of how not to be a poet in one's own time. The fourth is the apparently unwounded Oceanus. His advice that the Titans "stoop to truth" (II.178–80) directs us to the (relatively) impoverished Pope of *An Essay on Man*, though Oceanus' position is closer to that of Hazlitt, another advocate of disinterestedness, who renounced his art for criticism when he saw he could not hope to rival a Titian or a Rembrandt. Oceanus purports to have borne his own renunciation with equanimity, but Enceladus is present to afford quite a different perspective, reminding Oceanus of his "scalding in the seas" (II.320).

One Titan, "blazing Hyperion," is as yet undisplaced, still a practicing artist of sorts. Yet he too is victimized by temporal progress, an ancient undergoing the affliction of the moderns, suffering as well from a peculiarly Romantic disease of consciousness. Now that the spirit of the new age has encroached upon his pleasure palace he is in a mist, alienated from his surroundings and himself, not so much fallen as "falling continually ten thousand fathoms deep and being blown up again without wings and with all the horror of a bare shoulderd Creature." The foregoing, from the grand-march-of-intellect letter, describes the heat and fever of a life of "high Sensations" without knowledge, presumably Keats's own condition before he hit upon his doctrine of progress, the "great whole" toward which "every department of knowledge ... [is] calculated."

It is doubtful whether such knowledge would be of much use to Hyperion, since he is doomed to participate in a universe whose purposes are antagonistic to his own desires. Satan, his closest Miltonic counterpart, is similarly thwarted. But Hyperion is too innocent to understand that the horror he perceives is a hell within and too distraught to muster Satan's astonishing defenses, the will to declare himself unchanged and to take possession of his interior abyss. Like Satan, he curses; yet when he struggles for a heavier threat it sticks in his throat, whereupon he is subjected to his greatest torment:

> ... from the mirror'd level where he stood
> A mist arose, as from a scummy marsh.
> At this, through all his bulk an agony
> Crept gradual, from the feet unto the crown,
> Like a lithe serpent vast and muscular
> Making slow way, with head and neck convuls'd
> From over-strained might. . . .
>
> (1.257–63)

While not reducible to the pain of emergent self-consciousness, Hyperion's agony is clearly allied to it: the passage not only recalls Satan's serpentine incarnation but looks forward to the seizure of mortal knowledge Keats undergoes in *The Fall of Hyperion* (1.121–34). Hyperion, however, cannot learn from his experience. He seeks to allay his anguish by some objective action, attempting to assert himself by hastening the advance of the dawn:

> ... full six dewy hours
> Before the dawn in season due should blush,
> He breath'd fierce breath against the sleepy portals,
>
> Fain would he have commanded, fain took throne
> And bid the day begin, if but for change.
> He might not:—No, though a primeval God:
> The sacred seasons might not be disturb'd.
>
> And the bright Titan, phrenzied with new woes,
> Unus'd to bend, by hard compulsion bent
> His spirit to the sorrow of the time;
>
> (1.264–66, 290–93, 299–301)

His "radiance faint" (1.304), Hyperion has lost the power to create. Like Milton, he has presided over his final dawn.

Milton, of course, did dawn in "Lycidas," the opening of which Keats is quarreling with in the above passage. Milton's elegant pseudoapology for a premature harvesting of his art is not at issue here; Keats reads Milton more literally and profoundly than that. "Lycidas" begins with a crime against Nature. The violation of Nature's "seasons due" is a gesture prompted by Nature's violation of the higher principle of human life. If he does not quite make Nature afraid, Milton brings it to the bar, summoning and dismissing nature spirits like a magus in his efforts to account for the untimeliness of death, or any human loss. Although at the conclusion he returns to Nature with affection, he can do so only because it has been redeemed by the transcendent "might of him that walk'd the waves." Such transcendence, for Keats, is original imaginative sin. He would say, along with Wordsworth, "No more shall grief of mine the season wrong" ("Intimations Ode"). Portraying Hyperion as compelled to submit to natural process, he indicates what Milton's actual experience must have been, as opposed to his poetic representation of it, even as he suggests that Milton's initial trespass against process, like that attempted by Hyperion, is a blindly reflexive reaction to his subjective indeterminacy. Both Hyperion and Milton, in other words, are lacking in "Negative Capability," the ability to remain in uncertainties, doubts, and mysteries without nervously reaching after premature solutions.

The most uncanny feature of *Hyperion* is that whenever Keats aims his aggression outward it is also directed against himself. The poem reveals Keatsian negative capability for the defensive maneuver it often is: the will not to will can belie a mere inability or a failure of nerve. It is extravagant, but hardly an exaggeration, to identify Hyperion's impotent "over-strained might" and hysterical assault upon temporality with Keats's, not only in Books I and II but in the fragmentary third book as well. Here we encounter another failure to dawn and another premature attempt to lift the burden of the mystery.

Keats's project in Book III is clarified by reading in context the grand-march-of-intellect letter's most famous section and subtlest version of the progress theme. Milton, like the obsolete Hyperion, is trapped at a point just beyond the threshold leading from the "Chamber of Maiden-Thought." Wordsworth has transcended this stage of spiritual adolescence, exploring the mysterious dark passages that lie ahead. Keats adds that, "if we live, and go on thinking, we too shall explore them." And perhaps, in *Hyperion*, go beyond Wordsworth? Is it not golden Apollo's mission to advance or guide Keats beyond the dark passages to a final enlightened chamber, call it maturity or godhood? The hero of *Hyperion*, Keats says, is to be "a foreseeing God [who] will shape his actions like one."

Yet at the outset of Book III Apollo is a pathos-filled quester, and Keats is both a stumbling and a retrogressive poet. Though seeking an image of his own spiritual form—like Apollo, looking for himself, his own proper voice—he is working as closely with (and against) Milton as ever, tracing a developmental progress remarkably similar to Adam's in Book VIII of *Paradise Lost.* Whereas Hyperion is baffled by his loss of innocent consciousness, Apollo and Adam are frustrated by innocence itself, suffering a nonimmediate, reflective sorrow occasioned by their unsatisfied appetite for knowledge. Neither nature nor their own unassisted power can disperse this inner darkness, and both are roused by a timely visitation. God is Adam's guide, preparing him through discourse and a series of dream events for a recognition of who he is and what is to become of him. The guide in *Hyperion* is Mnemosyne, mother of the muses, under whose tutelage Apollo has been developing from his infancy. He too has been granted beneficent, prefigurative dreams, and once, awakening from a dream of his guide, had found a golden lyre by his side. Now beholding her substantially before him for the first time, he finds her name mysteriously upon his tongue, even as Adam, gifted with divine onomathesia, names the beasts of the field by "sudden apprehension." Hindered from self-realization by his "aching ignorance," Apollo confronts Mnemosyne with the same great questions Adam poses to his second heavenly guide and guardian, the angel Raphael: Are there not other regions than this isle? What are the stars? Where is power?

But if Keats's spiritual topography resembles Milton's, Apollo learns a lesson very different from Adam's. Raphael tells Adam that he may in time "turn all to spirit" (v.497), but such an advance upward along the hierarchy of being is possible only if he recognizes the contingency of all created forms, maintains his due station, and renounces too avid a quest for knowledge or power. Apollo, however, need not stand and wait; he "ascends wing'd" after a radically condensed period of development. Gazing into Mnemosyne's face, he is at once flooded by knowledge and deified:

> Knowledge enormous makes a God of me.
> Names, deeds, grey legends, dire events, rebellions,
> Majesties, sovran voices, agonies,
> Creations and destroyings, all at once
> Pour into the wide hollows of my brain,
> And deify me, as if some blithe wine
> Or bright elixir peerless I had drunk,
> And so become immortal. . . .
>
> (III.113–20)

Compare Adam and Eve's reaction to the forbidden fruit:

> As with new Wine intoxicated both
> They swim in mirth, and fancy that they feel
> Divinity within them breeding wings
> Wherewith to scorn the Earth.
>
> (IX.1008–11)

Their dizzying upward fall, an ironic initiation into the divine mysteries of good and ill, disrupts that generous continuity of natural and supernatural powers that had guided their previous advancement up the ladder of being, exiling them to the "subjected Plain" of our natural condition, where they must begin another, far more precarious progress toward the recovery of paradise within their own souls. Yet, as the chosen one in Keats's account of the survival of the fittest, Apollo suffers no loss of power coincident with his sudden access of knowledge. Unlike Adam, he neither knows a sympathetic relationship to external nature, spurning the green turf as hateful to his feet, nor cares about the "happier Eden" of love, having found a lyre rather than a helpmate by his side after his dream. Married to immortal verse and initiated by his muse into the mysteries that are to be the subject of his poems, Apollo becomes a god.

Having drastically narrowed the creative circumference of *Paradise Lost* in Books I and II of *Hyperion*, Keats again turns against Milton in Book III, turning as well against his earlier revisionary stance. Where Milton is expansive, Keats is contractive; where Milton is patient and humanizing, Keats is eager for flight, as much away from Milton as toward apotheosis. Falling away from Milton, he nevertheless keeps falling back into, or holding on to, Milton. The potentially Adamic Apollo is on his way to becoming simply a new old-style god. But although ascendant, he cannot dawn, and at the end of the poem Keats is swept up with him to a sublime height that is also a hallucinatory abyss:

> Soon wild commotions shook him, and made flush
> All the immortal fairness of his limbs;
> Most like the struggle at the gate of death;
> Or liker still to one who should take leave
> Of pale immortal death, and with a pang
> As hot as death's is chill, with fierce convulse
> Die into life: so young Apollo anguish'd:
> His very hair, his golden tresses famed
> Kept undulation round his eager neck.
> During the pain Mnemosyne upheld
> Her arms as one who prophesied.—At length
> Apollo shriek'd;—and lo! from all his limbs
> Celestial
>
> (III.124–36)

Engulfed by knowledge, Apollo anguishes. What is this knowledge (of "Names, deeds, grey legends, dire events, rebellions, / Majesties, sovran voices, agonies, / Creations and destroyings") if not the Miltonic legacy, mediated by Mnemosyne, or Memory, a representative of the old Titanic order who has forsaken her peers for prophecies of Apollo? Apollo's giant agony is Keats's epic venture.

Halted at the threshold, Keats cannot assert his independent presence, at least not in *Hyperion*. As Hyperion's displacer, Apollo seems to have nowhere to ascend to except the Titan's pleasure palace, an emblem of the Miltonic epic universe. From the "mirror'd level" of its pavement proceeds Hyperion's "gradual agony," Keats's "over-strained" reflection of *Paradise Lost*. Apollo, however, experiences a fortunate fall, into Keats in *The Fall of Hyperion*. Here Keats stands alone in the vast ruin that is Moneta's sanctuary, the "eternal domed Monument" of literary tradition. Striving to mount the immortal stairs leading to the muse's shrine, he relives his authorship of *Hyperion*:

> Prodigious seem'd the toil; the leaves were yet
> Burning—when suddenly a palsied chill
> Struck from the paved level up my limbs,
> And was ascending quick to put cold grasp
> Upon those streams that pulse beside the throat:
> I shriek'd, and the sharp anguish of my shriek
> Stung my own ears—I strove hard to escape
> The numbness; stove to gain the lowest step.
> Slow, heavy, deadly was my pace: the cold
> Grew stifling, suffocating, at the heart;
> And when I clasp'd my hands I felt them not.
> One minute before death, my iced foot touch'd
> The lowest stair; and as it touch'd, life seem'd
> To pour in at the toes:
>
> (I.121-34)

The chill rising from the pavement threatens Keats with voicelessness and a numbing of his hands. He explains his abandonment of the two *Hyperions*—really his failure to graft the original mythological fragment onto the *Fall's* completed autobiographical induction—as follows:

> There were too many Miltonic inversions in it—Miltonic verse cannot be written but in an artful or rather artist's humour. . . . It may be interesting to you to pick out some lines from Hyperion and put a mark X to the false beauty proceeding from art, and one || to the true voice of feeling. Upon my soul 'twas imagination I cannot make the distinction—Every now & then there is a Miltonic intonation—But I cannot make the division properly.

The shrieks of Apollo in *Hyperion* and of Keats in the *Fall* are a protest of the poet's voice, his word, against this bewilderment of mine and thine, the devastation of *poetic* death.

Hyperion is Keats's dying into life. Its very failure forcibly impresses upon him the full burden of the mysteries of self and vocation and leads him back, in his perplexity, to the energy and freedom of his own mind. In the great odes and in *The Fall of Hyperion* Keats recasts Milton's story of our fall into mortal consciousness in his own idiom, supplying as well whatever consolations such sadly limited consciousness can win. The specter of Miltonic influence is not exorcised, but it becomes less awesome and generally appears at Keats's bidding. Perhaps it is simply that the specter of Milton becomes more benign when Keats begins to be menaced by the specter of Wordsworth, the genius of "dark passages." However, his more knowing and successful wrestling with Wordsworthian influence can be attributed to his experience with Milton in *Hyperion*—the threshold he could not cross until he was compelled, by the poem itself, to acknowledge the precariously liminal condition of the modern writer.

LESLIE BRISMAN

Keats and a
New Birth: "Lamia"

*Even the wisest among you is only a disharmony and hybrid of plant and
phantom. But do I bid you become phantoms or plants? ... I conjure you, my
brethren, remain true to the earth, and believe not those who speak unto you of
superearthly hopes!*

—NIETZSCHE, *Thus Spake Zarathustra*

*To retranslate man back into nature, to master the many vain enthusiastic glosses
which have been scribbled and painted over the everlasting text, homo natura, so
that man might henceforth stand before man as he stands today before that other
nature, hardened under the discipline of science, with unafraid Oedipus eyes and
stopped-up Ulysses ears, deaf to the lures of the old metaphysical bird-catchers who
have been fluting in at him all too long that "you are more! You are superior!
You are of another origin!"—this may be a strange, mad task, but who could
deny that it is a task!*

—NIETZSCHE, *Beyond Good and Evil*

For the poet concerned about inspi-
ration and about his place in what Keats called "the grand march of
intellect," the ordinary march of nature seems to proceed with enviable
regularity. Overlooking the nature of human sexuality and generational
gaps, one sees "out there," in natural history, that season succeeds season,

---

era succeeds era, without the new having to justify its place and without the old threatening to occupy more than its place. In literary history succession is always problematic, both in terms of the individual poet's progress from one moment of inspiration to another and in terms of continuity from one poet to another. The problems are accentuated when one's precursor seems to have preempted even the awareness of the difference between natural and intellectual succession.

For Keats, Milton—even more than Wordsworth—was the great originator of that awareness. Milton wrote the central elegy about experiential loss and spiritual renewal, and he wrote *the* epic about man falling out with nature. Most important, he represented in his own person the alienation from the continuity of nature, lamenting that "with the Year / Seasons return, but not to me returns / Day" (*Paradise Lost*, III. 40–42). Like Wordsworth, Keats sought a counter to Miltonic discontinuity which would represent inspiration renewed as faithfully as are plants and seasons. The search for or appeal to such a countermyth of continuity not only underlies Keats's greatest work in the odes and Hyperion poems but justifies a studied lightness throughout the poetry—a lightness all his own—under the auspices of which new bursts of inspiration seem to spring up from the earth.

I

Written first of the five great odes in the spring of 1819, "Ode to Psyche" represents a new spiritual season. This ode not only comes up (crops up) first but is about firstness, about building a fane in some untrodden region of the mind, where the poet will be the new hierophant of a previously unworshiped goddess. Just what is implied by coming first is a question raised in many ways, especially in the central stanzas which announce and subvert a belatedness. But it is important that those stanzas are preceded by one that announces a natural origin for the succeeding burst of inspired self-proclamation. Cupid and Psyche are discovered on the earth, and as though they had sprung up from the earth. Of course to find a newly emerged infant, a presexual Cupid, would be to find no child of Venus—for whom sexuality is pre-everything; the lovers are sighted, rather, shortly after their sexual *regeneration*, after the moment which, in the myth of this poem and in the psychoanalytic myth of the mind generally, substitutes for an original generation. Keats's source for the myth of a reunited Cupid and Psyche is the late classical Apuleius; but the idea that the lovers are united here on earth, not in heaven (and especially the idea that they have just been reunited on earth), is original to Keats himself—or to the realm of nature to which sexual love is here found to belong.

When Pope claimed that Homer and Nature were the same, he expressed an orthodoxy according to which a poet's precursor not only represents an understanding of nature, but is understood to be absorbed into the general body of the given that we call nature. For Keats, the poet and nature are in a sense the same, and the precursor is encountered as a belated version of the same. If one regarded the opening verses of the "Ode to Psyche" as an allusion to or parody of the opening of Milton's *Lycidas*, then *Lycidas* would be an original text and the Ode a belated successor. But Keats's gentle phrasing, "sweet enforcement and remembrance dear," reminds us that Milton's "bitter constraint and sad occasion dear" were bitter and sad because nature had gotten there first and killed Lycidas before the uncouth swain was ready. Unlike "bitter constraint," Keats's "sweet enforcement" suggests a cooperation with nature, for the claims of love precede those of obligation and imply a closer tie to the one who is said to occasion the song—a tie in accordance with which claims of priority are laid aside.

If lovers in general know no first and last, this is all the more true of a poet-lover who is both stricken by the lady he "discovers" and intent on re-creating her. Cupid is appropriately the poet's original because he is traditionally the prime mover in matters of love and is himself victim as well as originator of blind desire for Psyche. In addition there were, in fact, two Cupids: the older god was identified with love in the sense of original motion, the gravitational force that attracts one physical body to another; the second Cupid was the youngest god of the pantheon, and Venus' son. In distinction from the Oedipus story, this bit of lore provided Keats with the material for a myth of originality without anxiety, of a belated youth who can be intellectually identified rather than set in emotional opposition to his original. Like the blinded Oedipus, Milton found himself "Presented with a Universal blanc / Of Nature's works to me expung'd and ras'd." Like the rejuvenated Cupid, Keats claims in this poem to "see, and sing, by my own eyes inspired." Is being inspired by one's own eyes the supreme originality or hopeless victimization by one's sexual nature? If the lure is erotic, Keats seems to be saying in the Ode, the difference dissolves, for nothing is as much one's own as one's desire, and to be inspired by what one sees is to be in touch with both the ultimate priority of nature—the primacy of eros or Cupid—and in touch with one's powers of creation—one's Psyche.

The turn on Milton's priority is redoubled, after this little invocation, by the ensuing narrative of the first stanza of the Ode. In *A Map of Misreading*, Harold Bloom finds the poet to occupy the position of Satan, who is not only cast out of heaven, but who comes upon the already ongoing sexuality of Adam and Eve and feels belated and excluded. Unlike Satan, who can speak his seductions in Eve's ear only when her relation to Adam is held in the suspension of sleep, the poet can sing in the ear of Psyche without disturbing the relation of Cupid to Psyche. Having no exterior or prior designs on the lovers, he had "wander'd in a forest thoughtlessly," and so his first thought can be no voyeuristic sense of exclusion but the pristine, newly begotten love of Psyche. The semiallegorical nature of Keats's myth gives him this advantage over Milton's Satan, for "the wingèd boy I knew" can involve a self-recognition in a way that Satan's sight of Adam cannot. To find Keats identifying with Satan's sexual deprivation is to see him doubly removed from the originality of the paradisal moment; but to see Keats, contra Satan, discovering his own eros is to see one way in which he is by no means "too late" but has, as far as his psyche is concerned, already embraced the muse.

In accordance with this anxiety-free reading, the often-cited original for the middle stanzas, Milton's Nativity Ode, becomes another text that Keats has preempted. The grand repetition or representing that takes place between stanzas two and three restores a priority not to a pagan over a Christian deity, but to this poem over preexistent poems. Milton seems like the belated Christian, while Keats, who claimed to be "more orthodox than to let a heathen Goddess be so neglected," reworks the myth (works it, in a sense, backward) to let in the warm love that marks the psychological priority of eros and the poetic priority of Keats.

II

The gay subversion of Milton's status and that of literary history generally is lavishly extended in *Lamia*. Like the "Ode to Psyche," this poem begins with an otherwise unnecessary prologue which plants the seeds of an irony about origins; the poem goes on to tell a story in which the characters' significance is a function of their relation to this irony. Lost "in the calmed twilight of Platonic shades," Lycius is an idealist, a believer in the romantic origin of ideas and things, who is lured when he finds himself outidealized in the subtle pinings of Lamia:

> Thou art a scholar, Lycius, and must know
> That finer spirits cannot breathe below
> In human climes, and live: Alas! poor youth,
> What taste of purer air hast thou to soothe
> My essence? What serener palaces,
> Where I may all my many senses please,
> And by mysterious sleights a hundred thirsts appease?
> It cannot be—Adieu!
>
> (I.279–86)

As both lady and text, Lamia makes the "taste of purer air" something that her admirer must reinvent. In *The Eve of St. Agnes*, Porphyro accepted an analogous challenge and offered a banquet for the senses to soothe the essence of Madeline awakening and descending from dreamy romance. Lycius, poor scholar, needs to be financed by the lady to keep her in the state to which she claims to be accustomed.

Perhaps on his example the reader borrows a hint from Lamia and wonders what he ("thou art a scholar") knows about finer spirits in human climes. If he goes back from Keats to Burton, Keats's source, he discovers only Lamia as serpent; literary, like biological, sources as such can represent natural origins in the poorest sense, not the riches of imagined preexistences. On the other hand, if he is impelled to look back to Milton, he finds he knows two things, or two sorts of antithetical things, about finer spirits and their mysterious sleights. In phrasing and ironically in situation, *Lamia* echoes *Comus*, and Lamia herself seems to appeal to Lycius with something of the residual resentment Milton's Attendant Spirit expresses when he first comes onstage. The Spirit belongs, he says, "In Regions mild of calm and serene Air, / Above the smoke and stir of this dim spot." Accustomed to the palace of Jove, he condescends because there are those ("and but for such, / I would not soil these pure Ambrosial weeds") who aspire to the Palace of Eternity. Milton's Spirit thus announces from the start his answer to the question Lamia raises about "what serener palaces" are to be offered in consolation. On the other hand, if we borrow not simply a luxurious resentment but a moral severity from the Attendant Spirit, we recognize in Lamia's question about palaces where all senses may be pleased a greater likeness to Comus than to Thyrsis. It is Comus who claims to be "of purer fire" and who offers to slake a hundred thirsts. Though it is very clear in the masque who is responsible for "fixing," who for liberating the lady, Keats's poem leaves morally ambiguous the power of Apollonius to fix his eye and fix the situation. This new area of uncertainty becomes the untrodden region of the mind—Keats's ground—on which the morally certain Milton seems a heavy-booted trespasser.

A similar ground of uncertainty and originality can be discovered by considering what knowledge *Paradise Lost* offers about the native home of finer spirits. In the most extended source passage, Eve's lament for lost paradise sets the pattern for Lamia's pining over the lost regions of air. Though Adam was created in Eden outside paradise, so that the soil and climate native to man is that of a lower world, Eve bewails the descent from Eden into obscure realms: "how shall we breathe in other air / Less pure, accustom'd to immortal Fruits?" (XI.284–85). Concern about purer air belongs to fallen beings, and re-presents in gentler form an anxiety about origins—about whether the self is continuous with the soul that had elsewhere its home. Belial projects this anxiety forward and takes comfort that though in hell their "purer essence then will overcome / Thir noxious vapor" (II.215–16); Satan turns against the self and is greeted—in a masterful irony—by the "purer air" of paradise (IV.153). The opportunity to conceive of one's native element without anxiety is offered by God when he brings all living creatures to Adam to be named but excepts the fish, who "cannot change / Thir Element to draw the thinner Air" (VIII.347–48). Later, Adam shows how he has internalized this qualification when he deprecates the sublimation of the Babel builder who attempts to climb "where thin Air / Above the clouds will pine his entrails gross" (XII.76–77). That the earth is native to man is a recognition (a re-cognition, something known, repressed, and then remembered) that comes with the fall.

For Keats, a more morally ambiguous forgetfulness or fall accompanies a more startling revelation about what turf one calls one's own. Attempting to undo her belatedness, Eve mistakes her native soil, just as Satan and Comus do. But is Keats's Lamia making a mistake about her history or with prescient strategy misleading Lycius when she challenges the youth to find in mortal experience an adequate counter for romantic origins? "What canst thou say or do of charm enough / To dull the nice remembrance of my home?" Her complaint that she must tread "this floor of clay, / And pain my steps upon these flowers too rough" may be more "charming" than Eve's lament for the flowers of paradise "That never will in other Climate grow." But is this a Comus-like charm of guile or a real feminine charm to evoke a concomitant verbal charm from Lycius and, ultimately, from Keats?

The charm can be broken, or at least understood for what it is, if one poses the riddle of Lamia's origin on the model of the child's question about chickens and eggs: Which came first, goddess, woman, or serpent? Though Apollonius would reply otherwise, Lamia appeals to Hermes with a firm conviction about where true charms lie: "I was a woman, let me have once more / A woman's shape, and charming as before" (I.117–18). In a sense a literary fiction was perpetrated on as well as by Lamia, and one must acknowledge the literariness of the story about origins in purer climes. The point is that either reduction ("Lamia is really a woman" or "Lamia is really a serpent") presents a formulaic demystification of literary fictions and a return to nature.

If statements about what Lamia "is" are antiromantic, reductive versions of statements about what Lamia was first, they could be said to supplant not only the romantic concerns of the opening Lamia-Hermes and Lamia-Lycius exchanges but the romance elements of Milton's poetry as well. Faced with the accusing Deity, Eve fully awakens from her dream of romantic origins, though she does not quite melt away the way Lamia does before Apollonius. Lamia is totally speechless, while Eve, though "with shame nigh overwhelm'd," speaks the single line "The Serpent me beguil'd and I did eat" (*PL*, X.162). For Milton the question of identity must take the form of a question about anteriority: after all, Eve's answer to God was already given in the Bible, and it is equally important for wholly internal reasons that Eve now acknowledge, whether as excuse or plain fact, the anteriority of the serpent. Such answers are defenses against the awesome anteriority of God, as God reminds—has already reminded—Adam before turning to Eve. But what about the answer, or rather the terrible silence, of Lamia when faced with Apollonius? If we borrow from Harold Bloom's *Map of Misreading* the association of defenses with tropes, then in place of Eve's criminal misprision, which makes her an ideological and temporal follower of Satan, we have Keats's literary misprision of Milton, and the conclusion of Lamia can be outlined like this:

The starting point is the recollection of a precursor exhibiting his strength. In *Comus*, Milton represented the Lady's song as being so efficacious "that even Silence / Was took ere she was ware," and Thyrsis is struck by those "strains that might create a soul / Under the ribs of earth" (ll. 555–62). In a mighty reaction formation, Keats conjures up a horrid presence to fill the vacancy left by the absence of Milton, and presents a Silence ravaging rather than ravished: "A deadly silence step by step increased / Until it seem'd a horrid presence there" (II.266–67). Then, in the impassioned cries of Lycius, this original reaction formation is represented as a reversal of the power of Milton's blindness and prophetic insight: the dreadful images of the Gods which "represent their shadowy presences" are invoked to threaten Apollonius with blindness and the isolation Milton bemoaned in the invocation to *Paradise Lost*, Book VII. Though the macrocosm—all the gods—is called down upon this one man, a counterforce is at work in the synecdoche of power—his eyes' ability to make the object of their glance wither. The dominant defense, the one controlling the basic action as well as the language, is the resulting *kenosis*, the isolation and undoing of Lamia. She whose presence filled the room—indeed, whose presence was the palatial room and all its décor—becomes a terrible emptiness. Not only are Lycius' arms "empty of delight"; the contiguity of metonymic language carries the emptied rhetorical structure across the enjambment to "as were his limbs of life." Characteristically, Bloom's map proves most indispensable at this point, guiding us from the limiting psychic defenses of isolation and undoing to the central artistic defense of repression. It may sound a bit weak to label as hyperbole Apollonius' resolution to the ambiguous ontology of Lamia: "Of life have I preserv'd thee to this day, / And shall I see thee made a serpent's prey?" But an otherwise weak identification becomes daemonized in its context, and if we feel the grotesque lowness not only of serpents but of "serpent" as an identity for Lamia, we are shocked simultaneously by the sublime, for these lines elevate the poem to the level of the stars and place it in a line from *Paradise Lost* to

The Auroras of Autumn—texts which pose "serpent" as grotesquely low and high sublime central figure. This achievement depends on the crucial repression of the fact that the "killing" irony is the power of the inner eye, or prophetic insight, purchased at the price of plain vision. Whether one believes the heart of repression to be a sexual instinct or recognizable fact, one could say that what is repressed here is the knowledge of serpent as *ananke*—the body of fate that condemns us all to sexual illusion. More immediately, as far as the rhetoric of the poem is concerned, what is repressed is the knowledge of the priority of the written word. "Serpent" is the Bible's first answer to the question of evil, and "serpent" is the answer Milton has inherited at the beginning of *Paradise Lost* but must "not know" long enough for the poem to grow. "Who first seduc'd them to that foul revolt? / The infernal serpent; he it was" (*PL*, I.33–34). Shifting for a moment from eye to ear, *Lamia* presents the sophist's speech as primary and accords to it the power of demystifying illusion while mystifying or remyst-ifying the charm-breaking word. What is left is quickly told. In a frightfully successful sublimation—the only successful defense, Freud claimed, but that is from the perspective of a reality principle—Lamia evaporates. Then, in a final *apophrades* or return of the dead coincident with the final word of the poem, serpent identity is "projected" on Lycius, "And in its marriage robe, the heavy body wound."

At this point, I realize, the anxiety-free myth of origins from the earth is in danger of being totally overwhelmed by evidence of Keats's engagement with Milton. Perhaps it would not be unfair to say that whereas mere borrowings deflate a myth of natural origins, the purpose as well as the uniqueness of psychic defenses makes consideration of them rather support a myth by which precursors have been ploughed under and the new poetry emerges from the native soil of one's own defenses. But in place of my metaphors, consider Keats's own from a letter concerned with Milton's significance:

> What a happy thing it would be if we could settle our thoughts, make our minds up on any matter in five Minutes and remain content—that is to build a sort of mental Cottage of feelings quiet and pleasant—to have a sort of Philosophical Back Garden, and cheerful holiday-keeping front one—but Alas! this never can be: for as the material Cottager knows there are such places as France and Italy and the Andes and the Burning Mountains—so the spiritual Cottager has knowledge of the terra semi incognita of things unearthly; and cannot for his Life, keep in the check rein—Or I should stop here quiet and comfortable in my theory of Nettles.

Even the "terra semi incognita of things unearthly" is imaged as being of this earth, a kind of "back garden" whose relation to a neater front garden would solve problems about cultivating one's originality. And the "theory of nettles" alluded to is a naturalized account of Miltonic power. Here is the passage immediately preceding the above:

> I have heard that Milton ere he wrote his Answer to Salmasius came into these parts, and for one whole Month, rolled himself, for three whole hours in a certain meadow hard by us—where the mark of his nose at equidistances is still shown. The exhibitor of said Meadow further saith that after these rollings, not a nettle sprang up in all the seven acres for seven years and that from said time a new sort of plant was made from the white thorn, of a thornless nature very much used by the Bucks of the present day to rap their Boots withall—This account made me very naturally suppose that the nettles and thorns etherealized by the Scholars rotory motion and garner'd in his head, thence flew after a new fermentation against the luckless Salmasius and occasioned his well known and unhappy end.

"Very naturally" he is led to the myth of rhetorical power originating from the earth. What Milton garnered in the meadow was not wholly wasted on Salmasius; newly "fermented" in Keats's brain, the figure emerges in *Lamia* as the crown of thorns appropriate to Apollonius-Milton: "Let spear-grass and the spiteful thistle wage / War on his temples" (II.228–29). From the extrapoetic turf of the letters comes this little confirmation that Keats identified Milton with the sage of cold philosophy. Or better: if we think of Apollonius' final words, "A serpent!" as Milton's opening answer in *Paradise Lost*, Apollonius seems not a redaction of Milton but his precursor. Milton's epic carries the burden of the "past"—of picking up where Apollonius at the end of *Lamia* left off; but Keats and the earth in which he makes his Milton roll—they come before, in his playfully "preposterous" but no less seminal victory over Milton's priority.

HELEN VENDLER

Stirring Shades
and Baffled Beams:
The "Ode on Indolence"

How happy is such a 'voyage of conception,' what delicious diligent Indolence! A doze upon a Sofa does not hinder it, and a nap upon Clover engenders ethereal finger-pointings.

—Letters, I, 231

"Ode on Indolence"
"They toil not, neither do they spin."

One morn before me were three figures seen,
  With bowed necks, and joined hands, side-faced;
And one behind the other stepp'd serene,
  In placid sandals, and in white robes graced:
They pass'd, like figures on a marble urn,
  When shifted round to see the other side;
    They came again; as when the urn once more
Is shifted round, the first seen shades return;
  And they were strange to me, as may betide
    With vases, to one deep in Phidian lore.

How is it, shadows, that I knew ye not?
  How came ye muffled in so hush a masque?
Was it a silent deep-disguised plot
  To steal away, and leave without a task
My idle days? Ripe was the drowsy hour;
  The blissful cloud of summer-indolence
    Benumb'd my eyes; my pulse grew less and less;

Pain had no sting, and pleasure's wreath no flower.
   O, why did ye not melt, and leave my sense
      Unhaunted quite of all but—nothingness?

A third time pass'd they by, and, passing, turn'd
   Each one the face a moment whiles to me;
Then faded, and to follow them I burn'd
   And ached for wings, because I knew the three:
The first was a fair maid, and Love her name;
   The second was Ambition, pale of cheek,
      And ever watchful with fatigued eye;
The last, whom I love more, the more of blame
   Is heap'd upon her, maiden most unmeek,—
      I knew to be my demon Poesy.

They faded, and, forsooth! I wanted wings:
   O folly! What is Love? and where is it?
And for that poor Ambition—it springs
   From a man's little heart's short fever-fit;
For Poesy!—no,—she has not a joy,—
   At least for me,—so sweet as drowsy noons,
      And evenings steep'd in honied indolence;
O, for an age so shelter'd from annoy,
   That I may never know how change the moons,
      Or hear the voice of busy common-sense!

And once more came they by:—alas! wherefore?
   My sleep had been embroider'd with dim dreams;
My soul had been a lawn besprinkled o'er
   With flowers, and stirring shades, and baffled beams:
The morn was clouded, but no shower fell,
   Though in her lids hung the sweet tears of May;
      The open casement press'd a new-leaved vine,
   Let in the budding warmth and throstle's lay;
O shadows! 'twas a time to bid farewell!
   Upon your skirts had fallen no tears of mine.

So, ye three ghosts, adieu! Ye cannot raise
   My head cool-bedded in the flowery grass;
For I would not be dieted with praise,
   A pet-lamb in a sentimental farce!
Fade softly from my eyes, and be once more
   In masque-like figures on the dreamy urn;
      Farewell! I yet have visions for the night,
And for the day faint visions there is store;
   Vanish, ye phantoms, from my idle spright,
      Into the clouds, and never more return!

The *Ode on Indolence*, which Keats left unpublished, is, as Blackstone says, the seminal poem for the other great odes. Though it was written down as late as May, perhaps just before the *Ode on a Grecian Urn*, since they share the same stanza (used afterward for the *Ode on Melancholy*), the experience which gave rise to it is related in March, in the 19 March section of Keats's journal-letter of 14 February–3 May 1819. The letter contains the imagery of the ode in little:

> This morning I am in a sort of temper indolent and supremely careless: I long after a stanza or two of Thompson's Castle of indolence...Neither Poetry, nor Ambition, nor Love have any alertness of countenance as they pass by me: they seem rather like three figures on a greek vase—a Man and two women—whom no one but myself could distinguish in their disguisement.

Keats later in the spring so reimagines himself into his March experience that he relives it among "the sweet tears of May"; nevertheless, the core of the ode remains his lassitude in March, his unwillingness to be roused out of his mysterious indolence by the three motives—Love, Ambition, and Poetry—which pass before him in Greek disguise.

The uneasy structure of *Indolence* enabled Charles Brown, copying probably from loose sheets, to propose an incorrect sequence for its stanzas, which he subsequently corrected; but only a poem peculiarly static could have offered the possibility of such a mistake. In fact, the poem seems to make no apparent progress at all; as it begins, Keats is indolent; as it ends, he is indolent; the visit of the disturbing figures seems to have left him unchanged, an embryonic poet refusing to be born, nestled in the womb of preconscious existence.

The *Ode on Indolence*, however, offers two conflicting structural shapes to our inspection: the first, attributable to the speaker, might properly be called by the Yeatsian name of vacillation; the second, a stronger shape of steady recurrence, attributable to the figures, counters the first. Though the ode does record a vacillation of Keatsian mood, ranging from languor to yearning, from self-reproach to self-indulgence (reinforced, as we shall see later, by its language), the stronger shape in the poem is the shape of recurrent return, as the three sculptural allegorical figures again and again intrude upon the varying Keatsian dream. In some ways the poem never recovers—never wishes to recover—from its sight of that spacious and unhurried Greek procession which entirely subdues the poet to its plastic grace:

One morn before me were three figures seen,
　　With bowed necks, and joined hands, side-faced;
And one behind the other stepp'd serene,
　　In placid sandals, and in white robes graced:
They pass'd, like figures on a marble urn,
　　When shifted round to see the other side;
　　　They came again; as when the urn once more
Is shifted round, the first seen shades return;
　　And they were strange to me, as may betide
　　With vases, to one deep in Phidian lore.

Everything in the opening stanza reinforces the persistence and power of these art-figures, who so resemble the three Graces. They come not alone but companioned; their hands are joined in a unity of self-presentation; their movements are done in unison; they are dressed identically; at first sight they even seem identical as to sex. The theme of return is insisted on: "One behind the other *stepped* . . . / They *passed* . . . / They *came again*; as when . . . *once more* / . . . the *first* seen shades *return*." The poem continues to repeat this magic hovering of appearance and return in several rhetorical ways—by addressing the figures; by repeating their returns; by enumerating them (once in presence, once in absence) as Love, Ambition, and Poesy; by twice bidding them farewell; by entreating them to fade; by adjuring them to vanish. The whole poem is constructed upon their steady reappearances; as I have said, they make it, structurally speaking, a poem of recurrence.

Though Keats's attitude toward these presences changes with his changing epithets for them (they are to him first "figures," then "shadows," next "ghosts," and finally "phantoms"), they remain the same steady Greek forms, becoming, as they finally reveal their countenances to Keats, creations like Wallace Stevens' hidalgo on the stair, "a hatching that stared and demanded an answering look." Though begged by the poet to return to their places on the urn, though commanded to vanish into the clouds, they show no inclination to disappear or to discontinue their haunting of the indolent visionary.

Keats here deliberately presents himself, as he does in *Psyche, Nightingale,* and *Urn,* as a poet. In this ode he speaks of his demon Poesy; in the others he refers to his "tuneless numbers," his "mused rhyme," and more generally in the *Urn* to "our rhyme." In *Indolence* the conflict between the claims of Poesy (accompanied by its motive, Ambition, and its subject, Love) and Keats's almost physical need for "indolence" seems insoluble. The figures, in their determination, are unpreventable and ungovernable, and cause recurrent agitation by each of their comings; and yet the claims of "indolence" are indisputable, and stubbornly reassert themselves against every reappearance of the Greek figures.

It is with the wisdom of hindsight—because we have read *Nightingale* and *Urn*—that we can see this conflict between form and indolence as if it were a battle between the two later odes. "Indolence" speaks with the tranced voice of the *Ode to a Nightingale*; the Greek figures, in their mute glance, evoke the language of the *Urn*; the one is the voice of the bower, the other the voice of the artifact. There is, of course, a third voice in *Indolence*—the voice which, awakened out of the bower and repudiating Greek gravity, speaks in the worldly-wise tones we associate with portions of *Lamia*:

> O folly! What is Love? and where is it?
> And for that poor Ambition—it springs
> From a man's little heart's short fever-fit.

We hear this affectedly cynical voice once more in *Nightingale*: "The fancy cannot cheat so well / As she is fam'd to do, deceiving elf." Keats rejected these defensive tones as unworthy in the later odes, *Urn* and *Autumn*; there, bitterness and regret, the emotions underlying those cynical expressions, are allowed their proper undeflected voice, in the remarks on human passion and its aftermath in the one, and in the nostalgia for the songs of spring in the other.

In *Indolence*, then, Keats tries the superposition of one structural shape on another; over the vacillating shape of the various resistances and yieldings of indolence to form, he places the steady recurrent shape of the rhythmic return of the Greek figures. Harold Bloom says very well that the three figures resembling the Graces are in fact Keats's Fates; we may therefore name the two rhythms as the rhythm of Fate superimposed on that of will. Each persists throughout the poem; but, as I have said, the inexplicable, prior, and beautiful appearance, at the opening of the poem, of the rhythm of Fate—for all the rebelliousness subsequently mustered against it—makes that rhythm in reality the eventual victor, or rather a victor whose eventual victory we find ourselves envisaging as the poem ends.

And yet—also with the wisdom of hindsight—we know that Keats had reason to prolong his state full of "visions for the night, / And for the day faint visions" (he changed the latter phrase to "waking dream" in *Nightingale*). It was during these waking trances and embowered sleeps that his powerful assimilations and creations first took on body and form. His hour of rendezvous with the urn has not yet come, he senses, and he wards it off, profitably, from March to May. The gestating indolence he insists on refuses any subjection to time; he is suspended in dream, as the sweet tears of May (later to fall in a weeping shower in *Melancholy*) remain suspended in cloud in the sky. The season does not advance; he does not stir. The silent but urgent imperatives for change—Ambition, Love, and Poesy—challenge his immobility: his defensive impulse will be, in subsequent poems, to immobilize them in return, placing immobile Love in the center of his *Ode to Psyche*, and immobile Love and Poesy at the center of the *Urn*.

In this ode, then, we see the unwilling fancy of the artist facing at once its mental and emotional stimuli and its eventual sculptural artifact. The sculptural figures long to take on life, but are banished—back to the dreamy urn or up to the clouds, it scarcely matters—for the time being. The three spirits, almost indistinguishable each from the other, represent the principal *dramatis personae* of *Endymion* replicated in outline: the ambitious youth flanked by two maidens, one Love, the other Poesy, must recall to us Endymion placed between the Indian Maid and Cynthia. (Keats's letter had referred to the figures as "a Man and two women": in the ode Love and Poesy are clearly female, while Ambition is presumably male.) In short, the Fates here are Keats's doubling of his own dilemma of vocation already debated in *Endymion*, and the poem represents a dialogue of the embryonic, unformed, languorous, dreaming poetic self with its later envisaged incarnation in accomplished form.

Keats will never again incarnate form, or figures to be venerated, as an allegorical trinity. Ambition occurs, but incorporated into the speaker's own natural self, in *The Fall of Hyperion*; Love and Poesy are coupled as Cupid and Psyche in the *Ode to Psyche*, which follows in inspiration the *Ode on Indolence*. The two sculptural figures in *Psyche* are no longer allegorical representations of the poet's faculties for love and poesy, but rather have taken on separate mythological existence, an existence which for Cupid lapses somewhat at the end (where the poet seems to prepare to substitute himself for the god) but which is allowed throughout to Psyche. As a pagan goddess, Psyche preexisted, in the realm of mythology, her poet, and does not depend on him for her essence, as do the Love, Ambition, and Poesy of *Indolence*. Keats's wish for an object of worship external to himself dictates several of his other later objects, henceforth single ones, of veneration—a bird, an urn, a season. Such choices, which go beyond an interest solely in an allegorical psychology of creation or in a mythological reading of existence, point, as I hope to show later, to Keats's interest in artifact, audience, and medium.

But in the *Ode on Indolence*, the speaker is the indolent, inward-turned Keats still in his pastoral chrysalis, projecting onto an urn-*Doppelgänger* his internalized ambition, love, and poesy. The urn-double is unaffected by the expostulations of the protesting speaker: its figures return ever the same, ever poised, rhythmic, imperturbable, pregnant with meaning, placid, serene. In the top of sovereignty, these figures envisage all circumstance and remain unchanged under Keats's flurry of salutation, query, repudiation, and satire; their single gesture, a reproachful one, is to turn their profiles full-face and force his acknowledgment of their acquaintance. And yet, in spite of the placidity of their circling, the figures are in themselves not entirely placid; pale-cheeked Ambition betrays the fatigue of long vigils (a link forward to Autumn's patient watching), and the demon Poesy is "most unmeek." One might say that, like a poem, they manifest recurrence of rhythm while encompassing interior agitation. In this dialogue of Keats's mind with itself, suffering finds no vent in action.

The poem turns on the visual pun between "idle" and "indolence." In the severe judgment of the expectant figures, Keats may be said to have an "idle spright"; in his own defensive judgment, he is merely steeped in summer "indolence." He wonders, seeing himself as a lily of the field, whether the emphasis of the figures on a "task" is not merely the Philistine advice of "busy common-sense." Conversely, in an apprehensive twinge of self-reproach, he even suspects them of deliberately muffling themselves up so that they might abandon him to his self-indulgence; he imagines them stealing away with hushed steps so as—in their fancied plot—to leave his "idle" days without a task to occupy them.

The preliminary passings of the figures allow such speculation. When the spirits seem not to be noticing him, Keats is piqued; when they *do* notice him, he feels—after a moment of wild yearning after them—that they have torn him from his obscurely necessary reverie. As we notice now the underlying shape—what I have called the shape of vacillation underlying the shape of figure-recurrence—the first thing we realize is that the language of Keats's indolence takes two forms, as he rebukes the soliciting figures: we may call these forms of language, for convenience, the *Nightingale*-form and the *Psyche*-form. The first speaks in terms of a swoon, a numbness, and an insensibility; it sounds like a conflation of the opening drowsy numbness of the nightingale ode with its subsequent blind sinking toward death:

> Ripe was the drowsy hour;
> The blissful cloud of summer-indolence
> Benumb'd my eyes; my pulse grew less and less;
> Pain had no sting, and pleasure's wreath no flower.
> O, why did ye not melt, and leave my sense
> Unhaunted quite of all but—nothingness?

In this mood, Keats praises "drowsy noons, / And evenings steep'd in honied indolence."

If this first exploration of indolence borrows the language of death, the second, in *Psyche*-language, borrows that of birth. The sleep, no longer one of oblivion, is instead one of rich dreams, growing flowers, a chiaroscuro of light and shade, all that "information (primitive sense)," as Keats called it in his last letter, taking place in a landscape of incipient emotion, open casements, new-leaved vines, budding warmth, and a singing thrush. The language of the open casement and the budding warmth is the language of *Psyche*, just as Keats's self-stationing, his head "cool-bedded in the flowery grass," resembles his stationing of Cupid and Psyche, "couched side by side / In deepest grass... / 'Mid hush'd, cool-rooted flowers." The happy casement in *Psyche*, open to let the warm Love in, will eventually become in *Nightingale* the magic casements framing no human figures, and opening on things perilous and forlorn; but here, in *Indolence*, casements are still inviting, opening to press a leafy vine—the vine not yet, as it will be later, loaded and blessed with fruit, but rather full of pure potentiality. The first, benumbed, variety of indolence is principally sketched from thoughts of death, insensibility, and dissolution; but the second, creative, indolence draws its imagery from thoughts of birth, humidity, emergence, and illumination. The second indolence is briefly anticipated in the opening adjectives of the first—"ripe" was the drowsy hour, "blissful" was the cloud; but then numbness and blankness supervene, and it is only later that the budding creative indolence is explored.

There are, in short, two indolent Keatses and one ambitious one in this poem. The first indolent one wishes to obliterate sensation and the senses, removing at one gesture both the sting of pain (and even the sting of death, whence he draws the phrase "pain's sting," we might guess, given the ode's biblical epigraph) and the flower of pleasure. But the second indolent Keats is overbrimmed with inner and outer sensations of the most exquisite sort, mixing the apprehension of May's tears with the luxuriating in flowers, budding warmth, light and shade, and the poetry of birdsong. The third Keats—the ambitious lover and aspiring poet—disturbs the repose of both his indolent selves, distracting the one from oblivion and the other from sensation and reverie. Each "indolent" objection to the admonitory figures is fully and satisfyingly voiced; but we see that the linked figures, beautiful as they are, have not yet found for themselves a language equal to the "indolent" poetry of sheathed sensation that in a single breath ensconces delicious feeling and embroidered dreams:

> My sleep had been embroider'd with dim dreams;
> My soul had been a lawn besprinkled o'er
>   With flowers, and stirring shades, and baffled beams:
> The morn was clouded, but no shower fell,
>   Though in her lids hung the sweet tears of May;
>   The open casement press'd a new-leaved vine,
>   Let in the budding warmth and throstle's lay.

Keats speaks so easily here of the fertile soul, its dreamy sleep and its germinating ground, intimate with such completions and interminglings, that the separate, austere, discarnate urn-figures can scarcely seem an intimate part of that soul or of its contents.

The "moral" argument of the ode pretends to see poetic ambition as a temptation toward praise, love as a temptation to sentimentality: "I would not be dieted with praise, / A pet-lamb in a sentimental farce!" But the weakness of the satiric writing betrays Keats's inability to dismiss the true and justified sense of his own genius, and the intensity of his own passionate temperament. What was preventing his acquiescence in the demands of the figures was—though he could scarcely have known it in March—the incompleteness of those early dreams (including this dream of a rather unimaginatively decorated urn) which would yield, in a few weeks, the great odes.

If we recapitulate Keats's state of feeling in March (assuming that the ode is a reconstruction of his mind at the time), we find that his most powerful feelings were those of rapturous sensations both mental and physical, which took the form of sensing things beginning and about to happen—flowers budding, shades stirring, sunbeams seeking a path, tears about to fall, opening windows, bare vines growing green, warmth, bird-song, the vague shapes of night visions and waking dreams in daytime. These feelings are combated by an unwillingness to feel such new stirrings, a wish to sink into insensibility (prompted, we might suppose, by the illness of Tom Keats and his death a few months earlier on 1 December). Keats is also tempted to repudiate as worthless all his dearest desires—for fame, for love, for poetry; and yet he feels a steady and unyielding pursuit of his attention by his poetic genius, which will not be denied no matter how often he refuses its solicitations and banishes it (together with all stirrings of ambition and love) from his presence. He senses his poetic genius as another self, moving in mysterious and separate recurrences quite without reference to earthly time, displaying always a dignity and serenity of purpose, and emerging somehow from the noblest examples of creation he had seen, the Phidian marbles. He feels irrepressibly his own vocation as artificer, worker in a medium, one whose destined creations have come from their matrix (here, from an as yet unrealized "dreamy" urn) to rebuke their creator for not yet having created them. They bear, for that reason, overtones of the haunting ghost of old Hamlet rebuking his son for not yet having entered upon action.

In spite of the beauty of the rich language of open casements, cloud-tears, dreams, a bird's "lay," and vegetative growth—a garden of Adonis for the odes later conceived—the single most memorable moment in *Indolence* comes, surprisingly, in the poet's penitent "How is it, shadows, that I knew ye not?" The pang of that self-address (since the qualities Keats "knew not" were his own) is the kernel of feeling from which the whole ode originates, representing the pain of the accusatory encounter which is the subject of the ode, and the pain that the poet feels at his own ignorance in the encounter. He did not know his own soul, not when it appeared before him in that strange trio conjoining a processional rhythm with maiden fairness, fatigued eye, pallid cheek, and demonic fancy. Not to know one's own soul is for Keats the most mortal of lapses; he cannot believe that he has not recognized himself in this objectified vision. It becomes clear in the course of the ode that he has not known the shadows because he did not wish to know them, and this refusal had been prompted on the one hand by an exhausted shrinking from all further experience, painful and pleasurable alike, and on the other by an inchoate, if deeply felt, need for a longer time of budding and ripening. The hint of deathliness in the three figures, as they are evoked by the successively more disembodied names of shadows, ghosts, and phantoms, points to the degree to which sensual life must be sacrificed in being mediated into art-figuration; but Keats is not yet willing to explore his instinct for the inseparability of creation and sacrifice.

If we turn to look more closely at the language of the ode, we see that it uneasily adopts at least four modes of speech: narration of a past event to a presumed reader ("One morn before me were three figures seen"); recollection of the past event in a dreamy self-reverie ("Ripe was the drowsy hour"); an address (in the present tense) to the figures seen in the past ("How *is* it, shadows, that I *knew* ye not?"); and agitated worldly interpolation, occurring in the latter half of the poem only ("O folly! What is Love? and where is it?"). There is a marked unsettling of consciousness as Keats passes from one form of speech to the other. It may be most visible in the affected Byronic dismissal of Love and Ambition, but it is no less disturbing, if better managed, in the transitions from narration to recollection, from recollection to direct address, and so on. The poem exhibits Keats's problems in composition, problems occasioned by a wish to be fair, at one and the same time, to all sides of his nature and his art. Once he has decided on the visionary *donnée* of the poem, he feels compelled to explain his ghostly procession to those not so privileged, thus generating the heavy-handed narration of the ode, so much more swiftly accomplished in its original allegorical and nonvisionary form in the journal-letter. In the letter he feels no obligation to claim any status as seer or sage; but to authenticate in the poem both his vision and his original bafflement, he feels it necessary to establish his *bona fides* as an interpreter of Greek figures (he is learned, he tells his reader, in statues, but has not yet progressed beyond "Phidian" lore to an expertise with vase conventions). All this narration and explanation is incurred for the benefit of a putative listener to Keats's flowery tale, since

Keats would not need to tell himself again how many times the figures passed, or why he did not recognize the iconography of vase decoration, or what his credentials in interpretation might be.

Quite another motive from the explanatory one lies behind the powerful and sensual recreation of the drowsy hour, the most successful "writing"—in the limited sense of "intense, magical, and profound use of language"—in the poem. It will be my aim . . . to insist on a larger sense of "writing" in Keats—a sense which will include the grander issues of poetic conceptualization and architectonics as well as "magical" language—but every reader's first response to Keats (and many readers' final response) rests on judgments of his success or failure at the level of intensity or adequacy of language at any given instant, and on that alone. At any given instant, however, besides finding the *mot juste*, Keats is also deciding on a means of conceptualization (as, here, he has decided for three figures, which change conceptually from figures to phantoms, and from profiled figures to full-face figures); and at any given instant, he is also deciding how to continue, delay, or complete the structure of his poem (here, by the device of successive apparitions). The invention of appropriate language, in short, is only one of many inventions. Two others, invention of concept and invention of structure, are equally important in the odes, even if they have so far, by comparison to "writing" *tout court*, been comparatively neglected in criticism.

Since the most adequate language Keats finds in *Indolence* is the language for private re-creation of the scene of indolence (the language of private memory and reverie, not directed to an audience), I take it as axiomatic that the kernel of the poem, as a crystallization of accomplished feeling, lies in these passages. This does not prevent the competing kernel—a crystallization, in the figures, of a will for future accomplishment—from claiming entire emotional authenticity as well; but it is an authenticity for which a style has yet to be found. The restless stirrings of the will for accomplishment motivate all modes of speech here except the re-creative indolent one. But it is to that re-creative one, with its two facets of deathliness and ripening, that I wish now to turn.

The note of re-creation enters with the blended richness of two Keatsian themes—growth and sleep—in "Ripe was the drowsy hour," a line apparently promising both fruit and dream-visions. But we are balked of both as the first facet of indolence is momentarily turned to us—the apparent death of the senses, as they sink into an unconsciousness of almost all stimuli, "unhaunted quite of all but nothingness." It is, as we know, the vision of the three figures which prevents the poet's senses from that absolute annihilation. Keats's language for the negation of sense in sleep is fatally contaminated here with the luxuriousness of sense: it is far from the withered sedge and from places where no birds sing. Something very rich in his indolence is struggling for expression behind these negations. If his eyes are benumbed, it is by a *blissful* cloud; his pulse lessens by *growing* (even if by growing less and less); the two interpolated "no's" can scarcely obliterate the main nouns clustered in "pain . . . sting . . . pleasure's wreath . . . flower"; and the sweet and joyful steeping of evenings in honeyed indolence cannot be thought to represent a "nothingness."

In passing to the second, more openly creative facet of indolence, the activities of the "soul" when we are laid asleep in body, Keats borrows from *Tintern Abbey* a Wordsworthian division of body and soul which will not, in the long run, prove congenial to him. The philosophical Wordsworthian language for what happens when we are laid asleep in body and become a living soul is an impossible idiom for Keats; his soul, in its activities, is indistinguishable from his senses. The promise in "Ripe was the drowsy hour" now becomes fulfilled in dream, blossom, and song, in the most accomplished lines of the ode. In this fifth stanza, the "dim dreams" of the indolent soul borrow their language proleptically from the "dreamy urn"; the "stirring shades" within the soul's garden are named almost cunningly from "the first seen shades" of the urn-figures; the "besprinkled . . . flowers" arise from the repudiated "flower" of pleasure's wreath; the "clouded" morn in the awakened, if dreaming, soul is born from the "blissful cloud" of summer indolence numbing the eyes of sense; and, in the most evident parallel of all, the "tears of May" gather above those unshed "tears of mine," as the poet calls them, which he would refuse to have shed at the adieu of the figures (or so he boasts), had they consented to retreat, and leave him undisturbed.

The invasion, then, of the diction of the deep soul-dream by the diction of externality (whether of the external figures or the surrounding landscape) is proof that the soul-dream cannot remain sheltered from the world of time (the changing of the moons) and human "annoy" (pain and pleasure alike). "The voice of busy common-sense" (which we may call a denigration of the voice of mind in its pragmatic mood) Keats will not here dignify by conceptualizing it into a figure. But he does conceptualize the three other figures of "annoy"—Love, Ambition, and Poesy—and the problems of conceptualization provoke equal problems of diction.

In the journal-letter, the figures are psychological motives, external-ized because at the moment they are being rejected, or defended against; and their allegorization comes in a simile of appeal and detachment at once; the motives are contemplated but they are inert, having no "alertness of countenance," and seeming "like three figures on a greek vase." The externality and lifelessness of the motives do not survive their poetic reification into visionary forms: though they begin in placidity and serenity, they quickly arrive at disquieting, if disguised, intent; and one, the "demon Poesy," takes on an "unmeek" power rather like that of Lamia, who seemed "some demon's mistress, or the demon's self" (*Lamia*, 1, 56). The changing vocatives to the figures, and the uncertainty of conceptualization, suggest that Keats was not entirely master of the evolution of the poem.

Keats's suspicion of the figures yields the first tentative conceptualization of their function. Have they muffled themselves to steal away from him unrecognized, and leave him unmanned, without a task? Are they plotters against him, disguising their deep and silent plotting? Beholding one's own former energizing motives while refusing to acknowledge their present claim is the experience described in the journal-letter: Keats's change of nonacknowledgment to nonrecognition compels an ascription of intent to the reified motives which is not, in terms of the fiction of the poem, entirely coherent, since Keats seems both to desire and to repudiate a task in one breath. As I have said earlier, it is the conflict of "idleness" (as both the voice of busy common-sense and the voice of the figures, if they had one, would seem to call it) and "indolence" (as the voice of creative patience would call it) which is in question; but the melodramatic and theatrical diction of muffled shadows engaged in a deep-disguisèd plot, while it may be summoned up by those memories of Shakespeare, particularly *Hamlet*, which lie behind several of the odes, is a diction wholly unsuitable as a mode of address to urn-figures, and it vanishes leaving not a trace behind.

The reproachful "haunting" which seems the main intent of the figures links them, for Keats, with the ghost of Hamlet's father, with his purposeful remanifesting of himself to his indolent son; the figures are therefore invoked in purgatorial epithets suitable to revenants or shades. On the other hand, they are also life-figures, secular motives from the world of pain and pleasure, and to describe them Keats borrows, in an explanatory fashion connected with his narration to a common reader, diction from the common stock of emblematic moral iconography, to which he will again resort in the *Ode to a Nightingale*. Love the "fair maid" and Ambition "pale of cheek, / And ever watchful with fatigued eye" belong to the same static frieze of commonplaces on which we can see palsy shaking "a few, sad, last gray hairs," and men sitting and hearing each other groan. These fixed emblems evoke in every case Keats's feeblest diction precisely because they are representative of fixed and received ideas. He cannot bring himself to resort to one of these emblems for Poesy, at least not here in the ode. In the letter, Poetry had been as inert as Ambition or Love; but here Poesy takes on incremental life; the more blame is heaped on her, the more Keats loves her, a process mimicked by the phrase "more, the more . . . , most" incorporated into the stanza.

Keats first conceptualized the figures as graceful unknown visitors, next as theatrical muffled plotters, next as reproachful revenants, and next as moral emblems of duty or desire; his last conceptualization of them, and in the event his governing one, is as deities. The figures become the gods who preside over the ode, refusing to be dismissed by the speaker, for all his adjurations to them to fade and vanish. Protests are in vain; Keats might say of them, as Yeats does of his Magi:

> Now as at all times I can see in the mind's eye,
> In their stiff, painted clothes, the pale unsatisfied ones
> Appear and disappear.

One of Keats's difficulties with the conceptualization of his unsatisfied ones is that they represent such different internalized objects of the self. Love represents the erotic object, Ambition the social object, and Poesy the creative object: these figures are at once self-projections (Keats as lover, as fame-seeker, and as poet) and internalized objects. Ambition belongs at least in part to the world of busy common-sense and sentimental farce; Love, Keats fears, belongs especially to the world where change the moons; and Poesy, he suspects, belongs to a world more demonic than pastoral. But besides being self-projections (Love and Poesy, by convention "unmanly," must be projected as female beloved and female Muse) and internalized objects, these figures are, in the Keatsian sense, "presiders," as Shakespeare was to Keats a presider. Their elevated state dictates Keats's elevated language of address, different from the conversational narration ("One morn before me") or the affectedly colloquial language of expostulation ("and, forsooth! I wanted wings") or the dreamy language of sensual luxury in spiritual germination (evoked by the "lawn besprinkled o'er / With flowers"). The elevated diction does not preclude intimacy ("How is it, shadows, that I knew ye not?"), accusation ("O, why did ye not melt?"), or defiance ("Ye cannot raise / My head cool-bedded in the flowery grass"). But each time Keats moves into direct address to the deities (away from description, recollection, or social expostulation), the temperature of the poem rises in what we may call odal fire, a very different temperature from the incubating vernal warmth of the re-creative stanzas. By reducing the number of persons addressed and by keeping direct address throughout, Keats made the later odes more coherent than *Indolence*, with its three addressees only intermittently addressed.

In its passages from first-person narration to second-person address and back again, *Indolence* is unique among the odes, as *Melancholy* is unique in never addressing its presiding deity, but rather being a second-person address to the poet's own self. In the other odes, the deity—whether soul-goddess (*Psyche*), artist (*Nightingale*), art-object (*Urn*), or season (*Autumn*)—is unfailingly the object of address. In fact, Keats's largest single aesthetic decision in writing the greater odes was to place them squarely in the poetic tradition of invocation and prayer, where he had placed the first of his ambitious odes, the hymn to Pan in the first book of *Endymion*. (The later ode sung by the Indian Maid to Sorrow, in Book IV, mixes narration and invocation, and includes, in its incorporated vision of a Bacchic procession, interrogations of attendant damsels and satyrs prefiguring the interrogation of the figures on the urn.) The second firm aesthetic decision Keats made in the later odes was to speak in *propria persona*—not through a dramatic character like the Indian Maid, not in the choral unison of worshipers as in the hymn to Pan, but in his own troubled and aspiring single voice. Even when he mentions "other woe than ours" or "breathing human passion," the voice that utters those words is not the voice of a chorus or of humanity in general but that of a single speaker. Keats's third great decision, having adopted his single speaker, was to minimize the role of that speaker in successive odes until, from the visible single poet in *Indolence*, *Psyche*, and *Nightingale*, he has become the self-effacing and anonymous speaker, not specified as a poet, of *Autumn*.

The Byronic language of irony, which, as I have said, appears briefly in *Indolence*, is motivated no less by Keats's defensive guilt at the approach of the figures than by his own leap of the heart as he wishes to follow them: "I burn'd / And ached for wings." The motive of self-distrust rarely yields good poetry in Keats, and will fade from the odes, but this instance of it heralds the later outbursts against the cheating Fancy, the cold Pastoral, and the inaccessible Melancholy (in the canceled first stanza of that ode). All of these testify to the hostile energies released (after an attempt at idealization, invocation, or transcendence) by the journey homeward to habitual self. Until the motive of these necessary journeys homeward can be incorporated into the motive of idealization itself (and this does not happen until the close of *Melancholy*), the intemperate diction of disillusion must, if Keats is to remain truthful to his own emotions, confront the ecstatic or worshipful or in any case invocational diction provoked by the divine or idealized object.

We can see, in the concluding stanza of *Indolence*, all of Keats's previously established modes of speech jostling each other in an uncomfortable medley—the invocational ("So, ye three ghosts, adieu!"), the indolent re-creative ("my head cool-bedded in the flowery grass"), the ironic and hostile ("A pet-lamb in a sentimental farce!"), the descriptive-narrative ("masque-like figures on the dreamy urn"), the deprecatory language critical of sensation ("my idle spright"), and the language for the as yet discarnate stirrings of the will ("I yet have visions"). Eventually his boast that "for the day faint visions there is store" will be abundantly manifest in *Autumn*, her "store" anything but faint; but for the moment the claim is asserted only, its fruit invisible.

I cannot forbear to add a note on sentence rhythm, because Keats is quickened into different syntactic rhythms by his different languages. The stately pentameter passage of the first quatrain of the ode is somewhat dulled in the rather pedestrian repetitions of the following four lines; a new note of beauty is not discovered until the re-creative series of clauses is ushered in with the medial trochaic inversion "Ripe was the drowsy hour," and a waywardness of phrasal rhythm (which I reproduce here) begins to please the ear:

> Ripe was the drowsy hour;
> The blissful cloud of summer-indolence benumb'd my eyes;
> My pulse grew less and less;
> Pain had no sting, and pleasure's wreath no flower.

Though this is not an exquisite progression, the last line being too sententiously phrased for the state of soul it wishes to express, there is a kinetic deployment of rhythm which turns the pentameter away from stateliness and into a pulse of breathing irregularity. A religious formality resumes with "A third time pass'd they by," and then rhythmic inventiveness flags in the entirely too programmatic enumeration of the allegorical figures, with one line given to Love, two to Ambition, and predictably three to Poesy, a pattern repeated in the subsequent repudiation of the figures, which again reserves one line for the refusal of Love, two for Ambition, and three for Poesy. Rhythmic inventiveness recurs only in the second scene of re-creation, after which Keats resorts to a rhythm more or less confined to simple pentameter, in which syntax is accommodated to metrical form.

The diction of re-creation, in which Keats, after his exercises in *Endymion*, is already wholly accomplished, is a sensual diction (even if it is used, as it is here, to describe a spiritual state in which the senses themselves are benumbed and the pulse is lessened). Its elements include, as in so many other passages we shall encounter, drowsiness, ripeness, honey, dreams, a chiaroscuro (here of "stirring shades, and baffled beams"), flowers, grass, moisture, clouds, a personified time (which can be a month or season, here May with her "sweet tears" and morn with her "lids" in which raindrops hang as tears), an open casement, leaves, buds, warmth, and birdsong. This moist, sensual complex exists in conjunction (sometimes in competition) with a complex associated with idealization; some of its elements include stone (here an urn; elsewhere an altar or steps), figuration (here the urn-shades), dance, masque, or procession (here the joined hands and the serene pace), wings (as here, Keats would need wings to follow the figures), and architectural enclosure. Clouds, as the source of natural moisture and the realm of divine habitation, are common to both clusters of imagery; and dreams or visions seem, though springing from the one realm of indolence, to engender the other, that of idealization. All of these images will recur, and be amplified, and reduced, and reaffirmed, and criticized, in the later odes.

Keats searches in *Indolence* for a proper mode of self-cognition. The speaking "I" wishes, for the moment, to know itself solely as a being still in gestation, one whose senses have been laid to sleep and whose soul is an indolent lawn full of restless glimmers, dreamy budding, warmth, and overheard song. It does not wish to know itself in its erotic role as lover, its social role as seeker for fame, or its creative role as poet. It arduously repudiates the possibility that it may incarnate itself in an artifact. These questions of self-definition—in roles passive, active, erotic, social, and creative—will persist through the odes. *Indolence* is too timid even to take credit for its own visions: the figures come not by being summoned but rather appear inconclusively veiled in the passive: "One morn before me *were* three figures *seen*.../ They pass'd, like figures on a marble urn, / When *shifted* round.../ They came again; as when the urn once more / *Is shifted* round." *Indolence's* dual projection of the Keatsian self—into drowsy vegetative nature and into stern Greek figures—will also recur in the odes, as tension, as problem, and ultimately as solution.

We are left, in the end, with the two rhythms of the poem. One of them, the recurrent processional stateliness (as, in the manner of a charm, three figures come three times), is the rhythm of an embodied art and a compelling Fate. It is counterpointed, no less intensely, by the other, fitful, rhythm of refusal—now refusing in a lethargic lessened pulse, now in a rather uneasy cynicism, now in a ripeness of sensation and faint vision. In spite of his putative indolence, the poet is forcefully drawn into a relation with the allegorical figures, abruptly and briefly in the first, disturbed, address, posing the profound question of self-cognition—"How is it, shadows, that I knew ye not?"—and, again in a more prolonged way, in the repeated farewells which close the poem:

> O shadows! 'twas a time to bid farewell!...
>
> So, ye three ghosts, adieu!...
>
> Fade softly from my eyes...
>
> Farewell! I yet have visions...
>
> Vanish, ye phantoms...

These farewells and adieux place the poet in the position of an impotent magus or a would-be Prospero summoning and dismissing spirits. We see that these spirits will not be dismissed, that Keats has raised himself, in his dispute with them, from indolence. He begins to command his spiritual world even in attempting to refuse it; though he has not yet conceptualized its demands (which he will later call Beauty and Truth), he has conceptualized its aims (to love, to be ambitious for greatness, to be a poet). He remains, for the moment, the artist shrinking from embodying his faint vegetative visions in anything resembling an artifact, refusing even the purely mental cultivation of Fancy (in which he will take such active pleasure in *Psyche*). In making the constitutive rhetorical figure of *Indolence* that of dialectic, or dispute, Keats proposes an art of inconclusiveness: the rhetorical shape of the poem is that of a stalemate—nothing, neither way. The budding warmth of spiritual sensuality refuses to the end the cold pastoral of art; but the very insistence of the pressure toward figuration makes the shape of dispute seem a disingenuous one. The language, too, offers an unresolved conflict between the deathly and the lifelike; one scarcely knows whether the figures are more or less alive than the throstle. What is clear is that the budding natural warmth of this ode does not at all yet see its way clear to becoming an aesthetic warmth, in "the way some pictures look warm," which will so mercifully enable the composition of *To Autumn*. Keats, like his later bees, hopes in this poem that warm days will never cease; but the figures—silent, gentle, but persistent—have come to tell him otherwise.

DAVID BROMWICH

Keats and Hazlitt

In making large claims for a critic better known to his contemporaries than to posterity, one faces the question whether this is a task of antiquarian history or part of the history of the present. About any such writer one wants to know who read him then, that we should read him now. With Hazlitt the answer can be simple and satisfying. He was read by a genius of the next generation, who pronounced Hazlitt's "depth of taste" one of the three things to be prized in that age—alongside Haydon's paintings and *The Excursion*—and sought his company in person, for conversation, for practical suggestions, and for theoretical counsel. In the story of Keats's development, biographers have always needed some event to advance him from the novice who took Hunt and Byron as his patterns, to the author who taught himself to admire Shakespeare and Milton and to enter the lists with Wordsworth. That event was his reading of Hazlitt; to a lesser extent, the informal meetings in which Hazlitt did not disappoint the expectations Keats had formed of him; and finally, Hazlitt's lectures on poetry at the Surrey Institution. This suggestion is not new, but the record of Hazlitt's influence is much fuller, more convincing and more subtly connected with the practice of Keats's poetry, than anyone has yet shown. The present chapter aims at an interpretation of the "Ode to a Nightingale" and "Ode on a Grecian Urn" in the light of Hazlitt's criticism. But I want first to exhibit several passages from Keats's letters, in the hope of demonstrating how his purpose and passion conspired with Hazlitt's. I need to admit at the outset that these imperfectly represent his letters as a whole: I chose the passages I thought would most plainly support my argument. Others could have served, however, with an empha-sis very slightly different. Except Wordsworth, and the friends with whom he corresponded regularly, there was no contemporary who was more often in Keats's mind. The conclusion I will be working toward is this: that the odes test an idea of the imagination which Hazlitt had proposed in his lectures and critical essays; and that they afford, for power and for sympathy, a space as accommodating as that of the personal essays later collected in *Table-Talk*, which Hazlitt started writing about the same time.

In December 1814 Keats wrote an adoring sonnet "To Lord Byron," whom he then thought an incomparable poet, an expert unraveller of "The enchanting tale—the tale of pleasing woe." When one sets this poem against the letters of 1817, and considers that in the intervening months he had been studying Hazlitt, one can see what the first effect was. Keats had lacked a deep past, and this Hazlitt gave him. With it came the fear that he had arrived too late, but also the humility necessary to great work. In many instances he comes close to repeating Hazlitt's words from the *Round Table* essay "On Classical Education": "By conversing with the *mighty dead*, we imbibe sentiment with knowledge; we become strongly attached to those who can no longer either hurt or serve us, except through the influence which they exert over the mind. We feel the presence of that power which gives immortality to human thoughts and actions." Byron, though living, had never been a resource of this kind; and the tone in which Keats now praises the mighty dead is stronger and steadier, even if more deferential, than the tone in which he can praise any living poet. "I am," he writes to Haydon, "very near Agreeing with Hazlitt that Shakespeare is enough for us." In September 1817, three books into *Endymion*, he becomes aware of the connection between his progress as a poet and the close study of Shakespeare, and seeks a way of recording how much this has owed to Hazlitt. So he writes to a mutual friend, J. H. Reynolds: "How is Hazlitt? We were reading his [Round] Table last night—I know he thinks himself not estimated by ten People in the world—I wishe he knew he is." Hazlitt's argument against egotism, which reached back to Shakespeare as a deeper source of poetic truth, seems to have calmed Keats's irritability and fortified his resolve in the pursuit of fame. It was always Hazlitt's lesson, from his abridgement of Tucker to "The Indian Jugglers," that genius works by unconscious exertions of power. Among the *Round Table* essays he had just been praising, Keats would have found the sentiment in "On Posthumous Fame": "Men of the greatest genius produce their works with too much facility (and, as it were, spontaneously) to require the love of fame as a stimulus to their exertions, or to make them deserving of the admiration of mankind as their reward. It is, indeed, one characteristic mark of the highest class of excellence to appear to come naturally from the mind of the author, without consciousness or effort." From this Keats took one of his "Axioms" of poetry, as sketched in a letter to John Taylor about revising *Endymion* for publication: "if Poetry comes not as naturally as the Leaves to a tree it had better not come at all."

Two received ideas about Keats still limit both the specialist's and the common reader's understanding of his character. First, that he was a sensitive man, easily wounded, deficient perhaps in the comic sense that can delight in smart repartees or revenges; and second, that he was skeptical about the intellect, and believed an "irritable reaching after fact & reason" was typical of the analytic mind: the part of him that laughed, and read books of philosophy, did not write his poetry, and to prove it he gave us *Lamia*, with the philosopher Apollonius who laughs into oblivion the thing of beauty that poetry has been vouchsafed by myth. Two comments from Keats's letters in the spring of 1818 will be of interest here. Writing to Haydon on March 21, he applauds Hazlitt's strength as a good hater—"Hazlitt has damned the bigoted and the blue-stockinged; how durst the man?! he is your only good damner, and if ever I am damn'd—damn me if I shouldn't like him to damn me"—and in a letter to Reynolds on April 27, he speaks of preparing "to ask Hazlitt in about a year's time the best metaphysical road I can take." That is, he has metaphysical ambitions like Hazlitt's own, and wants to embark on a program of reading and speculation, but will not venture to present himself at the door of so admired a preceptor until he feels sufficiently impressive.

A year later, in the winter and early spring of 1819, writing to his brother George and sister-in-law Georgiana, he copies out for their edification certain passages of Hazlitt's prose to set beside his own. One of these is a considerable stretch (five pages in a modern edition) of the "Letter to William Gifford." Hazlitt there exposed to public opprobrium the slanderers of the "Cockney school," and Keats would have seen it as an occasion of disinterested valor, at which he as a beneficiary was permitted to rejoice. In his journal-letter, even after laying down his pen for a day, Keats picks it up with no thought more pressing than to continue with Hazlitt: it is as important for George to hear from *him* as from the correspondent proper. The passage, copied out over two days, evokes Keats's comment, "The manner in which this is managed: the force and innate power with which it yeasts and works up itself—the feeling for the costume of society; is in a style of genius—He hath a demon as he himself says of Lord Byron." I quoted part of this [in another essay] as an allusion to *gusto*, but I think "yeast" is explained as well by Keats's letter to Benjamin Bailey of January 28, 1818: the "portion of good" which is all that even the best of men have, is "a kind of spiritual yeast in their frames which creates the ferment of existence—by which a Man is propell'd to act and strive and buffet with Circumstance."

By 1819, when the "Letter to William Gifford" was published, Hazlitt seemed to Keats almost an embodiment of the modern idea of genius.

Even more intriguing than this journal-letter is a slightly earlier one, which quotes a shorter passage of Hazlitt's. It is from the *Lectures on the English Comic Writers*, which Keats did not attend but had contrived to borrow in manuscript, probably through J. H. Reynolds. He quotes from the portrait of St. Leon—a hero of Godwin's fiction whom the lecturer rated second only to Falkland in *Caleb Williams*—and he adds his own emphasis.

> He is a limb torn off from Society. In possession of eternal youth and beauty, he can feel no love; surrounded, tantalized and tormented with riches, he can do no good. The faces of Men pass before him as in a speculum; but he is attached to them by no common tie of sympathy or suffering. He is thrown back into himself and his own thoughts. He lives in the solitude of his own breast,—without wife or child or friend or Enemy in the world. *His is the solitude of the Soul, not of woods, or trees, or mountains*— but the desert of society—the waste and oblivion of the heart. He is himself alone. His existence is purely intellectual, and is therefore intolerable to one who has felt the rapture of affection, or the anguish of woe.

Breaking off, with the idea of pursuing other matters, Keats then decides "as I am about it" to continue with Hazlitt's character of Godwin. It is followed by the comment, "This appears to me quite correct," and then by a transcription of Keats's "Bards of passion"—as the earlier quotation had been directly preceded by the poem, "Ever let the Fancy roam." Here again one is struck by the way Keats manages to interweave Hazlitt's thoughts and eloquence with his own. In the whole body of his letters he gives this sort of prominence to the words of no other writer. By itself, and without the passages he later quoted from "A Letter to William Gifford," there would still be something extraordinary about this quotation, flanked on either side by a poem from Keats himself, and presented to his brother as the work of a single hand. It is as if Hazlitt's description of St. Leon and his own new poetry had appeared to Keats, and were meant to appear to others, as a single continuous act of expression.

Hazlitt describes the solitude of one who finds "himself alone" intolerable, because his thoughts are still of society, the earth, all the common affections he has left behind. To such a figure egotism has become a *given* (however despised or regretted), and this Keats feared to be his situation as a poet. When in *The Fall of Hyperion* he set himself to endure whatever self-searchings were required to change his situation, he needed a second voice to dramatize the power of the accuser he faced, and it seems to have been his deliberate purpose to draw into the speech of the prophetess Moneta as many echoes as possible of Hazlitt's description. But the first echo is sounded by the poet himself. After his ascent to Moneta's shrine, he asks why the place of vision is deserted: "I sure should see / Other men here, but I am here alone." He is then told the strangeness of his fate:

> Thou art a dreaming thing;
> A fever of thyself—think of the earth;
> What bliss, even in hope, is there for thee?
> What haven? Every creature hath its home;
> Every sole man hath days of joy and pain,
> Whether his labours be sublime or low—
> The pain alone; the joy alone; distinct:
> Only the dreamer venoms all his days,
> Bearing more woe than all his sins deserve.

This is "the desert of society—the waste and oblivion of the heart," known to the man "thrown back into himself and his own thoughts," as Hazlitt had painted him. Keats's hope in *The Fall of Hyperion,* that something living may be salvaged from the desert, requires him to bear witness to a misery worse than his, that of the fallen Titans. What Hazlitt showed him was the interest of placing their drama within himself, and using it to open his sympathies. For he had found in writing the first *Hyperion* that as a tragic narrative, the story could not hold his attention. It touched him more nearly when he saw it as a motive for every exertion that the poet—like the Godwinian hero, always thrown back into himself—could undertake to heal the sickness of a "purely intellectual" existence. The character of St. Leon answers to the idea of himself which Keats cherished throughout his early life, as well as to the image of the artist, cast out by society to be preserved for immortality, which he bequeathed to a third and fourth generation of romantics. It is plain in his letters that this was also the way he saw Hazlitt. The discovery of a genius of criticism, isolated by genius as by politics, but possessed of a "demon" in all his trials, was for Keats the discovery of another self.

He first met Hazlitt in January 1818, and felt bold enough to call on him by December 1818. But Hazlitt would have known about Keats even before they met, not only from the poems Hunt showed him but from Keats's article "On Edmund Kean as a Shakespearean Actor," which appeared in the *Champion* of December 21, 1817, and contained a sentence easily mistakable for one of Hazlitt's: "There is an indescribable gusto in his voice, by which we feel that the utterer is thinking of the past and the future, while speaking of the instant." Once they were acquainted, Hazlitt gave Keats advice about writing for magazines and, what was far more important, noticed him in a generous aside of his *Lectures on the English Poets.* We know how this came about, again from the evidence of Keats's letters. To Bailey, on January 23, 1818, Keats wrote that he would be attending the lectures as they were first delivered. In the event he missed some, but he certainly heard the sixth, "On Swift, Young, Gray, Collins, etc.," which included a judgment of Chatterton: "He did not show extraordinary powers of genius, but extraordinary precocity. Nor do I believe he would have written better, had he lived. He knew this himself, or he would have lived." How Keats was affected by this dismissal may be guessed from the circumstances of his life; and he spoke of his response in the letter to George and Tom Keats of February 21, 1818: "I hear Hazlitt's Lectures regularly—his last was on Grey Collins, Young &c. and he gave a very fine piece of discriminating criticism of Swift, Voltaire And Rabelais—I was very disappointed at his treatment of Chatterton—I generally meet with many I know there." He arrived at an earlier lecture, as he told Tom and George, "just as they were coming out, when all these pounced upon me, Hazlitt, John Hunt & son, Wells, Bewick, all the Landseers, Bob Harris, Rox of the Burrough Aye & more." Beside the casual phrase, "I generally meet with many I know there," this seems to show that Keats was in the habit of conversing freely after the lectures, with Hazlitt and his circle. Some such conversation after the sixth lecture will account for Hazlitt's recognition of him in the seventh.

> I am sorry that what I said in the conclusion of the last Lecture respecting Chatterton, should have given dissatisfaction to some persons, with whom I would willingly agree on all such matters. What I meant was less to call in question Chatterton's genius, than to object to the common mode of estimating its magnitude by its prematureness. The lists of fame are not filled with the dates of births or deaths; and the side mark of the age at which they were done, wears out in works destined for immortality.

Hazlitt's later appreciations of Keats are generally of two kinds. First, he recognizes him as an independent voice, one who can command the tones of genius and is leagued with himself against the mob of government critics and court bards. Keats's "fine fancy and powerful invention," he writes in the *Edinburgh Review* article on "The Periodical Press," "were too obvious to be treated with mere neglect; and as he had not been ushered into the world with the court stamp upon him, he was to be crushed as a warning to genius how it keeps company with honesty, and as a sure means of inoculating the ingenuous spirit and talent of the country with timely and systematic servility." Second, and in a very different key, he simply quotes Keats, as a touchstone of the original note in poetry after Wordsworth. In *The Spirit of the Age* for example, after illustrating the pedantic puerility of Gifford's *Baviad* and *Maeviad*, he quotes "The Eve of St. Agnes" for the pleasure of its "rich beauties and dim obscurities." In the essay "On Reading Old Books," he adds that "the reading of Mr. Keats's Eve of Saint Agnes lately made me regret that I was not young again." But the best homage he pays Keats is the impulse with which, to relieve an uneventful moment of his *Journey through France and Italy,* he launches into a one-line quotation from a poem then hardly five years in the world, as if everyone he cared to have as a reader would know it: "Oh for a beaker full of the warm South!" He had already published, in the essay "On Effeminacy of Character," a more stringent verdict on the poems than these gestures of loyalty seem to indicate.

> I cannot help thinking that the fault of Mr. Keats's poems was a deficiency in masculine energy of style. He had beauty, tenderness, delicacy, in an uncommon degree, but there was a want of strength and substance. His Endymion is a very delightful description of the illusions of a youthful imagination, given up to airy dreams—we have flowers, clouds, rainbows, moonlight, all sweet sounds and smells, and Oreads and Dryads flitting by—but there is nothing tangible in it, nothing marked or palpable—we have none of the hardy spirit or rigid forms of antiquity. He painted his own thoughts and character; and did not transport himself into the fabulous and heroic ages. There is a want of action, or character, and so far, of imagination. . . . We see in him the youth, without the manhood of poetry.

But I suspect he wrote this before looking closely at the 1820 volume, with *Hyperion* and the odes. Besides, he was saying no more than Keats himself had admitted in his Preface.

> [My Preface] is not written with the least atom of purpose to forestall criticisms of course, but from the desire I have to conciliate men who are competent to look, and who do look with a zealous eye, to the honour of English literature.
>
> The imagination of a boy is healthy, and the mature imagination of a man is healthy; but there is a space of life between, in which the soul is in a ferment, the character undecided, the way of life uncertain, the ambition thick-sighted: thence proceeds mawkishness, and all the thousand bitters which those men I speak of must necessarily taste in going over the following pages.

Hazlitt's failure to review *Endymion* doubtless proceeded from a reluctance to say anything that might be wounding to its author. He kept the disappointment to himself while Keats was alive; gave his reputation several lifts following one skeptical delay after his death; and saved a final estimate for the section on Keats in *Select British Poets* (1824), where as Keats's first anthologist he had a chance to exhibit once more the depth of taste for which he had earned the lasting esteem of his subject. There are three passages from *Endymion*—including the Procession and Hymn in Honour of Pan (ending with the words "But in old marbles ever beautiful"), and the Indian Lady's Song—along with one from *Hyperion,* the "Ode to a Nightingale," "Fancy," and "Robin Hood." I have said that Keats found his second self in Hazlitt, and that he showed this particularly in the insistence that his brother read his verse beside Hazlitt's prose, as examples of kindred energies. Hazlitt was the older man in this friendship, and a comparable intensity of response could not be expected from him. But he wrote about Keats and appears also to have treated him as his equal in genius. No other encounter between poet and critic has been so fortunate for literature.

This does not strike me as the sort of influence—involving the spread of doctrine—which it has usually been supposed to exemplify. Keats understood Hazlitt's ideas till they became second nature to him; but the ideas were always inseparable from the tact of expression; Hazlitt's power, in every way, was *communicated*. This may be harder for us to see, and more paradoxical for us to ask questions about, than it would have seemed to romantic authors, for we find border-crossing expeditions between poetry and prose more difficult than they did. At any rate I think Hazlitt's effect on Keats can be traced to something so minute as the pace of his movement in verse, which is not the sinuous grace of Coleridge or the lapidary delibera-tion of Wordsworth, but the variable speed of uncommon thoughts, hurried along as each shift of subject permits a new accession of power. Keats has, in poetry as well as prose, the "fiery laconicism" he praised in Hazlitt—a very different thing from Byron's whirlwind truculence. *Lamia* is perhaps his closest approach to a middle style, and to Hazlitt's prose: its verse is lively, swift to digress and return, and at home in all the possible roles of a narrator.

> Love in a hut, with water and a crust,
> Is—Love, forgive us!—cinders, ashes, dust;
> Love in a palace is perhaps at last
> More grievous torment than a hermit's fast:—
> That is a doubtful tale from faery land,
> Hard for the non-elect to understand.
> Had Licius liv'd to hand his story down,
> He might have given the moral a fresh frown,
> Or clench'd it quite: but too short was their bliss
> To breed distrust and hate, that make the soft voice hiss.
> Besides, there, nightly, with terrific glare,
> Love, jealous grown of so complete a pair,
> Hover'd and buzz'd his wings, with fearful roar,
> Above the lintel of their chamber door,
> And down the passage cast a glow upon the floor.

Though the opening two couplets make an observant and not uncritical homage to Byron's style of worldliness, the disclaimer, "Hard for the non-elect to understand," and "He might have given the moral a fresh frown, / Or clench'd it quite," are pure Hazlitt, in their self-confidence and gusto, and freedom from self-regard. Yet Keats speaks as a moral narrator not in his poems, but in the aphorisms of his letters. These have made him, in a few sayings, the single most widely quoted authority on the program of romanticism, apart from Blake; and yet his aphorisms have the peculiarity that they are useless to those who respect less than the whole of their context. This was a quality of Hazlitt's aphorisms too, and it seems to belong more largely to the discursive genius of empiricism. Here I want only to remind the reader of four well-known observations for which Hazlitt's thought, as I have been tracing it, supplies a context even more satisfying than Keats's *Letters*.

The first, from a letter to Bailey of November 22, 1817, concerns the poet's freedom from the habitual or irritable demands of a single fixed identity, a set "character."

> Men of Genius are great as certain ethereal Chemicals operating on the Mass of neutral intellect—but they have not any individuality, any determined Character. I would call the top and head of those who have a proper self Men of Power.

Men of Power are great because there is no telling what will strike them: Wordsworth's attraction to the lichen on the rock, Rousseau's care for the lustres of his remembered life, as epitomised by the memory "*Ah, voilà de la pervenche*," are equally unpredictable from any individuality but theirs; whereas Byron is doubtless somewhere below the "top and head" of this class, having (only more fluently) the strange and picturesque imaginings that come to most men, when they put themselves in a strange and picturesque mood. Shakespeare on the contrary would rank highest among the "Men of Genius" whose individuality is dispersed through the invention of dramatic characters. Keats refers to nothing more than the mystery surrounding this dispersion, when he speaks of chemicals "operating on the Mass of neutral intellect": he makes no claim for the poet's detachment or impersonality.

John Middleton Murry thought the contrast between Shakespeare and Wordsworth must have been present to Keats's mind whenever he set men of genius against men of power. The special importance of Shakespeare as a foil to the man of power, and as an example of how the highest genius surpasses the egotistical, appears more clearly by the proximity of the foregoing remarks to some others about Wordsworth, offered after two months of further reflection, in the letter to Reynolds of February 3, 1818.

> It may be said that we ought to read our Contemporaries. That Wordsworth &c should have their due from us. but for the sake of a few fine imaginative or domestic passages, are we to be bullied into a certain Philosophy engendered in the whims of an Egotist—Every man has his speculations, but every man does not brood and peacock over them till he

makes a false coinage and deceives himself. . . . We hate poetry that has a palpable design upon us—and if we do not agree, seems to put its hands in its breeches pockets.

Once again it was Hazlitt who gave Keats the polemical assurance one feels at work here. His review of *The Excursion* was the incitement without which we should hardly be reading Keats today, and this letter was written soon after the lecture "On Poetry in General."

The dramatic poet according to Hazlitt had a scope for his imaginative energies denied to the lyric poet—as the man of genius has a *range* of powers denied to the man of power. Keats is still pondering the difference in a letter to Haydon, of April 8, 1818, on the subject of heroic painting. What he can never know intimately about an artist of genius, but always believes in the existence of, are "the innumerable compositions and decompositions which take place between the intellect and its thousand materials before it arrives at that trembling delicate and snail-horn perception of Beauty," the result of much careful exploring in "your many havens of intenseness." The immediate source is Hazlitt's lecture on Shakespeare, from a few weeks earlier, with its observation that in Shakespeare there is no "fixed essence of character" but "a continual composition and decomposition of its elements, a fermentation of every particle in the whole mass, by its alternate affinity and antipathy to other principles which are brought into contact with it." I have shown [in a previous essay] how Hazlitt adapted the same thought to a larger subject in the essay "On Imitation," where art "divides and decompounds objects into a thousand curious parts." The vocabulary of both Hazlitt and Keats in this instance, is pretty plainly Lockean, for Locke had spoken of the difficulty in "moral names" as peculiar to the associative process of composition and decomposition: "What need of a sign, when the thing signified is present and in view? But in moral names, that cannot be so easily and shortly done, because of the many decompositions that go to the making up the complex ideas of those modes." One may see this as part of the same difficulty that interested Hazlitt and Keats, by reflecting that moral names are nothing but the signs for Hazlitt's "moral quantities," that is, for the stuff of character itself. Coleridge too had a way of employing this vocabulary, but generally with disgust, as a thing appropriate to the fallen labors of the understanding: "The leading differences," he writes in Appendix C of *The Statesman's Manual*, "between mechanic and vital philosophy may all be drawn from one point namely, that the former demanding for every mode and act of existence real or possible *visibility*, knows only of distance and nearness, composition (or rather juxtaposition) and decomposition, in short the relations of unproductive particles to each other. . . . This is the philosophy of death, and only of a dead nature can it hold good."

Keats, however, as much as Hazlitt, believed it was a philosophy of life. He would have expected Haydon as a painter to understand in advance that the compositions and decompositions can never confidently be numbered or classified; but in employing the phrase nevertheless he went out of his way to adopt an Enlightenment view of his experiments in poetry.

Their understanding of the mind's compositions and decompositions had broad implications for the politics of both Hazlitt and Keats. The same sympathies by which a reader of literature was taken out of his habitual self, allowed to inhabit other characters, and encouraged to revise the story of his own life by the alternate affinities and antipathies that he chose, made any system unnatural which supposed that the boundaries of self and of continuous identity were more permanent in society than in the individual mind, as it traveled from thought to thought. Only in the absence of such imposed boundaries could the man of genius and the man of power reside together in a single body. "Man," Keats tells Reynolds, in a letter of February 19, 1818, "should not dispute or assert but whisper results to his neighbour, and thus by every germ of Spirit sucking the Sap from mould ethereal every human might become great, and Humanity instead of being a wide heath of Furse and Briars with here and there a remote Oak or Pine, would become a grand democracy of Forest Trees." Some days later, in the *Examiner* for March 7, 1818, Keats would have found a similar feeling in the first installment of Hazlitt's great manifesto, "What Is the People?"

> And who are you that ask the question? One of the people. And yet you would be something! Then you would not have the People nothing. For what is the people? Millions of men, like you, with hearts beating in their bosoms, blood circulating in their veins, with wants and appetites, and passions and anxious cares, and busy purposes and affections for others and a respect for themselves, and a desire for happiness, and a right to freedom, and a will to be free.

If the sound is fiercer than any we can imagine as native to Keats's grand democracy of forest trees, the reason is that Hazlitt was addressing those who must clamor and shout before they can be heard in whispers. But far from despising the quieter calling that Keats pursued, he was eager for its result, from the very start of a short career. The new voice was also an answering voice, and had for him the quality of a confirmation.

"ODE TO A NIGHTINGALE"

Negative capability was Keats's name for one elusive element that goes "to form a Man of Achievement especially in Literature, and which Shakespeare possessed so enormously." The emphasis on Shakespeare owes much to Hazlitt's criticism; so does the unorthodox notion that art's task of selection and construction must begin with a negative sort of triumph: a purging away of the interfering self, and of all its particles of irritability. Apart from *The Round Table*, "A Letter to William Gifford," and Hazlitt's two books of lectures, he likely read the *Essay on Human Action*; and his thoughts about dramatic poetry were made keener by the *Characters of Shakespeare's Plays*, of which he praised the chapter on *King Lear* for its "hieroglyphic visioning." What he found most useful were Hazlitt's doubts about the predominance of the self in modern poetry: the egotistical, Hazlitt taught, was only one version of the sublime, and a limited one. The highest poetry makes us forget the identity of the poet in the many identities he assumes; thus Shakespeare had "only to think of any thing in order to become that thing, with all the circumstances belonging to it." He seems to us in dramatic works, as he passes from one character to another, "like the same soul successively animating different bodies."

In a letter to Richard Woodhouse of October 27, 1818, Keats adopted this idea for his own ends, and turned it against Wordsworth.

> As to the poetical Character itself, (I mean that sort of which, if I am any thing, I am a Member; that sort distinguished from the wordsworthian or egotistical sublime; which is a thing per se and stands alone) it is not itself—it has no self—it is every thing and nothing—It has no character—it enjoys light and shade; it lives in gusto, be it foul or fair, high or low, rich or poor, mean or elevated—It has as much delight in conceiving an Iago as an Imogen. What shocks the virtuous philosopher, delights the camelion Poet. It does no harm from its relish of the dark side of things any more than from its taste for the bright one; because they both end in specula-tion. A Poet is the most unpoetical of any thing in existence; because he has no Identity—he is continually informing and filling some other Body.

Keats here is curiously more polemical than Hazlitt. The main thing he wants the poet to avoid is any aspiration to the "wordsworthian or egotistical sublime": without the parenthesis his injunction would read, "As to the poetical character itself...it is not itself." Self, the "thing per se," Wordsworth (as Hazlitt described him) taking a personal interest in the universe, is the enemy whom the sentence rounds upon. Wordsworth remains himself entirely too much of the time. Yet why should Keats have made an antagonist of the poet who had created in *The Excursion* another of the "three things" he thought would survive the age? Keats too aimed to be a poet of the sublime, and perhaps that is reason enough. His sublimity, when he came to know it, would be closely related to Wordsworth's, but to invent it at all and discover the strength to pursue it, he had to believe the difference was going to be tremendous.

He hoped to attain a point of view from which sublime emotions could be his as a more than temporary privilege. At the same time he needed to be invulnerable to the charge of egotism that he had brought against Wordsworth. He was reconciled to seeing the self dominate his poetry as much as it had Wordsworth's; but unlike Wordsworth he would leave the way open to feel as someone or something else. The change has to do with dramatic situation. The narrator of a Keats ode is always on the verge of becoming not quite himself, and he makes us believe that to remain so is to widen experience. But this sounds like what English critics have sometimes called "empathy"—translating the German *Einfühlung*—and I need to say why it is closer to what Hazlitt all along had been calling "sympathy." Empathy is the process by which a mind so projects itself into its object that a transfer of qualities seems to take place. Keats, on the other hand, was looking for a capability of so heightening the imagination's response to anything that the identities of both the mind and its object would grow more vivid *as what they are.* Nor had Wordsworth failed utterly to advance this quest for an intenser sympathy. His poetry struck Keats as evidence that there was a "grand march of intellect"—even Milton "did not think into the human heart, as Wordsworth has done." Yet the suspicion lingered with him that Wordsworth's poetry, though of a new kind, was not the most profound of its kind.

"To this point was Wordsworth come," Keats writes, in the letter I have just quoted: to this point, he means, and no further. For Wordsworth had remained content with what by Keats's lights was a constricting half-knowledge. He saw into his own heart only, and therefore the outward lesson of his poetry, which was the need for accommodation to the teachings of nature, made possible an inward deception. The accommodation really went the other way: nature, or a carefully selected aspect of it, was bent to the will of the poet. To a youthful admirer this could seem a betrayal of both poetry and nature, in the name of the human heart. Poetry, because Wordsworth by his choice of subjects and his limitation of tone, had contracted its scope so drastically; nature, because it now occupied the foreground of every poem, but was seen only through the distorting medium of poetry that had "a palpable design upon us." Keats's sense of disappointment is not what most readers can be expected to feel, when they read Wordsworth after Pope and Cowper, and beside Byron and Scott. But Keats had at this time a relentless narrowness of focus. He read Wordsworth after Shakespeare and beside Shakespeare.

Alison, and associationist critics generally, had argued that any object in nature could be expressive, because it had to be interpreted as an object of the mind, and would give back the mind's own expression as if from afar by awakening "trains of thought." If one takes this as a creed of individual life, and reads the associations of each mind as its signature, then associationism becomes a powerful sanction for the egotistical sublime. But if one supposes such trains of thought are interesting because they can be shared—if one concludes that the reader can be taught to recognize in them the workings of his own mind, and not encouraged to end in awe of the poet's—then associationism looks like the right intellectual groundwork for a poetry of sympathy. To the latter point Keats had come, by the time he wrote his odes: the reaction that his reading of Hazlitt fostered gives him more in common with Alison's American disciples like Bryant, than with Wordsworth after 1800. No single passage of Hazlitt's carries the force that the ideal of sympathy had to gather little by little in Keats's mind, through reading and reflection and the writing of new poems. Yet the conclusion of the essay "On Reason and Imagination"—written too late for Keats to have known it—gives an essence of the kind of understanding Keats was working toward, in his letters diffusely, and in his odes with an effect of such concentration that they make the ideal hard to name.

> Man is (so to speak) an endless and infinitely varied repetition: and if we know what one man feels, we so far know what a thousand feel in the sanctuary of their being. . . . As is our perception of this original truth, the root of our imagination, so will the force and richness of the general impression proceeding from it be. The boundary of our sympathy is a circle which enlarges itself according to its propulsion from the centre—the heart. If we are imbued with a deep sense of individual weal or woe, we shall be awe-struck at the idea of humanity in general. . . . If we understand the texture and vital feeling, we then can fill up the outline, but we cannot supply the former from having the latter given. Moral and poetical truth is like expression in a picture—the one is not to be attained by smearing over a large canvas, nor the other by bestriding a vague topic. . . . I defy any great tragic writer to despise that nature which he understands, or that heart which he has probed, with all its rich bleeding materials of joy and sorrow. The subject may not be a source of much triumph to him, from its alternate light and shade, but it can never become one of supercilious indifference. He must feel a strong reflex interest in it, corresponding to that which he has depicted in the characters of others. Indeed, the object and end of playing, "both at the first and now, is to hold the mirror up to nature," to enable us to feel for others as for ourselves, or to embody a distinct interest out of ourselves by the force of imagination and passion.

Hazlitt's "light and shade" necessary to a work of art—an associationist trope for the whole that is implied by the coexistence of opposite parts—appear also in Keats's sketch of the poetical character, and they will reappear in his last letter: "the knowledge of contrast, feeling for light and shade, all that information (primitive sense) necessary for a poem are great enemies of the stomach." As he prepared to write the "Ode to a Nightingale" in particular, he was pondering what it meant to write from a sanctuary of being, such as Hazlitt speaks of, and what course the imagination might trace from it. The "boundary of our sympathy," a "circle which enlarges itself according to its propulsion from the centre—the heart," was the region he hoped to explore in this poem.

Before discussing the poem I must add an unexpected link between the act of sympathy which it presents, and the argument for disinterested action in Hazlitt's *Essay*. On March 19, 1819, in the same journal-letter that had quoted the "Letter to William Gifford," Keats told his brother that the energies displayed in any natural activity "though erroneous . . . may be fine—This is the very thing in which consists poetry; and if so it is not so fine a thing as philosophy—For the same reason that an eagle is not so fine a thing as a truth." An eagle like a poem is beautiful quite apart from its moral qualities, moral truth not being understood here as a necessary condition of beauty. Yet it takes second place to a truth, as nature in our eyes takes second place to human society. The remark is partly explained by a passage earlier in the same letter which is not as well known.

> I perceive how far I am from any humble standard of disinterestedness—Yet this feeling ought to be carried to its highest pitch, as there is no fear of its ever injuring society—which it would do I fear pushed to an extremity— For in wild nature the Hawk would loose his Breakfast of Robins and the Robin his of Worms—The Lion must starve as well as the swallow.

Disinterestedness ought to be kept up: it is a finer thing than self-interest, and as Hazlitt had shown it seems harder to act from only because we are trained by habit to look first to ourselves. It is of our very humanity to be disinterested, as much as it is to be self-centered. But when we move from human society to nature the matter alters. The possibility of disinterested action then turns out to be a result of artificial arrangements which society brings into being. Reduced to a practice by the hawk, it would oblige him to lose his meal. The hawk and eagle are not expected to act from disinterested motives, any more than they are expected to feel sympathy. Do they in this resemble the poet?

Keats wrote his letter in an experimental mood. It took the Ode to show us that poetry is more impressive than the eagle of his comparison would allow it to be. In their freedom from care and sympathy alike, the eagle and hawk resemble only one of the singers in Keats's poem: the nightingale. Keats aims to feel as it does. Yet the difference between them remains his necessary human inheritance. Having once recognized this, one may call his expansive gesture of identification by the name of empathy or, as seems more in keeping with Keats's own vocabulary, sympathy, but in either case it will be understood that the poet carries out an imaginative action of which the bird is incapable. Indeed, the poet is only a poet by virtue of this gesture. He of all men feels in this way, even if he regrets the continual renewals of feeling and, with each wave, the sharper awareness that his subject is compounded of light and shade. So, in the course of the poem, those elements of the poet's character that belong to the irritable self, and can encounter nothing without palpable design, will vanish. The sort of personality that Keats still believes in is what Hazlitt described in his *Essay*, as "nothing more than conscious individuality: it is the power of perceiving that you are and what you are from the immediate reflection of the mind on its own operations, sensations, or ideas."

If one places those words from the *Essay* beside Keats's appreciation of a certain phase of Milton's poetry, where the reader feels the "Author's consolations coming thick upon him at a time when he complains most," one will have a fair sense of the intellectual allegiances he took for granted when he wrote.

> My heart aches, and a drowsy numbness pains
>   My sense, as though of hemlock I had drunk,
> Or emptied some dull opiate to the drains
>   One minute past, and Lethe-wards had sunk:
> 'Tis not through envy of thy happy lot,
>   But being too happy in thine happiness,—
>   That thou, light-winged Dryad of the trees,
>   In some melodious plot
> Of beechen green, and shadows numberless,
>   Singest of summer in full-throated ease.

One recalls the aphorism from "The Indian Jugglers," that "greatness is great power, producing great effects." In the "Ode to Psyche" Keats's reader might have been conscious of the effects without feeling certain of the power: what kind it was, and from what source it claimed its authority. Even the identity of that poem's speaker is indefinite, until he comes upon Cupid and Psyche, and can assume their energy as his own.

> I wander'd in a forest thoughtlessly,
>   And, on the sudden, fainting with surprise,
> Saw two fair creatures.

From this lucky diversion he gets his chance to make a poetry filled with sensations as well as thoughts. Still he draws all his strength from what he beholds; he cannot offer the sympathy of one distinct being for another, because he hardly exists before he unveils the lovers; he himself, it may be said, is created by the act of sympathy. There is thus a quiet irony in the powerful line, "I see, and sing, by my own eyes inspir'd."

The reader who moves from this to the "Ode to a Nightingale" is startled by the presence of a feeling "I." One knows a good deal about this speaker after five lines: that he is acquainted with griefs and their numb aftermath; that envy (a twisted sympathy) is a motive he wants to rise above; that he is not quite conquered by cares, but acquires a strange vigilance from the pressure of having to contemplate them. The rest of the stanza opens an ambiguity which the rest of the poem will dramatize: "being too happy in thine happiness" may refer either to the poet or the bird; but the bird is never fully present except through the poet. Something must correspond to the "Thou," and yet it remains spectral without the "I," syntactically and grammatically tenuous. When the stanza achieves a finality of place and feeling, in "some melodious plot / Of beechen green, and shadows numberless," one feels that this could belong to the nightingale only with the spirit that inhabits it in conversation.

Keats's second stanza opens with a private joke against himself, "O, for a draught of vintage." Claret had appeared in his letters among the accessories proper to the full life of sensations. Now it is lovingly described, but with an awareness that its effect is to dull sensation, and to obscure identity. The effect can be felt especially in the Miltonic inversions of the last two lines—"That I might drink, and leave the world unseen, / And with thee fade away into the forest dim." The poet wishes to be unseen; but the world, given his present state, will also be unseen by him. Were the assimilative logic extended much beyond this, the second stanza would leave Keats in the situation of the knight in "La Belle Dame sans Merci." But any such ending is held back by a vision of ordinary suffering in a world less fortunate than the nightingale's, the world without motion in which Keats had nursed his brother Tom through the days just before his death. Its mood is dictated by powers offstage—in the poem itself, by the "fade away" that still governs from the last stanza—and the actions it permits are all subordinate.

> Here, where men sit and hear each other groan;
> Where palsy shakes a few, sad, last gray hairs,
> Where youth grows pale, and spectre-thin, and dies;
> Where but to think is to be full of sorrow
> And leaden-eyed despairs,
> Where Beauty cannot keep her lustrous eyes,
> Or new Love pine at them beyond to-morrow.

Doubts of the real worth of poetry were crowding in upon Keats as he wrote this stanza; what at worst is done out of vanity may be judged by posterity to have been done in vain also. Is not every poet an egotist, compared to every nurse? How is Tom's death to be weighed in the balance with the composition of an ode?

From the burden of these questions Keats fancies for the moment that he can be released by an act of willed elation. The interjection, "Away! Away!" wards off the evil and, in the same breath, declares him bound for new regions. He is helped in this escape by the temporary artifice of a myth.

Yet the language in which he presents it—"haply the Queen-Moon is on her throne, / Cluster'd around by all her starry Fays"—is facile in the worst style of *Endymion*. The effect I think is deliberate: Keats had to hear these particular notes ring false before he could be delivered back to himself. Unlike the bird he cannot join the night's tenderness simply by doing what is in his nature. He can join it nevertheless, by looking with different eyes on what has surrounded him all along. This is the major transition of the Ode, and as he enters it Keats's impression is that he is dazed, and for the first time must move slowly.

> I cannot see what flowers are at my feet,
>   Nor what soft incense hangs upon the boughs,
> But, in embalmed darkness, guess each sweet
>   Wherewith the seasonable month endows
> The grass, the thicket, and the fruit-tree wild;
>   White hawthorn, and the pastoral eglantine;
>   Fast fading violets cover'd up in leaves;
>   And mid-May's eldest child
> The coming musk-rose, full of dewy wine,
>   The murmurous haunt of flies on summer eves.

Here the poet is "cluster'd around" like the Queen-Moon: what she boded only he can fulfill humanly. As in "To Autumn," the catalogue here follows the course of a season, the early growths separable and a little plain, the late ones replete and intertwined. The effortless naturalism of the writing suggests that the hope Keats expressed in a letter to Bailey, of a kind of immortality from "having what we called happiness on Earth repeated in a finer tone and so repeated," was both sincere and pure of hermetic intent. That version of heaven was for those who delighted in sensation rather than hungered after truth. But Keats avoided the word "heaven"; he cared more for "havens of intenseness," wherever the artist might find them: his own life would arrive at a spiritual repetition from the effort of sympathy to compass ever vaster subjects. In this stanza he seems to have found the resting place from which the effort can begin.

He does not pause long. The sixth stanza will require his largest act of identification—the embrace of death—and Keats has too lively a sense of surprise, and even here too keen a love of the sheer sport of the exertion, to collect all his thoughts before us. Two associations seem to control his movement: "embalmed darkness" with its subtle shock had left the expectation that his mood would be explained, or more fully encountered; and the flower-catalogue had lightly echoed a similar description in "Lycidas," where the poet's bier was strewn with "The Musk-rose, and the well-attir'd woodbine, / With cowslips wan that hang the pensive head, / And every flower that sad embroidery wears." Keats must have discovered by these associations that he was composing an elegy after all. It remained for him to give it the shape of an elegy for himself, but without grief. The triumph of his movement from this to the next stanza is that he makes an apparently egotistical turn of the Ode coincide with its farthest stretch of imaginative sympathy.

> Darkling I listen; and, for many a time
> I have been half in love with easeful Death,
>   Call'd him soft names in many a mused rhyme,
> To take into the air my quiet breath;
> Now more than ever seems it rich to die,
>   To cease upon the midnight with no pain,
>   While thou art pouring forth thy soul abroad
>   In such an ecstasy!
> Still wouldst thou sing, and I have ears in vain—
>   To thy high requiem become a sod.

With the phrase "Darkling I listen," an adjective probable only for the bird is appropriated by the poet; and it is understood that his readers will complete the exchange for themselves: "Thou wast not born for death, immortal Keats." Anti-sentimentalist critics have supposed that he was here confessing himself in love with death and, since there is something suspect in this, that he needed to shake free of the delusion before his poem was finished. Yet in calling death "easeful" he means, not "death, which is always easeful" but "one sort of death which has seemed easeful to me." This line, and all the lines that prepare for it, have an air neither of defiance nor of passive suffering and defeat. Death is in the poem, as a no longer terrifying allegorical figure, because death is where the full diapason of human identity must close. A sufficient motive for Keats's poise is the untroubled connection he makes, however hard we may find it, between death and immortality. He finds nothing strange in asking death to possess and continue his own wind of inspiration, "To take into the air my quiet breath."

The most perfect gloss I can imagine for the seventh stanza is Hazlitt's account of the dramatic strength in Shakespeare's poetry, which Keats heard him say aloud in the lecture-hall and never forgot: "The passions are in a state of projection. Years are melted down to moments, and every instant teems with fate. We know the results, we see the process." At the conclusion of another lecture, "On Thomson and Cowper," Hazlitt connected this "process" with listening, and not merely thinking and speaking: "The cuckoo, 'that wandering voice,' that comes and goes with the spring, mocks our ears with one note from youth to age; and the lap-wing, screaming around the traveler's path, repeats for ever the same sad story of Tereus and Philomel." In Keats's mind these two passages had now joined.

Thou wast not born for death, immortal Bird!
　No hungry generations tread thee down;
The voice I hear this passing night was heard
　In ancient days by emperor and clown:
Perhaps the self-same song that found a path
　　Through the sad heart of Ruth, when, sick for home,
　　　She stood in tears amid the alien corn;
　　　　The same that oft-times hath
　　Charm'd magic casements, opening on the foam
　　　Of perilous seas, in faery lands forlorn.

Listening to the "self-same song that found a path / Through the sad heart of Ruth," he projects himself in imagination into the prospect that stretched before her amid the alien corn. His success here makes anything possible, and so the casement becomes magic. Only after his venture into a human history, and by an effect best described, in the anachronistic language of the cinema, as *montage*, do we see the picture of Ruth give way to a kindred, equally generous but now visionary scene, opening "on the foam / Of perilous seas, in faery lands forlorn."

Keats, as J. R. Caldwell demonstrated in *John Keats' Fancy*, wrote many of his poems in a kind of trance-state, which he believed congenial to the high argument of psychological romance. This practice would free him from habitual trains of thought—he might be bad but he would not be second-hand—and it would allow his imagination the unchanneled freedom which gave a promise of enduring invention. Some unhappy poems were produced as a result, but his greatest poems, the "Ode to a Nightingale" among them, were evidently written in much the same way. What may puzzle us is not the strangeness of his practice, since later poets have made it familiar, but rather Keats's implicit reliance on an exalted idea of the unconscious. There was no source for this in the associationist writers he knew, and we seem to be left with the true but primitive explanation that he invented the beliefs he needed to carry conviction. I prefer instead to enlist Hazlitt's aid again, by quoting from his essay "On Dreams," but with the same limitation I placed on the passage from "On Reason and Imagination." In these cases unlike the lectures and *The Round Table*, we cannot suppose that he showed Keats the way to his own thoughts. "On Dreams" was written after the Ode, and its interest is that it presents a genius of comparable sympathies working through a similar course of speculations.

Nevertheless I believe the essay brings some sort of order to the apparently lawless drift of fancy that Keats encouraged in himself; and the following passage may be read as a commentary on Keats's preferred manner of composition from *Endymion* to the odes.

The *conscious* or connecting link between our ideas, which forms them into separate groups or compares different parts and views of a subject together, seems to be that which is principally wanting in sleep; so that any idea that presents itself in this anarchy of the mind is lord of the ascendant for the moment, and is driven out by the next straggling notion that comes across it. The bundles of thought are, as it were, untied, loosened from a common centre, and drift along the stream of fancy as it happens. . . . Thus we confound one person with another, merely from some accidental coincidence, the name or the place where we have seen them, or their having been concerned with us in some particular transaction the evening before. They lose and regain their proper identity perhaps half a dozen times in this rambling way; nor are we able (though we are somewhat incredulous and surprised at these compound creations) to detect the error, from not being prepared to trace the same connected subject of thought to a number of varying and successive ramifications, or to form the idea of a *whole*. . . . The difference, so far then, between sleeping and waking, seems to be that in the latter we have a greater range of conscious recollections, a larger discourse of reason, and associate ideas in longer trains and more as they are connected with one another in the order of nature; whereas in the former, any two impressions, that meet or are alike, join company, and then are parted again, without notice, like the froth from the wave. So in madness, there is, I should apprehend, the same tyranny of the imagination over the judgment; that is, the mind has slipped its cable, and single images meet, and jostle, and unite suddenly together, without any power to arrange or compare them with others, with which they are connected in the world of reality. There is a continual phantasmagoria: whatever shapes and colours come together are by the heat and violence of the brain referred to external nature, without regard to the order of time, place, or circumstance. From the same want of continuity, we often forget our dreams so speedily: if we cannot catch them as they are passing out at the door, we never set eyes on them again.

It is the conscious link between our ideas that organizes our experience into a consistent mass, and creates in us the abstract idea of self. We need this idea and this link if we are to be masters rather than servants of our associated ideas, and use the power of the imagination. Yet in sleep, or the kind of trance that slips the mind's cable, we are at the mercy of every chance link that may happen to connect our ideas, as they pass by each other and catch upon some salient point. We are thus robbed of the idea of a coherent self which seems to endow us with more than accidentally formed associations, and from which we gain the conviction of our power as agents. The waking imagination, no less than the judgment, requires the support of some such conviction, and Keats in his final stanza has to exorcise an impending tyranny of the dreaming imagination.

> Forlorn! the very word is like a bell
> To toll me back from thee to my sole self!

Adieu! the fancy cannot cheat so well
    As she is fam'd to do, deceiving elf.
Adieu! adieu! thy plaintive anthem fades
    Past the near meadows, over the still stream,
        Up the hill-side; and now 'tis buried deep
            In the next valley-glades:
Was it a vision, or a waking dream?
Fled is that music:—Do I wake or sleep?

The contrast between waking and dreaming imagination, or between the "continual phantasmagoria" of sleep and the habitual relations of the self, had been given a different shading in Book II of *Endymion*, where the return from wandering thoughts was seen as a compelled tribute paid by fancy to the repressive self.

There, when new wonders ceas'd to float before,
And thoughts of self came on, how crude and sore
The journey homeward to habitual self!
A mad pursuing of the fog-born elf,
Whose flitting lantern, through rude nettle-briar,
Cheats us into a swamp, into a fire,
Into the bosom of a hated thing.

The recurrence in the Ode both of "cheat," and of the self-elf rhyme, persuades me that the old passage was still in Keats's mind, but he had set himself to revise it thoroughly. A great difference of tone separates the "habitual self" of *Endymion*—into which fancy betrays us by its excess, and is blamed for doing so—and the "sole self" of the Ode. The latter is a necessary thing, in charge of the daylight world which Keats no longer regrets, and which has its own sympathies to ask of us. It is fancy as such and not its "journey homeward," that Keats now describes as a cheat, exhibiting in this a self-possessed humor with some affection for his own errors: the "deceiving elf" only acts up to its name, but in the "fog-born elf" of *Endymion* there had been something hellish. Keats in the Ode does not resent the obligation to reserve a space for less fanciful imaginings. As for the "sole self," it is what each of us has, in solitude, when for better or worse we do have the power to arrange and compare our ideas.

At the end of the Ode, dream images pass "out at the door," to adopt Hazlitt's words a last time. Keats himself remains fixed while the nightingale escapes "Past the near meadows, over the still stream, / Up the hill-side." The landscape has grown sober with the lucidity of daily things, and what survives the poem is a commitment to this mood as a final standard of comparison. And yet Keats is not oppressed by its demands, as he had seemed to be at the start of the poem. Out of the dream of truth in the middle stanzas has come the self-confidence of the egotist who is free of vanity because he has travelled outside himself for a time. "Do I wake or sleep"—it does not matter, because he is free to renew his journey, and to return again. The most nearly analogous emotion in literature is what one feels at certain moments of resolution in Shakespearean romance. One is made to believe that the ordinary must suffice but the ordinary too may be transfigured: as when, in A *Midsummer Night's Dream*, Helena speaks the lines that announce her contentment with what she can know but imperfectly, "And I have found Demetrius like a jewel, / Mine own and not mine own." Keats's poem ends like this not only because day follows night, but because the emotional extremes, being explored till they were exhausted, have at last left open a middle ground for the romance of realities.

One notices in rereading the Ode how deftly near the end it confirms Hazlitt's sense of the imagination's mastery over all associated impressions. Keats's use of the word "forlorn" has entered this poem at the suggestion of the same consonant group, f-l, which sounded in the phrase "faery lands." The adjective-noun pair was hopeful; the second adjective overcasts every hope: together, from the conformity of sounds alone, they exemplify the associative force of contrariety which was at work also in Keats's remarks about light and shade. By the end of the poem, however, he could afford to hear the low echo drawn out of high fancy, without contriving a miraculous escape. He is forlorn as a man untouched by irritations; his expansiveness and his skepticism here coincide. Imagination, he has seen, is the freedom to widen speculation; by making other things more vivid it contracts rather than expands the domain of self, though only for the moment; but what cannot ever be modified is the mind's liberty in forming new associations: to deny that would be, in Hazlitt's metaphor, "like supposing that you might tread on a nest of adders twined together, and provoke only one of them to sting you." Thus the narrowly sympathetic poetry of the Wordsworthian sermon and the Keatsian reverie have left room for a poetry that claims both the generosity and the privilege of a larger view. Long before this, in "Sleep and Poetry," in *Endymion*, and in sonnets dedicated to artists and art, Keats had written at the level he thought a modern could sustain. With the "Ode to a Nightingale" he had a poetry equal to what he loved.

"ODE ON A GRECIAN URN"

On this reading of the "Ode to a Nightingale," the poem has five distinct movements, the transitions being hard-won in each instance, and the constant sense of transition the necessary dramatic element in a poem that has one voice and yet means to shun the egotistical sublime. Keats begins by confessing his sickness of spirit; moves abruptly to dispel it, by his vow to "fly to thee" and join the Queen-Moon and her company, in what turns out to be a false effort of transcendence; finds nevertheless that this has led to an act of true imagination, with his embrace of death in "embalmed darkness"; by death is then reminded of the dead, and of another human sufferer of history or legend, whom the nightingale once soothed; and at last returns to life and the world of common realities, larger-spirited than the man who had begun, "My heart aches...." These particulars need to be remembered because there has been a tendency among critics to read the "Ode on a Grecian Urn" as a companion poem, with a similar plot. The poems do seem to me to work together, but they were evidently written from very different impulses, and in the later poem it would be hard to trace any movement comparable to the one I have just proposed. Even the formal differences which separate them are not trivial. The urn is silent where the nightingale poured forth its song; static, where the nightingale was free to move and finally to depart from the poem. Keats might allow himself to "be intense upon" a creature he knew could not be captured. But the urn *can* perhaps be captured and somehow contained, whether by description or moralizing commentary, and Keats's effort to avoid doing so begins with his title. To address his poem "to" the urn would imply a degree of presumption about its identity; he writes merely "on" it. His tone through most of the poem, in keeping with the same downward modulation, is tentative and coaxing, and the exclamations of the "Ode to a Nightingale" are replaced by questions. The scenes depicted on the urn interest him to the point of excluding the artist who fashioned it, and this emphasis accounts for some of Keats's uneasiness about the sort of answer he wants. His ideas about the "poetical character" were by this time very clear, his ideas about the character of a poem much less so, as his abortive experiments with *Hyperion* had lately shown. The "Ode to a Nightingale" was a poem about the poet (warm, and adaptable to many identities) whereas the "Ode on a Grecian Urn" is about the poem (cold, and beyond interrogation). To Keats himself the first must have seemed an act of sympathy, and the second an act of power.

What readers most honor in the "Ode on a Grecian Urn," and are at the same time made uneasy by, is its dividedness of purpose. In spite of the task it assumes, it does not manage to exclude the warm strivings of life, or the troubled sympathies of the poet: he cannot finish the poem without trying to imprint on the urn the pathos of these things. By doing so he reduces the distance between himself and a chosen object of power, and implies that there are special dangers in our admiration for its cold remoteness and its grandeur above humanity. Since the object itself seemed to warn him of such dangers, Keats felt nothing wrong in allowing the object to instruct us concerning them, with a motto about the right use of art. Hence the inscription "Beauty is truth, truth beauty" which has perplexed much commentary on the poem. It is the third and fourth stanzas, with their scenes of "breathing human passion," that disturb commentators as not quite belonging there; but the weight of the protest falls on the concluding motto, which in retrospect seems answerable for every awkward fact. If he had written the poem without those stanzas, offering as complete stanzas 1, 2, and 5, we would regard it as a well-managed sublime poem on the order of Collins's "Ode to Evening." It would be more perfect and it would move us less. A recent critic of the Ode, Patrick Parrinder, writes that Keats "expresses the full allure of aestheticism, without quite taking the leap into vulgar commitment." This is just perceptive enough to be irritating. Keats registers the allure only to reject it firmly, and to show an appreciation of art in which there is no want of keeping between art and humanity.

What did Keats feel when he saw before him an urn several centuries old? We have his testimony from one comparable occasion, the visit to the Elgin Marbles about which he wrote two sonnets in the spring of 1817. "On Seeing the Elgin Marbles for the First Time" seems to me the more conclusive in its statement of awestruck deference.

> My spirit is too weak—mortality
>> Weighs heavily on me like unwilling sleep,
>> And each imagined pinnacle and steep
> Of godlike hardship tells me I must die
> Like a sick eagle looking at the sky.
>> Yet 'tis a gentle luxury to weep
>> That I have not the cloudy winds to keep
> Fresh for the opening of the morning's eye.
> Such dim-conceived glories of the brain
>> Bring round the heart an undescribable feud;
> So do these wonders a most dizzy pain,
>> That mingles Grecian grandeur with the rude
> Wasting of old time—with a billowy main—
> A sun—a shadow of a magnitude.

The poem exhibits a poet's aspiration to compete with the grandeur of an art different from his, and greater by virtue of its duration. He hopes to find in himself a spirit as sublime as what he contemplates, yet the picture he gives of his failure is not sublime but pathetic, almost maudlin—"Like a sick eagle looking at the sky." Instead of the energy of mind that ought to reveal the poet's high contest with a nature informed by just such energy, he can show only "an undescribable feud," "a most dizzy pain." It looks as if, from a poem that began with the stock materials of the sublime—imagined pinnacles, cloudy winds—Keats were backing into a confession of defeat, which aims to move us by its sincerity. And yet the poem ends with impressive dignity in spite of its loss of heart. The new quality emerges from the sudden awareness of distance, in a mood so unexpected by Keats that he can approach it only by telegraphic dashes, and the reticence of the indefinite article: "a billowy main— / A sun—a shadow of a magnitude." The movement from an undescribable feud round the heart, to the acknowledgement of an alien strength, already suggests what Keats would mean in the "Ode on a Grecian Urn," when he spoke of being teased out of thought. His unhappier thoughts are of the soul's incompetence to gain these heights while the body still lives. But such thoughts come from our inability to be the contemporaries of our own greatness—which Keats, until the end of the poem, confuses with our inability to match the greatness of a past age. The last lines present the clearing away of that confusion. Nothing in the marbles themselves, Keats realizes, but rather the abyss that time has wrought between them and himself, brings the sensation of an incommensurable grandeur that he feels in looking at them. Cured of his weakness, he is able to participate in their glory at last, though it is experienced as something cold and inhuman. We may ponder this a moment longer in the light of all the elements that compose the resolution of the "Ode on a Grecian Urn." Here as in the later poem, the character of his feeling changes with the recognition that time itself creates sublimity, by robbing art of its signature and making it mysteriously natural. So old marbles can affect us "as doth eternity." Here too, mingled admiration and horror is a natural response to an object about which one can feel with a half-resentful certainty that "When old age shall this generation waste, / Thou shalt remain." Notwithstanding the strength of these associated feelings, there is no sense here that the sublime object could ever be "a friend to man."

Between the composition of this poem and the "Ode" two years later, Hazlitt had given his lecture "On Poetry in General," which we have good reason to suppose Keats read. The lecture included a comment on the relations between painting and poetry, and the remoteness of painting from human affections which only language can suggest. Raphael's cartoons are mentioned as proof of the rule, since their effect is inconceivable without our knowledge of the biblical texts; for contrast, Hazlitt calls to mind the "pure" beauty of Greek statues, and the phrase "marble to the touch" extends his criticism to the Elgin Marbles.

> Painting embodies what a thing contains in itself: poetry suggests what exists out of it, in any manner connected with it. But this last is the proper province of the imagination. Again, as it relates to passion, painting gives the event, poetry the progress of events: but it is during the progress, in the interval of expectation and suspense, while our hopes and fears are strained to the highest pitch of breathless agony, that the pinch of interest

lies. . . . It is for want of some such resting place for the imagination that the Greek statues are little else than specious forms. They are marble to the touch and to the heart. They have not an informing principle within them. In their faultless excellence they appear sufficient to themselves. By their beauty they are raised above the frailties of passion or suffering. By their beauty they are deified. But they are not objects of religious faith to us, and their forms are a reproach to common humanity. They seem to have no sympathy with us, and not to want our admiration.

Hazlitt concludes by regarding the marbles as instances of power rather than sympathy: they are a kind of Coriolanus among art objects. This, with an attendant sense of their cold self-sufficiency, was the conclusion Keats had reached in the last lines of his sonnet. He reaches it once more in the "Ode on a Grecian Urn," and one's suspicion that his reading of Hazlitt strength-ened an earlier sentiment of his own is confirmed by the paraphrase, "All breathing human passion far above," which he makes of Hazlitt's "they are raised above the frailties of passion or suffering." The sharp "hopes and fears" that Hazlitt sees as special to poetry, "strained to the highest pitch of breathless agony," also have their answering interval in Keats, whose lovers are "For ever panting" and strained to the pitch of "A burning forehead, and a parching tongue."

In such intervals alone lies the hidden story that interests us when we look at works of art. But can an unspeaking object be relied on to tell the story unaided? Hazlitt thought not, and made his objection the more memorable by an allusion to Wordsworth's great line, "By our own spirits are we deified." As said by the poet in "Resolution and Independence," this had meant that only human sympathies give us a human immortality, in the minds of others. Yet as repeated by Hazlitt, and in its new form, "By their beauty they are deified," it bears witness to everything about the marbles that makes them gods above our humanity. Because the only religion we care for is the religion of humanity, this beauty renders them "not objects of religious faith to us." The irony of the allusion is directed against the marbles, and puts Hazlitt for the moment in accord with Wordsworth. When he came to write this Ode, Keats was searching for a more generous view of such objects, in which they would appear necessarily as a friend to the common affections. His problem was to do that in a poem which first acknowledged the coldness and strangeness of the object. He would thus be required to expand the interval in which, as Hazlitt said, "the pinch of interest lies," but without cheating, or somehow crediting the object with a pathos only language can express. Judged in these terms, the end of the Ode is a victory for art, but not for the urn; it is much closer to Hazlitt's distinction between poetic and plastic expression than Keats would have liked to come; for it shows the urn being rescued into meaning by the poet who speaks. The Ode is a marriage between the urn, plastic art, beauty, the "unravished bride of quietness"—and the poem, poetic art, truth, the master of verbal expression. At its consummation the urn is released into words, though of a sort possible only to writing or inscription, and not to oral speech. Decorum is thus preserved, but one feels that the poem's final weight of authority belongs with truth, without which beauty would remain cold to the touch as to the heart.

To test the argument beyond these preliminaries I have to quote the poem.

> Thou still unravish'd bride of quietness,
>   Thou foster-child of silence and slow time,
> Sylvan historian, who canst thus express
>   A flowery tale more sweetly than our rhyme:
> What leaf-fring'd legend haunts about thy shape
>   Of deities or mortals, or of both,
>   In Tempe or the dales of Arcady?
>   What men or gods are these? What maidens loth?
> What mad pursuit? What struggle to escape?
>   What pipes and timbrels? What wild ecstasy?
>
> Heard melodies are sweet, but those unheard
>   Are sweeter; therefore, ye soft pipes, play on;
> Not to the sensual ear, but, more endear'd,
>   Pipe to the spirit ditties of no tone:
> Fair youth, beneath the trees, thou canst not leave
>   Thy song, nor ever can those trees be bare;
>   Bold Lover, never, never canst thou kiss,
> Though winning near the goal—yet, do not grieve;
>   She cannot fade, though thou hast not thy bliss,
>   For ever will thou love, and she be fair!

A poem written entirely in the key of the first four lines of these stanzas—the key of temperate and paradoxical satisfaction—would be very tedious to the merely human reader. But the relation which obtains here between the first four lines and the last six will be carried through the entire poem. First, the paradox is stated, with an air of ironic calm and good cheer; but in every case a deep distress has been held back, which needs the rest of the stanza to bring out its painful character. The relation between the two parts of each stanza is this, that the thought of immortality leads to the thought of death: the transition will be most astonishing in the final stanza, where the fourth line is not set off from the fifth by an end-stop—"Thou, silent form, dost tease us out of thought / As doth eternity," which I would paraphrase: "Your cold stillness shows us what silence all our thoughts end in, as for that matter our own deaths will show us." The not wholly agreeable surprise that Keats feels almost electrically across the line break is registered by the exclamation mark at "Cold Pastoral!" But about this phrase I will say more presently.

The thought which the opening lines of the first stanza hope to suppress is that the urn was not always an orphaned thing. It now seems the "foster child of silence and slow time" because, though it had its human parentage, all trace of this has disappeared. Its silence, the absence of a signature, imparts mystery to the urn, and that mystery by the passage of time is transformed into sublimity. But the loss of any known author, and with it the loss of personal pathos, trouble Keats more than calling the urn its own author, "Sylvan Historian," would seem to imply. One has some sense of the violence of the exclusion in the queer pun on "express": as if the figures on the urn were straining against their condition, and pressed outward toward articulate life, in spite of the formal constraint that forbids them any verbal expression. The questions that follow are not a bit complacent—not content as rhetorical questions are, to be subdued to the silence that is their element—but rather tongue-tied, with the stammering of children not yet sure of their right to speak. In the last lines of the second stanza, Keats moves to reconcile the lover to the frozen gesture in which he finds himself trapped so near the goal. The over-insistent concern which he feels on the lover's account is chiefly evident in his repeated denials: "canst not," "nor ever," and to close off the last hope, "never, never." But Keats has to add, "do not grieve": poetry by its nature deals in "the flowing, not the fixed," as Hazlitt put it; and if sculpture deals in the fixed, may it not offer the consolation that its permanence is that of a paradise without death? The unfamiliarity of this thought provokes him to write two more stanzas confirming its beauty, and they are among the saddest he ever wrote.

> Ah, happy, happy boughs! that cannot shed
>   Your leaves, nor ever bid the spring adieu
> And, happy melodist, unwearied,
>   For ever piping songs for ever new;
> More happy love! more happy, happy love!
>   For ever warm and still to be enjoyed,
>   For ever panting and for ever young;
> All breathing human passion far above,
>   That leaves a heart high-sorrowful and cloy'd,
>   A burning forehead, and a parching tongue.
>
> Who are these coming to the sacrifice?
>   To what green altar, O mysterious priest
> Lead'st thou that heifer lowing at the skies,
>   And all her silken flanks with garlands drest?
> What little town by river or sea shore,

> Or mountain-built with peaceful citadel,
>   Is emptied of this folk, this pious morn?
> And, little town, thy streets for evermore
>   Will silent be; and not a soul to tell
>   Why thou art desolate, can e'er return.

It is Keats himself whose cries of "happy, happy" must end in a breathless panting. And it is this happiness, more cloying than any sorrow, that makes us think of "breathing human passion" with relief. The ambiguous syntax, too, appears temporarily to set breathing human passion above anything the urn can depict; even when we read the syntactical inversion correctly—"These things, being above all human passion"—we may still be struck by the logical inversion that follows; for it would have been sounder practice, if the poem really wished us to forget the burning forehead and parching tongue, to place them somewhere other than the strong rhetorical position they now occupy at the end of the stanza.

But Keats at this period of his life must have counted himself among the lovers coming to the sacrifice, and sincerity compelled him to mention their pains in close conjunction with the question about their identity which opens the next stanza. The opening four lines describing the life of the town, however, are free of personal concern. In his effort to describe it without sympathy, and bounded by the speechless decorum of the urn itself, he approaches a Byronic pleasure in the picturesque. He writes of what is sublime, not because it is a work of man, but because it is a work of man overthrown; and yet he writes as if art alone, without any communion between the creating mind and the human passions it regards, could supply the terms in which we feel enlarged by such sublimity. If the poem had ended in this style, it might be included in Ruskin's general protest against the picturesque as a heartless ideal. In the second part of this stanza, however, Keats associates the urn's choice of an empty town to depict with his own readiness to empty the poem of all that concerns the town's inhabitants. The connection is between the urn-maker's choice to free his representation of persons, and what it would be for Keats to deprive his poem of feelings: the poem he thought he should aspire to make would be in this sense desolating. Keats was incapable of arriving at such a recognition without tremendous regret; and with his regret comes pity: "And, little town, thy streets for evermore / Will silent be." This is the only sentence, of all those following his questions, that even sounds like an answer. No soul can return, of course, except someone like Keats, a poet who does not accept the limits of the picture-making historian.

After the implicit equations have settled, of silence with apathy, and speech with pathos, the way open for the Ode as a poem was the way Keats took: to coax the urn, by compliment and salutation to conjure it into speech, and so to give it the sympathies of poetry. Yet he had to accomplish this in a manner that would reassure the urn that its condition as a silent and anonymous thing was not being violated.

> O Attic shape! Fair attitude! with brede
>   Of marble men and maidens overwrought,
> With forest branches and the trodden weed;
>   Thou, silent form, dost tease us out of thought
> As doth eternity: Cold Pastoral!
>   When old age shall this generation waste,
>   Thou shalt remain, in midst of other woe
>   Than ours, a friend to man, to whom thou say'st,
> "Beauty is truth, truth beauty,"—that is all
>   Ye know on earth, and all ye need to know.

Of many readers who felt uncomfortable with this ending, Robert Bridges was the first to object to "Attic shape! Fair attitude!" as an embarrassing pun. Others have followed him; and yet this is the language of conjuring: it is not more forced than "Abra Cadabra." The stanza affords much other evidence of a workmanship of style the reverse of negligent. The use of "overwrought" is the loveliest single instance, where the several meanings— "elaborately worked over"; "inlaid and intertwined"; "excited to the point of forgetting one's manners"—all converge in our sense of the maker's pains, the visible signs of his labor, and the vivid intensity of men and maidens on the brink of going too far. This was the sort of idiomatic play on words, incorporating both etymology and common usage, which Keats could manage like nobody else. Wordsworth can return to and revive the power of a word's origin, while allowing us to read it in some commoner way at first, as in his use of "consecration" and "distress" in the Peele Castle elegy; Coleridge is adept at finding grotesque juxtapositions for a word's original and colloquial meanings, though he often turns out to have half-invented one of them, as in his etymology of "atonement" (at-one-ment); but Keats sometimes liberates all the suspended senses of a word, to the advantage of all, with a lack of fuss that would cause equal delight to a parliamentary orator and a coffee-house politician. The implications of this freedom for a poem that has affected to renounce speech entirely will be felt in the progress of the stanza.

The great turn occurs at "Cold Pastoral!" H. W. Garrod argued that it need imply no change of heart, because Keats's admiration for such coldness has in fact been less pronounced all along than the reader supposes. Some of Hazlitt's strictures on Benjamin West are pertinent to the difficulty: in particular his objection that Death in West's painting had "not the calm, still, majestic form of Death, killing by a look,—withering by a touch. His presence does not make the still air cold." Coldness like this, a possible attribute of the sublime and also of death, would have governed Keats's understanding of the word in the context he was building; and he had prepared readers to admire the sublime chill in just the way Garrod warns them against, in a whole series of passages. One recalls especially, from "Sleep and Poetry," the immortals on display at the home of Leigh Hunt:

> Round about were hung
> The glorious features of the bards who sung
> In other ages—cold and sacred busts
> Smiled at each other. Happy he who trusts
> To clear futurity his darling fame!

In the more skeptical mood of *The Fall of Hyperion*, shortly after the Ode, there is the chill Keats feels on the steps of Moneta's temple, and her cold lips, and her face "deathwards progressing / To no death": monitory sensations, but assisting the poet on his quest, with a privation that starves his illusions. It may be difficult to admire but we can reasonably expect that Keats, when he describes the urn as cold, will be saying so in a tone of admiration. Yet "Cold Pastoral!" is said much more in a tone of shock, and even of rebuke. This comes partly of the *memento mori* that has just startled him across a line-break. Eternity does not tease us out of thought into something finer (a life of sensations) but rather out of thought and out of life.

"Tease us out of thought" therefore seems to me the real enigma. An earlier use of the phrase, from the verse epistle "To J. H. Reynolds, Esq."— "Things cannot to the will / Be settled, but they tease us out of thought"— promises much but turns out to be no solution. It asserts that the insights of art have nothing to do with acts of the will, and about this one is hardly in doubt after four stanzas of the Ode. The urn is silent; it is we alone who have thoughts, and must be teased out of them: the poem still leaves us to guess what our thought is here. Yet, for the sense of vocation which chiefly interests us, there seem to be just two alternatives: (1) We are thinking of art's superiority to life and nature, its freedom from their pains, and its satisfying permanence; (2) We are thinking of the debt art owes to life and nature, which can never be repaid, but which it can sufficiently acknowledge in an expressive moment of sympathy.

In the poem Keats set out to write—about an ancient relic sublimely above our humanity, and indifferent to our pains—we would have been teased out of the second thought, and into a point of view congenial to the first though without being obliged to think it. But the effort to be honestly inclusive has worked into the poem so fully, and so shaken its structure with the climactic phrase "Cold Pastoral!", that the teasing moves us in the opposite direction. It is the purist defense of plastic art that now seems merely abstract and speculative, a matter of thought rather than of sensation; while the communicative work of language, with all its associations, shows us how art can be "a friend to man." The urn teases us out of thought as art makes us go beyond art. Keats needed a reversal this strong and this assured to support the magnanimity that he almost hides with the ease of his qualifying syntax, when he says "Thou shalt remain, in midst of other woe / Than ours, a friend to man." In that other woe, a future poet will be looking at Keats himself as one of the figures on the urn, coming to the sacrifice, with a burning forehead and a parching tongue—and the apology for art which he in turn composes had better not be too fluent, or find too happy a retreat in the paradox of a career perpetually arrested before the goal. Nor ought it to deify as a thing of beauty what was once also a thing of pain. The poet of "other woe than ours" will be using the urn as a friend to man if he imagines Keats much as Keats in the "Ode to a Nightingale" had imagined Ruth.

"What the imagination seizes as Beauty must be truth": this, from a letter of November 1817—nine months after the Elgin Marbles sonnet, but eighteen months before the Ode and several strata earlier in the story of Keats's development—has often seemed an irresistible help in deciphering the Ode's conclusion. But even then it was only one of Keats's "favorite speculations," and on its most obvious construction I do not think the great poem will admit it: what strikes us as beautiful for the moment is not, even for the moment, the sum of all we need to know. I have given what seems to me a useful aid from Hazlitt's essay "On Imitation," in the statement that "to the genuine artist, truth, nature, beauty, are almost different names for the same thing"; but another statement by Hazlitt, from the "Letter to William Gifford" which Keats was copying out for his brother a few weeks before the Ode, seems to me an even stronger source. Replying to the objection that he was a florid writer, Hazlitt said: "As to my style, I thought little about it. I only used the word which seemed to me to signify the idea I wanted to convey, and I did not rest till I had got it. In seeking for truth, I sometimes found beauty." Here truth carries the main stress, as it must also in the poem Keats's Ode has become by its penultimate line. But there is a special logic in the *sequence*, "Beauty is truth, truth beauty," which Hazlitt's writings on associationism help to explain. One needs to recall the tendency of any association to evoke its opposite: so light suggests shade; pleasure suggests pain; heat suggests cold; life suggests death. The process may always be reversed to conform to a different mood, as when Hazlitt writes in his essay "On the Fear of Death": "Perhaps the best cure for the fear of death is to reflect that life has a beginning as well as an end." If one grants the associationist premise that all our ideas are interrelated, it follows that by certain trains of thought, each of our experiences may imply every other, and that we come to know an experience not in itself but by its relation to every other.

When he imagined reading on the urn, "Beauty is truth, truth beauty," I think Keats was committing himself to the kind of sentiment that the urn, after his experience of it, might be supposed to say by inscription. And yet he was doing more than that. Truth, in the associationist chain that he was exploring, meant "Everything that is the case," the sum of our experience; beauty meant the part of experience that art selects to represent the whole: but "is" still plays fast work with his purposes unless we read it discriminatingly. *Beauty implies truth, truth entails beauty.* Or, to adapt Emerson's more responsive paraphrase, "There is no fact in nature which does not carry the whole sense of nature," and no fact of which our understanding is not modified by the whole sense of nature: this seems to me the expression of faith on which Keats's poem came to rest. We are asked to recognize that art excludes nothing of our experience, but finds in any part a sufficient clue to the whole, and in the whole the necessary modifications of each part. Keats thus ends by declaring that he values in art what Hazlitt valued in a "second nature." Beauty, truth, art, are to him almost different names for the same thing. Nor does the shift of a term imply any substantial dissent. Keats only refuses—as Hazlitt after "On Imitation" would generally refuse—to employ nature itself as an honorific name for the highest sort of art. He is, one may say, still surer than Hazlitt in his awareness of, and still more emphatic in communicating, the *work* art must do to make its selection.

Keats's sonnet on the Elgin Marbles came in spring 1817, Hazlitt's passage on them in "On Poetry in General" in spring 1818, and the "Ode on a Grecian Urn" in spring 1819. But the sequence is nicely progressive in something other than the dates. The sonnet had tried to find the marbles admirable precisely because they do not sympathize with us, and found the strain almost insupportable. Hazlitt replied in his criticism that one ought to search elsewhere for the effects of a human beauty and grandeur, because the marbles excluded on principle the moment of "breathless agony," the interval of suspended progress in which "the pinch of interest lies." The Ode deviated from its apparent theme to include that moment, and to consider it unstintingly, at the expense of concluding with an utterance more pertinent to English poetry, and what happens in this poem, than to the urn or Greek marbles for anything they show in themselves. The record would be incomplete without a final piece of evidence, from the same 1822 articles on the Elgin Marbles which [have been mentioned previously]. Hazlitt is more generous about them now, and I believe one thing that made him generous was Keats's poem. At all events he closes his account, as he had closed the chapter on *King Lear* several years earlier, with a set of propositions on the morality of art. There are ten of them, mostly too elementary in the assertion, and too elaborate in the justification, to add anything to the argument. But excerpts from the fifth, sixth, and tenth will certainly interest the reader who has come this far.

> Grandeur consists in connecting a number of parts into a whole, and not leaving out the parts.

> As grandeur is the principle of connexion between different parts; beauty is the principle of affinity between different forms, or their gradual conversion into each other.

> Truth is, to a certain degree, beauty and grandeur, since all things are connected, and all things modify one another in nature.

If Keats's apology for art seems to apply more directly to poetry than to sculpture or ceramics, still the sympathy and power with which, in looking at an object, he widened speculation about its ground in human life, showed a way for the right use of any art. Hazlitt in this article was availing himself both of what he had taught Keats, and of what Keats had taught him in return.

More broadly, by helping Keats to revise his own idea of the imagination, Hazlitt altered the course of modern poetry. Keats opened up the romantic lyric from within, and by doing so lengthened its endurance. With *Hyperion*, mastered by an epic ideal, he had ended in disappointment, with an abrupt dismissal of his Miltonic experiment: "English ought to be kept up." All along Hazlitt had been moving him in the direction of Shakespeare, and if one looks in romantic poetry for a Shakespearean fullness, and a Shakespearean gusto in dialogue, the place to find them is nowhere in the poetic drama of the period, but in Keats's odes. For the odes have answering voices that are not merely echoes: Keats had come to a new understanding of how a writer's voice might implicate a reader's fate. When one considers his immense influence on the Victorians, and counts the long poems they wrote in any case, one may wonder whether the lyric need in fact have become their dominant mode, and whether it could have done so had he not enlarged its scope. Besides, there was another element of Keats's genius that made him attractive to his successors: he had found a place in poetry for the disagreeables. Not to be dispelled, evaporated, or reconciled, but to be named as part of truth, and belonging to a larger part. Hazlitt alone could have attached him to this faith, for though Keats might have sought it from Coleridge, there was, as Empson says in his essay on "Beauty is Truth," "remarkably little agony in Coleridge's theory of Imagination . . . whereas Keats was trying to work the disagreeables into the theory." Keats's aims in poetry and Hazlitt's in criticism place both in accord with a concern for dramatic form that modern poets have been unwilling to disclaim. Other forces, other personalities, of course intervened, but the periods of literary history are never as inviolable as we make them to speed our thinking, and one reason we read lyric poems today, and not epics or romances of solitary life, is that between 1815 and 1820 Hazlitt convinced a very young man born into a great age of poetry that something still remained to be done.

Chronology

1795   Born October 31, at 24 Moorfields Pavement Row, London.

1803   Sent to Clarke School at Enfield.

1804   Keats's father falls off a horse and dies.

1810   Keats's mother dies; his grandmother, Alice Jennings, sets up a trust fund for the Keats children.

1811   Keats removed from school and apprenticed to Thomas Hammond, an apothecary and surgeon in Edmonton, north of London.

1814   Keats writes his first poems at age 18 or 19.

1816   First published work in May; journeys to Margate on the coast to write; returns to London and meets Leigh Hunt and Benjamin Robert Haydon; writes sonnet on Chapman's Homer in October.

1817   First volume appears in March. Keats begins *Endymion*; visits Benjamin Bailey at Oxford; finishes *Endymion* in November. Writes "Negative Capability" letter, and sees Wordsworth, Lamb and others at Haydon's "Immortal Dinner."

1818   Reconsiders his entire career from January-June. Writes new Shakespearean sonnets, and writes "Isabella" (March and April). Visits ill brother Tom (March to early May); returns to London; walking tour of Northern England with Charles Brown; returns to find his brother in worsened condition. Angry reviews of *Endymion*. Begins "Hyperion" (September), nursing Tom until he dies (December 1). Meets Fanny Brawne (November). Keats rents his rooms from Charles Brown in Wentworth Place, Hampstead.

1819   From January to February writes "The Eve of St. Agnes," at Chichester and Bedhampton. Returns to Hampstead, writes "The Eve of St. Mark." Meets Coleridge in April; the Brawnes move next door; writes "Vale of Soul-Making" letter, "La Belle Dame Sans Merci," and "Ode to Psyche."

Writes odes—Nightingale, Grecian Urn, Melancholy and Indolence, in May. From June until August: on Isle of Wight, with Charles Brown; writes first half of "Lamia," and part of "The Fall of Hyperion"; begins writing love letters to Fanny Brawne. Writes "Otho the Great" with Brown. In September finishes "Lamia," gives up on "The Fall of Hyperion"; writes ode "To Autumn," and returns to London. Becomes ill in October. Begins engagement with Fanny Brawne; writes Fragment of "King Stephen," and "The Cap and Bells."

1820 In February Keats, now gravely ill with tuberculosis, has a hemorrhage and remains confined for months. Moves (May–August) to Kentish Town, when Brown rents his house to others. Third book is published—*Lamia, Isabella, The Eve of St. Agnes, and other Poems.* On September 18 he sails for Italy with Joseph Severn, arriving at Naples on October 31. In Rome, he finds rooms in 26 Piazza di Spagna (now the Keats-Shelley Memorial House).

1821 Dies on February 23. Buried in the Protestant cemetery in Rome.

Contributors

HAROLD BLOOM, Sterling Professor of the Humanities at Yale University, is the author of *The Anxiety of Influence, Poetry and Repression,* and many other volumes of literary criticism. His forthcoming study, *Freud: Transference and Authority,* attempts a full-scale reading of all of Freud's major writings. A MacArthur Prize fellow, he is general editor of five series of literary criticism published by Chelsea House.

WALTER JACKSON BATE is University Professor of English at Harvard. He is renowned for his critical biographies of Dr. Johnson and Keats.

The late PAUL DE MAN was Sterling Professor of Comparative Literature at Yale. His influential work in critical theory includes *Blindness and Insight* and *Allegories of Reading.*

MORRIS DICKSTEIN is Professor of English at Queens College and the author of *Gates of Eden.*

STUART M. SPERRY is Professor of English at the University of Indiana, and writes extensively upon Romantic literature.

GEOFFREY HARTMAN is Karl Young Professor of English and Comparative Literature at Yale. He is best known for his writings on Wordsworth, and for his work in critical theory, including *Beyond Formalism, Criticism in the Wilderness,* and *Saving the Text.*

PAUL SHERWIN is Dean of Humanities at the City College of the City University of New York, and the author of *Precious Bane: Collins and the Miltonic Legacy.*

LESLIE BRISMAN, Professor of English at Yale, is the author of *Milton's Poetry of Choice and its Romantic Heirs.*

HELEN VENDLER, Professor of English at Boston University and at Harvard, is widely known for her books on Yeats and Stevens, as well as her book on contemporary poetry, *Part of Nature, Part of Us.*

DAVID BROMWICH, Associate Professor of English at Princeton, has written extensively on modern poetry, as well as on Hazlitt.

Bibliography

Allott, Miriam, ed. *The Poems of John Keats*. New York: Norton, 1970.

Bate, Walter Jackson. *John Keats*. Cambridge: Belknap/Harvard University Press, 1963.

————, ed. *Keats: A Collection of Critical Essays*. Englewood Cliffs, N.J.: Prentice-Hall, Inc., 1964.

Bloom, Harold. *The Visionary Company*. New York: Doubleday and Company, 1961.

Brisman, Leslie. *Romantic Origins*. Ithaca: Cornell University Press, 1978.

Bush, Douglas. *John Keats: His Life and Writings*. New York: Macmillan Company, 1966.

————, ed. *Selected Poems and Letters by John Keats*. Boston: Houghton Mifflin Company, 1959.

Caldwell, James R. *John Keat's Fancy: The Effect on Keats of the Psychology of His Day*. Ithaca: Cornell University Press, 1945.

Colvin, Sidney. *John Keats: His Life and Poetry, His Friends, Critics and After-Fame*. London: Macmillan Company, 1925.

de Man, Paul, ed. *The Selected Poetry of Keats*. New York: Signet, 1966.

Dickstein, Morris. *Keats and His Poetry: A Study in Development*. Chicago: The University of Chicago Press, 1971.

Ende, Stuart A. *Keats and the Sublime*. New Haven: Yale University Press, 1976.

Evert, Walter H. *Aesthetic Myth in the Poetry of Keats*. Princeton: Princeton University Press, 1965.

Fogle, Richard Harter. *The Imagery of Keats and Shelley*. Hamden, Conn.: Archon Books, 1962.

Forman, Maurice Buxton, ed. *The Letters of John Keats*, 4th ed. London: Oxford University Press, 1952.

Gittings, Robert. *John Keats*. Boston: Little, Brown and Company, 1968.

Goldberg, M.A. *The Poetics of Romanticism: Toward a Reading of John Keats*. Yellow Springs, Ohio: Antioch Press, 1969.

Hewlett, Dorothy. *A Life of John Keats*. London: Hutchinson and Company, 1970.

Hilton, Timothy. *Keats and His World*. New York: Viking, 1971.

Jones, James Land. *Adam's Dream: Mythic Consciousness in Keats and Yeats*. Athens, Ga.: University of Georgia Press, 1975.

Jones, John. *John Keats's Dream of Truth*. London: Chatto and Windus, 1969.

Little, Judy. *Keats as a Narrative Poet*. Lincoln, Neb.: University of Nebraska Press, 1975.

Lowell, Amy. *John Keats*. Hamden, Conn.: Archon Books, 1969.

Murry, John Middleton. *Keats and Shakespeare*. London: Oxford University Press, 1951.

_____. *Keats*. New York: The Noonday Press, 1955.

_____. *Studies in Keats*. New York: Haskell House, 1966.

_____, ed. *The Poems and Verses of John Keats*. London: Eyre and Spottiswoode, 1949.

O'Neill, Judith, ed. *Critics on Keats: Readings in Literary Criticism*. London: George Allen and Unwin, Ltd., 1967.

Ridley, M.R. *Keats's Craftsmanship: A Study in Poetic Development*. New York: Russell and Russell, Inc., 1962.

Rollins, Hyder Edward, ed. *The Keats Circle*, 2 vols. Cambridge: Harvard University Press, 1965.

Sheats, Paul D., ed. *The Cambridge Edition of The Poetical Works of Keats*. Boston: Houghton Mifflin Company, 1975.

Slote, Bernice. *Keats and the Dramatic Principle*. Lincoln, Neb.: University of Nebraska Press, 1950.

Sperry, Stuart M. *Keats the Poet*. Princeton: Princeton University Press, 1973.

Stillinger, Jack. "The Hoodwinking of Madeline: Skepticism in 'The Eve of St. Agnes'," in *Studies in Philology* 58 (1961): 533–55.

_____, ed. *John Keats: Complete Poems*. Cambridge: Belknap/Harvard University Press, 1982.

Thorpe, Clarence D. *The Mind of John Keats*. New York, 1926.

Trilling, Lionel, ed. *The Selected Letters of John Keats*. New York: Farrar, Straus and Young, Inc., 1951.

Vendler, Helen. *The Odes of John Keats*. Cambridge: Belknap/Harvard University Press, 1983.

Ward, Aileen. *John Keats: The Making of a Poet*. New York: Viking, 1963.

Wasserman, Earl R. *The Finer Tone: Keats's Major Poems*. Baltimore: Johns Hopkins University Press, 1967.

Weller, Earle Vonard. *The Autobiography of John Keats, Compiled from His Letters and Essays*. Palo Alto: Stanford University Press, 1933.

Acknowledgments

"Introduction" from *From Sensibility to Romanticism*, edited by Frederick W. Hilles and Harold Bloom, copyright © 1965 by Oxford University Press. Reprinted by permission.

"Negative Capability" by Walter Jackson Bate from *John Keats* by Walter Jackson Bate, copyright © 1963 by the President and Fellows of Harvard College. Reprinted by permission of Harvard University Press.

"The Negative Road" by Paul de Man from *Selected Poetry of John Keats*, edited by Paul de Man, copyright © 1966 by Paul de Man. Reprinted by permission.

"The World of the Early Poems" by Morris Dickstein from *Keats and His Poetry* by Morris Dickstein, copyright © 1971 by The University of Chicago Press. Reprinted by permission.

"The Allegory of *Endymion*" by Stuart M. Sperry from *Keats the Poet* by Stuart M. Sperry, copyright © 1973 by Princeton University Press. Reprinted by permission.

"Poem and Ideology: A Study of 'To Autumn' " by Geoffrey Hartman from *Literary Theory and Structure*, edited by F. Brady, J. Palmer and M. Price, copyright © 1975 by Yale University Press. Reprinted by permission of Yale University Press.

"Keats: Romance Revised" by Harold Bloom from *Poetry and Repression* by Harold Bloom, copyright © 1976 by Yale University Press. Reprinted by permission.

"Dying into Life: Keats's Struggle with Milton in *Hyperion*" by Paul Sherwin from *PMLA* (May 1978), copyright © 1978 by the Modern Language Association of America. Reprinted by permission of the Modern Language Association of America.

"Keats and a New Birth: *Lamia*" by Leslie Brisman from *Romantic Origins* by Leslie Brisman, copyright © 1978 by Cornell University Press. Reprinted by permission.

Index